ACCORDING TO MATTHEW

A COMMENTARY ON
THE GOSPEL OF MATTHEW

DR A. T. BRADFORD

Thanks are due to D Perrem for his editorial work, M Leader for his help with layout and, as always, to my wife Gloria.

Cover art based on the Greek Orthodox icon 'St Matthew the Apostle'

Published by Templehouse Publishing, London, England.

www.templehouse-publishing.com

ISBN 978-0-9564798-3-9

The author may be contacted via: info@templehouse-publishing.com

Contents

According to Matthew

Forward

This book represents an attempt to restore the Jewishness of Jesus to his biographical writings of the first century. Three out of the four 'gospels' (Greek: *'euaggelion'* - the 'good news') [1] were written by Jews. Mark (who is believed to have written his first), appears to have had Jesus' close associate Peter as his source. John was, with Simon Peter, one of Christ's closest friends and disciples. Matthew's Gospel is the longest of all the Gospels, and was written apparently with a Jewish audience in mind. Hence Matthew is a Jew writing about a Jew for the Jews, and his gospel is laid out in our Bibles as the first of Christ's four biographers. I started out planning to write about Luke's Gospel, using my medical knowledge to illustrate the Roman physician's painstakingly detailed account of Jesus' life and teaching. But then 'The Jesus Discovery' happened,[2] and the revelation that God gave me about the Jewish humanity of his beloved Son, and also Jesus' adoptive father Joseph, spilled over largely into Matthew's gospel, and Luke is still waiting. As a doctor too, I'm sure he would have understood.

This book is written from the well recognised view that our Bibles are two languages removed from the words Jesus and his contemporaries spoke (Aramaic and Hebrew translated to Greek, then to English). To fully grasp the meaning it is necessary to peel back the English translation and tackle the Greek 'original' text, in addition to considering the historic and social context, behavioural and especially Jewish human psychology, with a large dose of common sense and an eye for Matthew's (and Jesus') Jewish sense of humour. To date, translations have based themselves on traditional views (e.g. that he was an uneducated itinerant man). Such a view is at odds with the Jewish environment in which Jesus ministered, His enemies among the parties of the Pharisees and Sadducees despised such people (as John 7:49 shows - 'This mob that knows nothing of the law - there is a curse

4

on them' - NIV), yet they never describe Jesus as either uneducated or as an itinerant person - something that they would have been quick to do had that been the case. This commentary will challenge some of these traditional views with alternatives based on the methods of analysis described above.

The commentary that follows is a verse by verse attempt to get beneath the surface of the Gospel narrative. Where helpful for explanation, the writings of the three other Gospels will be quoted, because their detail is useful to fill out the overall picture that Matthew is painting. The commentary has been written from a perspective informed by an understanding that the Scripture is the living and active word of God (Hebrews 4:12), that it's largely Jewish authors wrote in a manner true to their society and historic context, and that this context is described by non-Biblical historians such as Josephus Flavius.[3] I hope that through reading it the Jesus of the first century will become clearer and closer to the reader.

The Gospel According To Matthew

Introduction

Matthew, one of the twelve apostles of Jesus, originally worked as a tax-collector for the occupying Roman army (Matthew 9:9) in Capernaum on the north-western shore of Lake Galilee, in the jurisdiction of the Roman client-king Herod Antipas, son of King Herod the Great. As such, he would have been a wealthy man, but one labouring under the guilt of being a traitor to the spiritual heritage of his people, Israel. As an educated Jew, he had an extensive knowledge of the Hebrew Scriptures and used it widely in his writings in order to convince his Jewish audience of Jesus' identity as the Messiah. At the time that he wrote his eye-witness account of Christ's life the Roman hostilities that began in AD 66 and culminated in the destruction of the Temple had not yet commenced. The second century bishop Irenaeus (a disciple of Polycarp who was a disciple of the Apostle John), recorded that Matthew wrote 'among the Hebrews in their own language, while Peter and Paul were preaching in Rome',[4] which dates Matthew's writing to around AD 63.

Because Matthew is writing primarily for the benefit of his fellow Jews, he begins by establishing Jesus' lineage as a true Israelite. For the Jews, their family history was of the first importance because their heritage and salvation depended on their membership of the people descended from Abraham - with whose descendents God had made promises ratified by a solemn covenant. Genesis 17:7-8 records: 'I will establish my covenant between me and you and your descendants after you throughout their generations for an everlasting covenant, to be God to you and to your descendants after you. I will give to you and to your descendants after you, the land of your sojournings, all the land of Canaan, for an everlasting possession; and I will be their God." The priesthood, so essential for the performance of the ritual sacrifices that dealt with the problem of their sins, had been given to Moses' brother,

Aaron, and his sons (Exodus 28:41), and it was a legal requirement that all priests be able to prove their lineage.[5] The family trees were housed in the Temple under the supervision of the Sanhedrin and were available for public consultation so that they could be checked; the absence of any criticism of Matthew's content by detractors shows that they were undisputed matters of public record. Matthew is not seeking to enumerate every single ancestor in this lineage of Jesus via his earthly father, Joseph, rather he selects three groups of fourteen ancestors to show that Jesus is descended from Abraham via King David (a necessary part of his claim to be the Messiah), and then that his lineage continued despite the exile to Babylon up until Matthew's day. Unlike Luke (who lists forty generations from Mary), Matthew's purpose was to establish the fact of succession from David, particularly noting prominent ancestors, to establish a legal claim to David's throne.

Luke is evidencing Jesus' humanity (back to Adam), and starts with Heli, understood to be the father of Mary, not Joseph. The Greek only mentions Joseph parenthetically: 'Jesus... the son (so it was thought, of Joseph), of Heli'. Women were rarely included in Jewish genealogies (hence Mary is not named), but Luke is dealing with the unique case of a virgin birth and the difficulty of tracing the physical descent of one who had no human father. Luke reinforces this exception by starting with Jesus and ascending up the list of ancestors rather than the usual manner of descending. Mary's genealogy (via David's son Nathan) by-passes Jeconiah (Coniah), who had the curse of 'recording as childless' (Jeremiah 22:30). This obviates the otherwise insurmountable difficulty that the natural descendants via David's son Solomon faced in regard to inheriting kingship. Matthew records the virgin birth of Jesus but avoids using the term 'Joseph (*a descendant of Jeconiah*) begat' (*italics mine*). Instead he records Joseph as 'the husband of Mary, of whom was born Jesus'. In the Greek, 'whom' is the feminine singular and can refer only to Mary (who was not a descendant of Jeconiah). Humanly speaking, Jesus was born of Mary only, with Joseph as his legal and adoptive father.

7

1-6: 'The record of the genealogy of Jesus the Messiah, the son of David, the son of Abraham: Abraham was the father of Isaac, Isaac the father of Jacob, and Jacob the father of Judah and his brothers. Judah was the father of Perez and Zerah by Tamar, Perez was the father of Hezron, and Hezron the father of Ram. Ram was the father of Amminadab, Amminadab the father of Nahshon, and Nahshon the father of Salmon. Salmon was the father of Boaz by Rahab, Boaz was the father of Obed by Ruth, and Obed the father of Jesse. Jesse was the father of David the king.'

Jesus was fully a man of his people, Israel, as well as being God in human form. His Jewish ancestry reflects the chequered nature of that people, from men of great faith, such as Abraham and Isaac, to Jacob (who conspired to cheat his older brother Esau of his blessing), and also foreigners who were added from outside the covenant with Abraham and his descendants. Then there was Judah, who fathered Perez and Zerah by taking his daughter-in-law Tamar for a shrine prostitute after having refused to provide his son for her to marry (Genesis 38). Amminadab was the father of Elisheba, the wife of Aaron (Exodus 6:23), and Nahshon was the ruler of the tribe of Judah (Numbers 2:3), and his son Salmon married Rahab, the foreign brothel / guest-house keeper of Jericho (Joshua 2:1). Obed's mother was also a foreigner: Ruth the Moabite (Ruth 1:4).

6-11: 'David was the father of Solomon by Bathsheba who had been the wife of Uriah. Solomon was the father of Rehoboam, Rehoboam the father of Abijah, and Abijah the father of Asa. Asa was the father of Jehoshaphat, Jehoshaphat the father of Joram, and Joram the father of Uzziah. Uzziah was the father of Jotham, Jotham the father of Ahaz, and Ahaz the father of Hezekiah. Hezekiah was the father of Manasseh, Manasseh the father of

Amon, and Amon the father of Josiah. Josiah became the father of Jeconiah (Jehoiachin) and his brothers, at the time of the deportation to Babylon.'

Jesus was qualified to take the Messiah's title, 'Son of David', because it could be shown that he was a direct descendant of that greatest of Jewish kings. Whereas Luke's genealogy follows David's son, Nathan (see Introduction), Matthew's follows Solomon's line to Joseph, and Matthew does not hesitate to remind his Jewish audience of David's adultery with Bathsheba and the murder of her husband Uriah (2 Samuel 11). Rehoboam's arrogance caused the kingdom of Israel to be divided (2 Chronicles 10), and idolatry to flourish (1 Kings 14:23), idolatry which his son Abijah perpetuated, and which Asa revoked. The nation's spiritual well-being improved further under Jehoshaphat; however, some idolatry persisted (1 Kings 22:43). Joram 'did evil in the sight of the Lord' (2 Kings 8:18), Uzziah was struck with leprosy for burning incense in the manner of the Priests (2 Chronicles 26:19), Jotham rebuilt a city gate but failed to suppress idolatry (2 Kings 15:34), and Ahaz was an idolater who sacrificed his own son (2 Kings 16:3).

The main bright spot was the reign of Hezekiah, who 'trusted in the Lord, the God of Israel; so that after him there was none like him among all the kings of Judah, nor among those who were before him. For he clung to the Lord; he did not depart from following him, but kept his commandments, which the Lord had commanded Moses' (2 Kings 18:5-6). His son, Manasseh, however, was an idolater, who 'filled Jerusalem with innocent blood' (2 Kings 21:16) and his son, Amon, also 'did evil in the sight of the Lord' (2 Kings 21:20). The boy-king, Josiah, took after Hezekiah and: 'did right in the sight of the Lord and walked in all the way of his father David' (2 Kings 22:2), as he repaired the Temple and renewed the covenant. This was not enough to turn back God's judgement, however; Josiah was killed in battle with Pharaoh Neco of Egypt (2 Kings 23:29) and his son, Eliakim, replaced him, having been re-named 'Jehoiakim' by Pharaoh. Jehoiakim's son, Jehoiachin (also known as Jeconiah and Coniah), then succumbed to the Babylonian invasion under Nebuchadnezzar and was taken into exile to Babylon (2 Kings 24:15), in an act of judgement of God.

12-17: 'After the deportation to Babylon: Jeconiah became the father of Shealtiel, and Shealtiel the father of Zerubbabel. Zerubbabel was the father of Abihud, Abihud the father of Eliakim, and Eliakim the father of Azor. Azor was the father of Zadok, Zadok the father of Achim, and Achim the father of Eliud. Eliud was the father of Eleazar, Eleazar the father of Matthan, and Matthan the father of Jacob. Jacob was the father of Joseph the husband of Mary, by whom Jesus was born, who is called the Messiah. So all the generations from Abraham to David are fourteen generations; from David to the deportation to Babylon, fourteen generations; and from the deportation to Babylon to the Messiah, fourteen generations.'

The process of spiritual restoration began again with the humbling of the Jewish people associated with the deportation to Babylon between 597 and 587 BC. Zerubbabel returned to oversee the rebuilding of the Temple in conjunction with Ezra the Priest, who taught the people the Law of Moses (Nehemiah 8). Little is known about the men of this period, but they endured the time of Greco-Macedonian sovereignty and the Syrian oppression, with the Maccabean uprising, before the Roman invasion of 63 BC; which set the scene for the life of Joseph, the husband of Mary. Matthew has arranged Jesus ancestors in groups of fourteen (the numerical values of the Hebrew letters in the name of David totals fourteen), but the last group finishes on thirteen, with Jesus. Matthew may have been indicating that the last generation after Christ is not yet closed, being made up of Jesus' spiritual offspring.

18-19: 'Now the birth of Jesus Christ was as follows: when his mother Mary had been betrothed to Joseph, before they came together she was found to be with child, by the Holy Spirit. And Joseph her husband, being a righteous man and not wanting to disgrace her, planned to send her away secretly.'

In Jewish culture, betrothal was a binding commitment to marriage occurring a year before the wedding ceremony, and sexual infidelity during this time period was punished by stoning to death at the town gates, as was laid down in Deuteronomy 22:24. This was an even more severe punishment than that for adultery, which the Mishnah laid down as 'death by strangling'.[6] The Mishnah consisted of Rabbinic commentary on the Mosaic Law, and was considered to be equally binding. Joseph, rather than falsely claim the baby to be his, intends to save Mary by moving her to another place. The Greek here ('*apoluô*') can also mean divorce; however, a divorce would not have saved Mary's life unless Joseph acknowledged the baby as his, in which case he would not have had grounds to divorce her. A divorce alone would have only put off the inevitable public knowledge of her pregnancy by a few months. Joseph, a devout man, was not prepared to lie about his part in the conception; however neither is he prepared to leave Mary facing the inevitable and deadly consequences that her pregnant state placed her in out of wedlock. The only solution is what has happened in many societies in similar situations since - a change of geographical location to a place where the personal history of the mother-to-be is unknown. Mary, Luke tells us (1:40) goes to stay with her relative Elizabeth, who is herself pregnant with John the Baptist.

Joseph is described as a 'righteous *man*', however the word 'man' is not present in the Greek text. He is simply described as '*dikaios*', which means 'one who obeys the divine Laws',[7] and is often translated as 'devout' or 'righteous'. Its root is the Greek word '*dikh*', meaning 'a judicial hearing, judicial decision, especially a sentence of condemnation, and the execution of a sentence or punishment'.[8] For the Jews in Jesus' day, the way to right relationship with God was through keeping the Law, just as Moses had told their ancestors: 'The Lord commanded us to observe all these statutes, to fear the Lord our God for our good always, and for our survival, as it is today. It will be righteousness for us if we are careful to observe all these commandments before the Lord our God, just as he commanded us' (Deuteronomy 6:24-25).

'Righteous' people were those who kept the Torah, including the Oral Law - the Mishnah - which was not written down until 220 AD. The only way, therefore, to know the Mishnah well enough to be said to be keeping it was to study with the Rabbis (who recommended 8 hours every day). Joseph is thus being described as an educated man. His designation as '*dikaios*' or 'just' is further supported by the title that one of his other sons, James, was known by - James 'the Just'.[9] James would have derived that title from his father Joseph - a 'just' person himself. It is possible that this designation, which by necessity involved rabbinic scholarship, means that Joseph may even have been a Rabbi, that is, one who taught the Torah in an unpaid capacity alongside a secular occupation. Rabbis were ordained men, but were otherwise indistinguishable from ordinary Israelites in having a family and an ordinary job by which they supported themselves, since the work of a Rabbi was not remunerated financially.

20-25: 'But when he had considered this, behold, an angel of the Lord appeared to him in a dream, saying, "Joseph, son of David, do not be afraid to take Mary as your wife; for the Child who has been conceived in her is of the Holy Spirit. She will bear a Son; and you shall call his name Jesus, for he will save his people from their sins." Now all this took place to fulfill what was spoken by the Lord through the prophet: 'Behold, the virgin will be with child and shall bear a son, and they will call his name Immanuel', which translated means, 'God with us'. And Joseph awoke from his sleep and did as the angel of the Lord commanded him, and took Mary as his wife, but kept her a virgin, until she gave birth to a Son; and he called his name Jesus.'

12

Joseph is reassured in his plans by the coming of an angel, who gives the common Jewish name of Jesus ('*Yehoshua*') to the baby, meaning 'Jehovah is salvation'.[10] The word 'salvation' includes the concept of rescuing of his people from the consequences of their sin. The angel quotes the promise of Isaiah 7:14, that as a sign from God one called Immanuel would come and dwell with men, and that the baby would be born of a virgin, since the Greek word '*parthenos*' signifies that a virgin birth is meant.[11] While the Hebrew of Isaiah ('*almâh*') can be equally well translated as 'young woman', the Greek (Septuagint) version of the Old Testament also translates the Hebrew as '*parthenos*'. This is important because the Jews held that the consequences of Adam's sin were passed on via the father, hence it was necessary for Jesus to be born of a virgin (with no human biological father) in order to be a perfect sacrifice for sin.

Chapter 2

1-3: 'Now after Jesus was born in Bethlehem of Judea in the days of Herod the king, Magi from the east arrived in Jerusalem, saying, "Where is he who has been born King of the Jews? For we saw his star in the east and have come to worship him." When Herod the king heard this, he was troubled, and all Jerusalem with him.'

Joseph had to travel to his family's home in Bethlehem, where Jesus was born, for the census ordered by Caesar Augustus (Luke 2:1). Luke records (2:7) that he was laid 'in a manger, because there was no room for them in the '*kataluma*'.' This is generally translated as 'inn', however it is the word for 'guestroom' in both Mark and Luke's description of the room used for Jesus final Passover meal. The word for 'inn' used in the parable of the good Samaritan (Luke 10:34) is '*pandocheion*', meaning a 'house for the reception of strangers'.[12] Bethlehem was a small village (Micah 5:2), too small for several inns, especially since the short distance (6 miles) to Jerusalem meant that many travellers had no need of one. Joseph went there because his family home was there, and in any event it is highly unlikely he would have taken Mary to an inn to give birth rather than to his family home. The Roman census meant that other relatives were there as well; the 'guest room' was consequently full. However, most family residences had an alternative place that offered warmth and the privacy required for a mother's first labour and delivery. Either immediately adjacent to the house, or when built on slopes excavated beneath the ground floor, was a space where the family's livestock was stabled. It combined ease of access with security for the animals, and the warmth created by the animals helped provide heating for the house itself. When the infant was delivered and wrapped in bandages, there was a warm, convenient place nearby to lay him in - the manger that the animals were fed from. The region was ruled by the Roman client-king, Herod the Great. Earlier, in around 40 BC the neighbouring Parthian Empire had invaded

Jerusalem, forcing Herod to flee to Rome seeking reinforcements. The Parthians ruled from the eastern cities of Babylon and Susa, where their Empire was guided by a priestly sect called the Magi, of whom the Jewish prophet Daniel had become a leader (Daniel 5:11). This sect studied astronomy and had identified a sign in the heavens as a portend of the birth of a great king in Israel. They were very likely to have been following prophetic guidance given by Daniel himself, and were acting therefore as converts to Judaism as disciples of Daniel and not the Zoroastrianism practiced by other Magi.

Herod was not of Jewish blood - his father Antipater was a descendant of Edom (a people Judas Maccabeus had forcibly converted to Judaism), and his mother was an Arab from Petra in Jordan. He had been given the title 'King of the Jews' by the Roman Senate under Octavian and Marc Antony while seeking the reinforcements needed to re-capture Jerusalem. When the Parthian Magi arrived, (undoubtedly with a military escort given their importance and their impudent confidence, bordering on rudeness, in making their inquiry of Herod in full knowledge of Rome's title), they ask for the one '**born** King of the Jews'. The paranoid Herod would almost certainly have taken this to be the first part of a take-over plan to again displace him with someone of more genuine Jewish lineage. Fearing another invasion, the people of Jerusalem as well as Herod were naturally deeply concerned over what would happen next. The arrival of the Magi was no small occasion.

4-8: 'Gathering together all the Chief Priests and Scribes of the people, he inquired of them where the Messiah was to be born. They said to him, "In Bethlehem of Judea; for this is what has been written by the prophet: 'And you, Bethlehem, in the land of Judah, are by no means least among the leaders of Judah; for out of you shall come forth a ruler who will shepherd my people Israel.'" Then Herod secretly called the Magi and determined from them the exact time the star appeared. And he sent them to Bethlehem and said, "Go and search carefully for the child; and

15

when you have found him, report to me, so that I too may come and worship him."

Having no knowledge of Micah 5:2, where Bethlehem is identified as the place of the Messiah's birth, Herod asked the rulers of the Jews for this information and they duly enlightened him. He then seems to have wanted to keep the Magis' news of the birth to himself, as he held a secret meeting with the Magi to discover the time when the star that they thought announced the birth had appeared. By this time, he appears to have ascertained that the Magi were there in an unofficial capacity as genuine worshippers and not on a political mission. He was already planning to murder this new threat to his rule. However, he appears to have been too scared, presumably of their escort, to accompany them himself, and so he opened the way for Joseph, Mary and Jesus to escape his grasp.

9-12: 'After hearing the king, they went their way; and the star, which they had seen in the east, went on before them until it came and stood over the place where the child was. When they saw the star, they rejoiced exceedingly with great joy. After coming into the house they saw the child with Mary his mother; and they fell to the ground and worshipped him. Then, opening their treasures, they presented to him gifts of gold, frankincense, and myrrh. And having been warned by God in a dream not to return to Herod, the Magi left for their own country by another way.'

Whereas the initial sighting of the star 'in the East' may well have been a planetary conjunction of Jupiter and Saturn believed to have occurred in 6BC, the re-appearance of the star and its movement towards the birthplace of Jesus appears to be a form of miraculous guidance that cannot be explained astronomically. The Magi were continually guided by God; using many means both natural (such as dreams and the advice of the Priests and Scribes) and supernatural. The reverence of their

16

worship shows that despite their non-Jewish origins they had a real understanding of who Jesus was, an understanding that was almost certainly founded on their knowledge of the legacy of the prophet Daniel. All of the gifts they brought were very valuable; gold as for a king, frankincense as for God or for a priest and myrrh (*'smurna'* - as in the city of Smyrna in Asia Minor) for it's anti-septic, perfume and embalming uses, signifying Christ's humanity and future death. The Magi were wealthy men, and these gifts, surely given in kingly quantity (the 'treasures' that they open is *'thesauros'*, meaning caskets) [13] as well as in quality, would have made Joseph and Mary wealthy too, providing for their journey to Egypt and beyond. (See 2 Corinthians 8:9, where the Apostle Paul records that Jesus had chosen to become poor from a position of wealth).

13-15: 'Now when they had gone, behold, an angel of the Lord appeared to Joseph in a dream and said, "Get up! Take the child and his mother and flee to Egypt, and remain there until I tell you; for Herod is going to search for the child to destroy him." So Joseph got up and took the child and his mother while it was still night, and left for Egypt. He remained there until the death of Herod. This was to fulfill what had been spoken by the Lord through the prophet: 'Out of Egypt I called my son'.

Joseph's prompt obedience kept him a step ahead of Herod's murderous intentions; he left his family home and took the caravan route to safety in Egypt, helped in the journey and the stay there by the valuable gifts he had just received. The date of Herod's death is known to be 4BC, and Jesus is now being referred to as a 'child' (*'paidion'*),[14] not a baby, probably about a year old, if a one year rough margin for error was allowed for by Herod in his orders to kill the male infants in Bethlehem. Hence, Christ was almost certainly born in 5 - 6 BC. When Matthew quotes from Hosea 11:1 ('When Israel was a youth I loved him, and out of Egypt I called my son'), he is making an important messianic point in likening Christ to Moses, who himself prophesied that God would send a 'prophet like me' (Deuteronomy 18:15). Like Moses (who was raised as a highly educated prince in Pharaoh's court), Christ would become a significant and highly educated figure of authority in Jewish society within the Temple life of his day, able to teach in the Temple courts and even clear the Temple market without interference. Both Moses and Christ were rejected by their own people, but they later both returned (from exile in Moses' case and death in Christ's case) to continue their respective missions of salvation.

16-18: 'Then when Herod saw that he had been tricked by the Magi, he became very enraged, and sent and slew all the male children who were in Bethlehem and all its vicinity, from two years old and under, according to the time which he had determined from the Magi. Then what had been spoken through Jeremiah the prophet was fulfilled: 'A voice was heard in Ramah, weeping and great mourning, Rachel weeping for her children, and she refused to be comforted, because they were no more.''

Herod was a highly paranoid individual who thought nothing of murdering his third wife Mariamne and three of his sons whom he perceived as being a threat to his throne. His 'slaughter of the innocents' is quite in keeping with what is known of his character. Matthew quotes from Jeremiah 31:15, 'Thus says the Lord, 'A voice is heard in Ramah, lamentation and bitter weeping. Rachel is weeping for her children; she refuses to be comforted for her children, because they are no more.' This prophecy was first fulfilled at the time of the exile of Israel to Babylon in 586 BC, when the Israelite captives were held in Ramah (Jeremiah 40:1) which is near Bethlehem. Rachel (wife of Abraham's grandson Jacob and matriarch of Israel) was buried in Bethlehem (Genesis 35:19), and stands, figuratively, for the Jewish mothers whose young sons Herod had murdered in his desire to kill Jesus. Bethlehem was a small village, and the number of male infants below age 3 would not have been great, hence the atrocity does not rank high in comparison to some of Herod's other misdemeanours.

18

19-21: 'But when Herod died, behold, an angel of the Lord appeared in a dream to Joseph in Egypt, and said, "Get up, take the child and his mother, and go into the land of Israel; for those who sought the child's life are dead." So Joseph got up, took the child and his mother, and came into the land of Israel.'

Herod died a particularly unpleasant death, described by the Jewish Roman historian Josephus in this way: 'The sickness affected his whole body, and greatly disordered all its parts with various symptoms. He had a slight fever and an unbearable itching over all the surface of his body, and constant pains in his lower bowel, and swelling in his feet as with dropsy, an inflammation of the abdomen, and a putrefaction of his genitals, that produced worms, as well as difficulty in breathing, and he could not breathe but when he sat upright, and had a convulsion of all his limbs. The diviners said those diseases were a punishment upon him for what he had done to the Rabbis. Yet did he struggle with his numerous disorders, and still had a desire to live, and hoped for recovery, and considered several methods of cure. Accordingly, he went over Jordan, and made use of those hot baths at Callirrhoe, which ran into the Dead Sea, but are themselves sweet enough to be drunk. And here the physicians thought proper to bathe his whole body in warm oil, by letting it down into a large vessel full of oil; whereupon his eyes failed him, and he came and went as if he was dying; and as a tumult was then made by his servants, at their voice he revived again.'[15] Josephus also states that Herod had a hacking cough.

From a medical perspective, Herod was clearly suffering from symptoms of heart failure (ankle swelling and difficulty in breathing especially when lying flat, with coughing), while the association with widespread itching points to advanced renal failure, something which is notoriously difficult to treat. Herod's physicians' remedy of lowering him into warm oil only caused Herod to faint. Both renal failure and heart failure are commonly caused by diabetes mellitus, and Herod, whose diet would have been high in sweet foods and the sweet wines of the region, would have been a good candidate for developing this condition. The presence of diabetes as a factor is also indicated by what happened to Herod's genitals. It is highly probable medically that their 'putrefaction' as described by Josephus was a case of Fournier's gangrene, a condition first clinically documented in 1883 by Jean Fournier, a French venereologist, who described a rapidly progressive gangrene of the penis and scrotum. This condition is linked to diabetes mellitus and alcohol excess, and is associated with extreme skin irritation and itching. Herod's multiple sexual partners placed him at risk of sexual disease; his multiple building projects may have been a sign of the grandiose ideas associated with cerebral syphilis.

22-23: 'But when he heard that Archelaus was reigning over Judea in place of his father Herod, he was afraid to go there. Then after being warned by God in a dream, he left for the regions of Galilee, and came and lived in a city called Nazareth. This was to fulfill what was spoken through the prophets: 'He shall be called a Nazarene.''

After Herod's death, Caesar Augustus divided the territory between Herod's sons. The oldest surviving son, Archelaus, inherited one-half of the kingdom, but was given the title of 'ethnarch' rather than king - a lesser title signifying one who rules without independence. He governed Judea, Samaria and Idumaea, which were considered the most important parts of the region, and he was renowned for his cruelty, a trait for which Augustus later banished him to Gaul. His younger brother, Antipas, was made tetrarch (ruler of one quarter of an area) of Galilee and Perea; and Philip, their half brother from Herod's fifth wife, was made tetrarch of Trachonitis, Gaulonitis and Paneas. Joseph considered it safer to return to his original home town of Nazareth in Galilee, on the caravan route from Egypt to the east. Matthew quotes 'the prophets' rather than any one specific verse; indeed, Scripture does not contain this exact phrase. However, 'Nazarene' came to mean a despised person, which Isaiah 53:3 records the Messiah to have been.

Chapter 3

1-3: 'Now in those days John the Baptist came, preaching in the wilderness of Judea, saying, "Repent, for the kingdom of heaven is at hand." For this is the one referred to by Isaiah the prophet when he said, 'The voice of one crying in the wilderness, "Make ready the way of the Lord, make his paths straight."' Now John himself had a garment of camel's hair and a leather belt around his waist; and his food was locusts and wild honey.'

Matthew now introduces John the Baptist. Jesus' mother Mary and John's mother Elizabeth were 'kinswomen' (Luke 1:36); hence, John was related to Jesus. His diet suggests that he was living in the desert, the term given to the area of lightly populated grazing land east of Jerusalem around the river Jordan. While locusts were 'clean' legally (Leviticus 11:22) and could be eaten; the Greek here can also mean locust beans (the pods of the indigenous Carob tree *Ceratonia siliqua*, which resemble a locust) and which were much more readily available than the insect itself. The Jews had a practice of ceremonial washings to deal with ritual uncleanness (Leviticus 22:6) should they come into contact with something that the Law held to be unclean. John began his ministry by extending this practice to address what was God's underlying intention - a turning away from sin. To baptize something carried the meaning of an irreversible change occurring, and was the term used for the permanent dyeing of cloth with a colour which could not be extracted.[16] Hence baptism was an outward expression of an internal reality.

John is announcing a coming kingdom, and, by extension, a coming king, which in that day and age would mean a straight road being built for the king's use (the Roman army would move earth and forests to build their roads). The outworking of 'repentance' ('*metanoeô*' - 'to change one's mind about something')[17] meant that there would be a change of life that allowed the life of the kingdom to be seen. (Luke 3:

11-14 provides some real life examples of this, such as the sharing of goods with those in need.) John's dress is similar to Elijah's (2 Kings 1:8: 'a leather girdle bound about his loins') who was believed to be the forerunner of the Messiah, and he is quoting Isaiah 40:3, which foretold the revealing of the 'glory of God', something that would also have had a Messianic connotation for his listeners.

7-10: 'But when he saw many of the Pharisees and Sadducees coming for baptism, he said to them, "You brood of vipers, who warned you to flee from the wrath to come? Therefore bear fruit in keeping with repentance; and do not suppose that you can say to yourselves, 'We have Abraham for our father'; for I say to you that from these stones God is able to raise up children to Abraham. The axe is already laid at the root of the trees; therefore every tree that does not bear good fruit is cut down and thrown into the fire."'

The Pharisees were the religious lawyers who interpreted the Law of Moses, whereas the Sadducees were the priests who controlled the sacrificial offerings in the Temple. Both had become corrupted (the Pharisees had become legalistic while the Sadducees exploited the profit opportunities the sacrifices gave them), and so John asks for proof of repentance by action before baptizing them, likening them to snakes seeking to escape a desert fire. The ancient claim to lineage from Abraham was popularly believed to exempt the Jews from God's judgement. However, John quickly points out that this is not the case; in fact, God's judgement is very close, a message echoed by Jesus himself in his prediction of the destruction of the Temple. (See Matthew 24:2).

11-12: 'As for me, I baptize you with water for repentance, but he who is coming after me is mightier than I, and I am not fit to remove his sandals; he will baptize you with the Holy Spirit and fire. "His winnowing fork is in his hand, and he will thoroughly clear his threshing floor; and he will gather his wheat into the barn, but he will burn up the chaff with unquenchable fire.'"

A Jewish slave was legally exempt from being compelled to perform the menial act of washing feet; John appears to be saying that in comparison with Christ he is not even fit to remove Christ's sandals, let alone wash his feet. Unlike John, who baptized in water for cleansing from sin, Christ's baptism was to be with the Holy Spirit for empowerment (as seen from the Day of Pentecost onwards) as well as for cleansing. The later part is represented by the baptism of fire, just as the fire of judgement will consume unworthy works leaving only those honouring to God. (See 1 Corinthians 3:13). The winnowing fork was a type of shovel used to throw the threshed wheat into the air, allowing the wind to blow the grain's coating of lighter chaff aside. After this, it would be swept up and burned, an image of the judgement of hell where, as Isaiah 66:24 states, 'the fire is not quenched'.

13-17: 'Then Jesus arrived from Galilee at the Jordan coming to John, to be baptized by him. But John tried to prevent him, saying, "I have need to be baptized by you, and do you come to me?" But Jesus answering said to him, "Permit it at this time; for in this way it is fitting for us to fulfill all righteousness." Then he permitted him. After being baptized, Jesus came up immediately from the water; and behold, the heavens were opened, and he saw the Spirit of God descending as a dove and lighting on him, and behold, a voice out of the heavens said, "This is my beloved Son, in whom I am well-pleased."'

Jesus' coming to be baptized shocks John, who understood baptism as a sign of repentance, however, Jesus (who was sinless and so had no need of repentance) was about to embark on his public priestly ministry which would result in his offering up his life as the ultimate sacrifice for sin. The High Priest had to undergo ceremonial washing and anointing before entering the Most Holy Place to offer sacrifices there.

Jesus was ceremonially washed by John and anointed by the Holy Spirit (in the form of a dove), before offering himself for sin in the manner described by the Apostle Paul: 'For what the Law could not do, weak as it was through the flesh, God did, sending his own Son in the likeness of sinful flesh and as an offering for sin' (Romans 8:3). God's righteous commands were perfectly met in Christ, his beloved son. Jesus' obedience continually pleased his Father, who spoke from heaven acknowledging and announcing his public ministry.

The priests (Numbers 4:43) served in the tabernacle of the congregation from age 30, and the Mishnah denotes this age as that of authority in public ministry.[18] Hence Jesus at age 30 leaves the confines of rabbinic scholarship within the Court of Israel in the Temple and embarks on the public ministry of teaching, preaching and the many signs associated with the message of his Father's Kingdom. But not without a prior test.

Chapter 4

1-4: 'Then Jesus was led up by the Spirit into the wilderness to be tempted by the devil. And after he had fasted forty days and forty nights, he then became hungry. And the tempter came and said to him, "If you are the Son of God, command that these stones become bread." But he answered and said, "It is written, 'Man shall not live on bread alone, but on every word that proceeds out of the mouth of God.'"

Luke and Matthew both describe Jesus as 'full of the Holy Spirit' for his first mission, (Luke 4:1), which was to do battle with the devil (the Greek is '*diabolos*' - 'accuser' or 'slanderer'; '*Satan*' is a Hebrew word meaning 'adversary'[19] found in Zechariah 3:1). The devil is a created being, a fallen angel alluded to in Isaiah 14:12 and Ezekiel 18:11-19, and Jesus prepared for this ordeal by praying and fasting. To 'tempt' is '*peirazô*', meaning a 'test' or 'examination', which God the Father would use to strengthen his Son. Jesus had laid aside his omnipotence in becoming human, and the weakness of his body through fasting threw him onto reliance in his Father to provide the strength needed to overcome temptation. Jesus' disciple John, who wrote in 1 John 2:16, describes temptation as functioning in three ways: the lust of the flesh, the lust of the eyes and the pride of life. These were the ways in which the devil tempted Eve. We read in Genesis 3:6: 'The tree was good for food (satisfying the desire of the flesh), a delight / pleasure to the eye (satisfying the lust of the eyes), and desirable for gaining wisdom' (satisfying the pride of life). Jesus, too, is tempted along these lines. The first of these temptations that Jesus encountered was: 'Tell these stones to become bread' - the lust of the flesh to take an unnatural shortcut towards having his natural human needs (in this case hunger) met. Jesus responds by saying that dependency on God is what is important - the provision of manna to the Israelites in the desert taught the people on depend on God in his provision for their lives.

5-7: 'Then the devil took him into the holy city and had him stand on the pinnacle of the Temple, and said to him, "If you are the Son of God, throw yourself down; for it is written, 'He will command his angels concerning you, and on their hands they will bear you up, so that you will not strike your foot against a stone.'" Jesus said to him, "On the other hand, it is written, you shall not put the Lord your God to the test.'"

The temptation here was to take a shortcut in God's timetable for recognition (achieved through death on a cross) by attempting to jump from the gallery on the south side of the Temple. This was 150 feet above the Temple floor and 700 feet above the floor of the Kidron valley, and would have been a kind of self-fulfilment of Malachi 3:1, which promised that the Messiah would suddenly come to his Temple. Here, Satan twists the Scripture by quoting Psalm 91:11-12, but conveniently leaving out the second half of verse 11 '…to guard you in all your ways', that is, in all your normal actions, not acts of deliberate recklessness, performed to satisfy 'the pride of life'. Satan also appeals to any possible sense of pride that he may have thought that Jesus felt in being 'the Son of God'. Jesus replies by quoting Deuteronomy chapter 6 verse 16. He would not misuse God's power but would subject the use of his gifts to whatever was God the Father's will.

8-11: 'Again, the devil took him to a very high mountain and showed him all the kingdoms of the world and their glory; and he said to him, "All these things I will give you, if you fall down and worship me." Then Jesus said to him, "Go, Satan! For it is written, 'You shall worship the Lord your God, and serve him only." Then the devil left him; and behold, angels came and began to minister to him.'

The idea of the second Person of the Trinity, who had participated in the creation of all things, worshipping one of the spiritual creatures he had made, is as preposterous as it is ludicrous and Jesus dismisses

26

Satan in the manner of a failing court jester with the words of Deuteronomy 6:13 which forbade idolatry. The temptation was to take a shortcut through sinning to something that was Jesus' by right - all the kingdoms of the earth, which Psalm 2:8 states are promised him by the Father, and, in showing them to him, Satan appeals to the 'lust of the eyes'. Satan, however, is simply a usurper who had taken over humankind's tenancy of the world by means of deception. This is rather like a hijacker offering to give back the thing he has stolen in return for promotion. Having undergone three rounds with the devil, Jesus, now exhausted with hunger, has his needs attended to by some of the angelic beings who had not joined with Satan in rebelling against serving God.

12-17: 'Now when Jesus heard that John had been taken into custody, he withdrew into Galilee; and leaving Nazareth, he came and settled in Capernaum, which is by the sea, in the region of Zebulun and Naphtali. This was to fulfill what was spoken through Isaiah the prophet: 'The land of Zebulun and the land of Naphtali, by the way of the sea, beyond the Jordan, Galilee of the Gentiles - the people who were sitting in darkness saw a great light; and those sitting in the land of the shadow of death, upon them a light has dawned.' From that time Jesus began to preach and say, "Repent, for the kingdom of heaven is at hand."'

Herod Antipas was tetrarch of Galilee and Jesus apparently deliberately went there to continue the ministry begun by John, settling in Capernaum on Lake Galilee, north of Herod's capital of Tiberias, a part of Israel made up of and surrounded by many foreigners and Gentiles. Galilee was at the crossroads of two trade routes and so many people passing through would have heard of Jesus' ministry. Matthew sees in this a fulfillment of Isaiah 9:1-2, which tells how the Lord would 'honour Galilee of the Gentiles' by allowing them to see 'a great light', which refers to the ministry of Jesus Christ - someone who was not to be put off by the murder of his cousin, John. Jesus called the people to turn and change their minds about sin ('repent' - *'metanoeô'*) [20] so that their behaviour could change as well.

18-20: 'Now as Jesus was walking by the Sea of Galilee, he saw two brothers, Simon who was called Peter, and Andrew his brother, casting a net into the sea; for they were fishermen. And he said to them, "Follow me, and I will make you fishers of men." Immediately they left their nets and followed him.'

John (John 1:35) records that Andrew had been a disciple of John the Baptist, whom he had heard refer to Jesus as the 'Lamb of God'; Andrew had immediately gone to find his brother Peter and tell him, 'we have found the Messiah'. Jesus appears to be already a figure of repute as a Doctor of the Law in the religious Jewish society of that time; an invitation to be the disciple of such a person was not something that they would have thought twice about accepting; it led to education in their beloved Torah and a high degree of social standing.

21-22: 'Going on from there he saw two other brothers, James the son of Zebedee, and John his brother, in the boat with Zebedee their father, mending their nets; and he called them. Immediately they left the boat and their father, and followed him.'

Zebedee's wife is believed to have been Salome, the sister of Jesus' mother Mary; hence James and John would have been cousins of Jesus and therefore would have been well acquainted with his rise to prominence as a senior Jewish religious teacher. They too accepted immediately the invitation to the prestigious position of disciple, one that would give them an opportunity to be trained in the Torah and the newer message Jesus was bringing of the Kingdom of God. John's gospel (John 3:2) describes how Jesus was at that time addressed by the title of '*Didaskalos*' - 'Doctor' [21] (of the Law) - by no less an authority than the ruling Sanhedrin council member Nicodemus, who is himself addressed with that title. Disciples of such a high ranking member of

Jewish legal and theological society would have had the privilege of representing his teaching in years to come, with significant social and even material advantages.

23-25: 'Jesus was going throughout all Galilee, teaching in their synagogues and proclaiming the gospel of the kingdom, and healing every kind of disease and every kind of sickness among the people. The news about him spread throughout all Syria; and they brought to him all who were ill, those suffering with various diseases and pains, demoniacs, epileptics, paralytics; and he healed them. Large crowds followed him from Galilee and the Decapolis and Jerusalem and Judea and from beyond the Jordan.'

Jesus the Rabbi and Doctor of the Law was legally authorised in his society to teach in the synagogue as well as in the Temple courts; he also demonstrated his spiritual authority by means of miraculous signs and healings, and so extended spiritual light to those Gentiles in Syria in the north. The densely populated region from the ten Greek-speaking cities around the Jordan yielded large crowds from the east of Lake Galilee, and as far south as Jerusalem.

Chapter 5

1-2: 'When Jesus saw the crowds, he went up on the mountain; and after he sat down, his disciples came to him. He opened his mouth and began to teach them.'

Jesus now moved up onto a hillside in order to more particularly teach his disciples rather than simply the crowds. He was about to teach them what God, his Father, is really like - 'blessed' or 'happy'- and what it would take for them to be the same way. Twice, Paul wrote to Timothy of God being 'happy', which is the meaning of '*makarios*' (often translated as 'blessed').[22] For example, in 1 Timothy 1:11, 'the glorious gospel of the blessed God', and 1 Timothy 6:15, 'Who is the blessed and only Sovereign, the King of kings and Lord of lords'. This term is used not in the sense of meaning 'praised' ('*eulogetas*', e.g. 1 Peter 1:13 - 'Blessed be the God and Father of our Lord Jesus Christ'), but rather as possessing a condition of happiness or blessedness.

3: 'Blessed are the poor in spirit, for theirs is the kingdom of heaven.'

'Poor' here is '*ptochos*', meaning beggarly or destitute,[23] derived from '*ptosso*', which means 'to crouch',[24] as a roadside beggar would - a common first century sight. Those who are poor in spirit recognise their own human condition of spiritual impoverishment, of one who is in great need and who, unless his need is met, will die. 'Spirit' is '*pneuma*', indicating our spiritual life, particularly related to God's Holy Spirit and, in this case, how much of that we have in and of ourselves - i.e. none, apart from what he has given us. Jesus was saying that the 'happy' ones, who inherit the life of his Kingdom (now, on this earth, to a significant degree, as well as in heaven) are those who can recognise their own spiritual beggarliness from a human perspective and do not have any pretensions about their own status or knowledge, and so are not filled with pride.

30

4: 'Blessed are those who mourn, for they shall be comforted.'

'Mourn' is *'pentho'* from *'penthos'* - 'sorrow' or 'mourning', of a general nature but, especially in the New Testament, the response to the effects of sin and its negative effects on us and others. The use of the word elsewhere maintains this meaning, e.g. 2 Corinthians 12:21, 'I am afraid that when I come again my God will humble me before you, and I will be **grieved** (*mourn*) over many who have sinned earlier and have not repented of the impurity, sexual sin and debauchery in which they have indulged.' Jesus was speaking in spiritual terms, just as in the previous verse regarding being 'poor in spirit'. He was not talking about mourning the dead, which was an elaborate part of Israelite culture at the time (e.g. Matthew 9:23-24 - 'When Jesus entered the ruler's house and saw the flute players and the noisy crowd, he said, "Go away. The girl is not dead but asleep."')

'Comforted' is *'parakaleo'*, from which the word Jesus used for the Holy Spirit ('Comforter' - *'parakletos'*) is derived. It means 'one called alongside' [25] (to help), which was the common term for a legal barrister and used in a court of justice to denote 'a legal assistant, counsel for the defense, an advocate; generally, one who pleads another's cause as an intercessor'.[26] Jesus was saying that, when we repent from sin, we are 'blessed' - 'happy' because our sins are forgiven.

5: 'Blessed are the meek, for they will inherit the earth.'

'Meek' is an extremely misunderstood word in the modern West. It is used commonly as meaning weak-spirited - a tendency to be used as a doormat. The Greek here is *'praus'*, from which the fruit of the Spirit (meekness) is derived. As W.E. Vine says, 'in Scripture, it consists not in a person's 'outward' behaviour only; nor yet in his relations to his fellow-men... Rather, it is an inwrought grace of the soul; and the exercise of it is firstly and chiefly towards God. It is that temper of spirit in which we accept his dealings with us as good, and therefore

31

without disputing or resisting; it is closely linked with the word humility, and follows directly upon it.' [27]

Meekness toward God 'stems from trust in God's goodness and control over the situation'.[28] In the Old Testament, the meek are those wholly relying on God rather than their own strength to defend them against injustice'.[29] This relates closely to verse 39 (not resisting an evil person). The quality of meekness was used to describe a horse that, with all its strength, is responsive to the rider because it has been trained to be instead of having a responsive attitude naturally. Its strength is therefore now both under its own control and also that of the rider, thereby greatly increasing its effectiveness.

Jesus was meek. As Matthew 11:29 reads, 'Take my yoke upon you, and learn of me; for I am meek and lowly in heart: and you shall find rest unto your souls.' But Jesus was certainly not weak, and a good example of that fact is his overturning the Temple money-changers' heavy wooden tables laden with coins. The meek will inherit the earth, literally. Jesus presents this as a simple statement of fact. When mankind has finished ruining the earth then God will re-make it anew and give it to those who have demonstrated this kind of trust in him to look after them (Revelation 21:1).

6: 'Blessed are those who hunger and thirst for righteousness, for they shall be satisfied.'

'Hunger' here is '*peinao*' - 'to suffer want' - 'to be in need of food and basic provisions'.[30] 'Thirst' is '*dipsao*' figuratively, those who are said to thirst who 'painfully feel their want of, and eagerly long for, those things by which the soul is refreshed, supported, strengthened'.[31] Jesus, as in verse 3, is speaking of those who are in desperate need spiritually and who are acutely aware of that need. They have come to the often painful realization that to rely on themselves and their own abilities, good and God-given though they may be, is futile, because when

32

dependence is shifted off God and onto self, our reliance is no longer fully on God.

The word for righteousness here is '*dikaiosune*', which has two common meanings. Firstly, it describes the only condition of mankind that is acceptable to God. Secondly, it describes the visible out-workings of that condition (godly fruit in our personal lives, good works God gives us to do for him, etc).[32] In the context of the rest of Jesus' teaching, its use here most probably means the first type - being in right relationship with God, something that requires an action from God to achieve because it is impossible for us to do so. That action was the death of Christ on the cross. This is what allows us to be re-connected to and fed spiritually by God. As we feed we become strengthened - we are filled ('*chortazo*' - 'to fulfil or satisfy the desire of any one').[33]

7: 'Blessed are the merciful, for they shall receive mercy.'

'Merciful' is '*eleos*', that is, 'the outward manifestation of pity; it assumes need on the part of him who receives it, and resources adequate to meet the need on the part of him who shows it.'[34] It comes from '*eleeo*', meaning 'mercy' - 'to feel sympathy with the misery of another'[35] such that it leads to an action that helps someone. If we have this attitude towards others we will receive the benefits of this attitude from God in our own lives. If we do not have this attitude we restrict the benefit we get. This is a very similar spiritual principle to that taught by Jesus about forgiveness in Matthew chapter 6 and encapsulated in verse 15 as 'But if you do not forgive others, then your Father will not forgive your transgressions.'

8: 'Blessed are the pure in heart: for they shall see God.'

Pure here is '*katharos*', meaning 'to cleanse', often with fire so as to be refined.[36] In Scripture, the heart is seen as the seat of the will. If our wills are set upon doing God's will then we will see God both when we die and more immediately in our lives as they personify him in the present.

9: 'Blessed are the peacemakers, for they shall be called sons of God.'

'Peacemaker' is '*eirenopoios*' from '*poieo*' ('to make') and '*eirene*' ('peace'), the Greek equivalent of Shalom (in Hebrew, 'wholeness'). '*Eirenopoios*' is 'one who loves to make peace',[37] specifically a covenant of peace. God loves to make peace, so much so he was willing to come himself and die on the cross in a painful and sin-laden death. Our happiness will be in direct proportion to how much peace we make. Spiritual peace is attained through the death of Christ on the cross and bringing ourselves and others into all the good that his sacrifice accomplished in becoming free from the curse of sin.

10: 'Blessed are those who have been persecuted for the sake of righteousness, for theirs is the kingdom of heaven.'

Jesus is the ultimate example of one who was persecuted because of right behaviour, all the way to Calvary. The behaviour that God the Father describes as right is not always appreciated by the world. For Jesus, it included spilling other people's coins onto the Temple floor and chasing their Jewish owners away with a whip. But when persecution occurs as a result, we can be happy enough about it if we also experience the authority of the King we serve changing things to reflect his nature. This is a very different thing from being persecuted for simply being obnoxious!

11: 'Blessed are you when people insult you and persecute you, and falsely say all kinds of evil against you because of me.'

In the upside-down world of God's kingdom values, happiness has some strange looking causes. If we know ourselves to be obedient to Christ's teaching we also know his approval, and there is no greater source of joy. If we are reproached 'because of Christ' (rather than for our own sins or mistakes) we are to a small extent sharing in his sufferings, with the promise of his Spirit and glory resting upon us and an eternal reward (see 1 Peter 4:14) .

12: 'Rejoice and be glad, for your reward in heaven is great; for in the same way they persecuted the prophets who were before you.'

'Rejoice' is a happy greeting, '*chairo*' being a kind of first century form of 'Yo!' 'Glad' is a stronger form yet - '*agalliao*' from '*agan*', 'much', and '*hallomai*', to 'jump up' [38] in the manner of the healed cripple of Acts 14:10. In the same way those prophets whom God had inspired and used in earlier times were chased away and maltreated (persecuted).

13: 'You are the salt of the earth; but if the salt has become tasteless, how, can it be made salty again? It is no longer good for anything, except to be thrown out and trampled underfoot by men.'

Wet salt, with the water soluble sodium chloride leached out and leaving only the unpleasant residue of potash, was good only for walking on. Jesus' followers are called to retain their own distinctive flavour of Christ-likeness.

14-15: 'You are the light of the world. A city set on a hill cannot be hidden; nor does anyone light a lamp and put it under a basket, but on the lampstand, and it gives light to all who are in the house.'

'Hill; here is '*oros*', which more commonly means 'mountain'. Here we see Jesus using humour to make his point. How can a mountain-top city be hidden? It is an absurd a concept as putting a measuring bucket over the much valued source of household light.

16: 'Let your light shine before men in such a way that they may see your good works, and glorify your Father who is in heaven.'

When the works that God is doing in and through us become visible to others, the opinion in which our heavenly Father is commonly held will be enhanced (glorified) - they will make God 'look good' to those observing their lives for signs of genuine spiritual life.

17: 'Do not think that I came to abolish the Law or the Prophets; I did not come to abolish but to fulfill.'

'Abolish' ('*katargeo*') means to 'render inoperative' and 'bring to an end'.[39] To 'fulfill' means to cause God's will (as made known in the Law of Moses) to be obeyed as it should be, and God's promises (given through the prophets) to receive fulfillment [40] in the sense of allowing the completion of the purpose of the Old Testament, pointing towards the One who was to come and cause God's Spirit to be an indwelling reality. The fact that the Old Testament remains the true and inspired word of God, with much that has yet to be fulfilled (such as the second coming of Christ), is reinforced in the next verse.

18: 'For truly I say to you, until heaven and earth pass away, not the smallest letter or stroke shall pass from the Law until all is accomplished.'

The jot, the smallest Hebrew letter ('*iota*'), and the smallest mark ('*keraia*') is not to be removed until the next age, a remark lost on many modern Christians who seem to regard the Old Testament has some kind of obscure historic artefact rather than the majority part of the living and active word of God.

19: 'Whoever then annuls one of the least of these commandments, and teaches others to do the same, shall be called least in the kingdom of heaven; but whoever, keeps and teaches them, he shall be called great in the kingdom of heaven.'

'Annuls' ('*luo*') [41] means to 'loose', in the sense of unbinding or releasing from constraints, something that many modern day Bible teachers seem to be doing in their disregard and negation of the Old Testament. The fact that we are now, in Christ, no longer under the Law in no way diminishes the sacred nature of the God-breathed text. Rather, Jesus calls for the Old Testament to be taught in such a way as to make the underlying spiritual messages be lived out in daily life. He who does so will be called 'great' ('*megas*'), meaning a 'person eminent for ability, virtue, authority and power'. [42]

20: 'For I say to you that unless, your righteousness surpasses that of the Scribes and Pharisees, you will not enter the kingdom of heaven.'

The Scribes and Pharisees lived out the Old Testament Law to the maximum possible degree. But their legalistic attitude missed the real purpose of the Law, which was to reveal sin and disclose the futility of our best human efforts to help ourselves. Far from diminishing the importance of the Law, Jesus is about to practice what he preached by demonstrating in the subsequent verses the way that the Law was but a shadow of God's intentions. Hebrews 10:1: 'For the Law having a shadow of good things to come, and not the very image (*i.e. Christ*) of the things, can never with those sacrifices which they offered year by year continually make the comers thereunto perfect.' The righteousness that Christ would· offer was his own - one based on a perfect relationship with his Father; he offers those that follow him this same relationship through the gift of his Holy Spirit.

21: 'You have heard that the ancients were told, 'You shall not commit murder' and 'Whoever, commits murder shall be liable to the court."

Murder would be a good example of something that most would agree is wrong from any moral standpoint. To commit murder is sufficient crime to bring upon oneself the authority of the courts.

22: 'But I say to you that everyone who is angry with his brother shall be guilty before the court; and whoever says to his brother, 'Raca,' shall be guilty before the supreme court; and whoever, says, 'You fool,' shall be guilty enough to go into the fiery hell.'

Jesus raises the bar ever so slightly! 'Angry' here is *'orgizo'* which takes its root from *'orge'* which carries the meaning of the agitated movement of violent emotion.[43] Jesus, being aware of the holistic link between primary emotion and eventual outcome, draws out the link to the boiling-over kind of rage and the murders that have resulted on many occasions down the centuries. But anger is not indicted alone. *'Raca'* is an example of the Aramaic language in daily domestic use by the Jews of first century Palestine, and is a term of complete contempt, literally meaning 'empty-headed'.[44] Being therefore pre-meditated and spiteful, it is a worse offense against God than the uncontrolled and often demonized bubbling over of rage that leads to murder.

Jesus now builds the point he is making to the third and final level. 'Fool' (*'moros'*, from *'musterion'*, meaning 'mystery',[45] perhaps because the workings of the mind of such a person are often a mystery, even to themselves), means a morally worthless and willfully bad person - a scoundrel, a more severe charge than merely being empty-headed on, simply, an intellectual level. For such a gross accusation, Jesus reserves his greatest condemnation - the fire of the rubbish tip of hell, *'Gehenna'*, derived from the Hebrew words meaning 'narrow gorge' and 'lamentation' or 'wailing'.[46] This originated from the gorge of Hinnom, south of Jerusalem, where the filth and dead animals of the city were cast out and burned; becoming therefore a fitting symbol of the future destruction of the wicked.

In Gehenna the fire truly never went out - just when it might have done fresh rubbish would get thrown down on top. The gorge was not naturally watered, and the rubbish conditions attracted an unpleasant type of worm referenced twice by Jesus in his description in Mark chapter 5, verses 29 and 30. It is truly a dreadful place to spend eternity, and best avoided through simply trusting in the saving power of Christ's death and resurrection.

23-24: 'Therefore if you are presenting your offering at the altar, and there remember that your brother has something against you, leave your offering there before the altar and go; first be reconciled to your brother, and then come and present your offering.'

Having explained the nature of this sin, Jesus then instructs those guilty of having fallen into it to put it right, even before doing something 'holy' such as offering a gift to God. God is more concerned about the quality of our relationships than in receiving a gift or an offering.

25-26: 'Make friends quickly with your opponent at law while you are with him on the way, so that your opponent may not hand you over to the judge, and the judge to the officer, and you be thrown into prison. Truly I say to you, you will not come out of there until you have paid up the last penny.'

Jesus extends his advice on getting right in relationships with people you have offended in legal matters too. His advice is to try and settle out of court if you are in the wrong. You never know what the judge might say!

27-28: 'You have heard that it was said, 'You shall not commit adultery'; but I say to you that everyone who looks at a woman with lust for her has already committed adultery with her in his heart.'

Jesus extends the same spiritual principle (that sin starts in the area of feelings and emotions) to the area of illicit sexual relations. Just as boiling anger is linked to murder, lust is linked to passion (*'epithumeo'* is derived from *'thumos'*, meaning firstly, 'passion, angry heat, anger forthwith boiling up and soon subsiding again' and secondly, 'glow, ardour, the wine of inflaming passion'.[47] This either drives the drinker mad or kills him with its strength. Both are pertinent to the feelings of the heart that often precede adultery - an uncontrollable boiling over of passionate lust, linked times innumerable in literature with the imagery of wine intoxicating in strength with frequently disastrous outcomes for human relationships - from lines being crossed that should have never even been approached. No wonder Paul said, 'Flee fornication!' (1 Corinthians 6:18). Jesus says that it is looking in a particular way that is the issue. The Greek here is *'blepo'*, meaning 'to look' physically with the eye or to look metaphorically.[48] Given Jesus' subsequent comments about the ripping out of the eye and the absence of any indication that any of his presumably normal red-blooded male followers ever actually did this, it can be fairly reliably considered that he was speaking metaphorically and not literally. Strong's Dictionary defines *'blepo'* in this way: 'to turn the thoughts or direct the mind to a thing, to consider, contemplate, to look at, to weigh carefully, examine'. Jesus is saying that a lustful glance is not the issue; that is not mental adultery. It is the look that carefully plans the seduction and can see its way clear to the final act itself that is the sin in question, not the quick admiring look that normal men give an attractive woman. Many women like to be admired - while this may be by unhelpfully gaining male attention, that attention is not necessarily the mental sin of adultery.

29-30: 'If your right eye makes you stumble, tear it out and throw it from you; for it is better for you to lose one of the parts of your

40

body, than, for your whole body to be thrown into hell. Where their worm dies not, and the fire is not quenched.'

To 'stumble' (KJV reads 'offend') is '*skandalizo*' (from '*skandalon*', 'a trap'),[49] 'to put a stumbling block or impediment in the way'; '*skandalon*' being 'the trigger of the trap or snare itself to which the bait was attached'.[50] If there is such a dangerous item lying around in your vicinity, Jesus instructs you to 'tear it out' - '*exaireo*' it, (from '*haireomai*'), meaning to 'choose by vote to get rid of it',[51] in a deliberate decision of the will over and above the emotions.

Hell is a subject that Jesus was not at all shy of teaching about. Gehenna was the rubbish dump of the city of Jerusalem, a deep and steep sided gorge in the valley of Hinnom, south of the city, where the debris and dead animals of the city were cast down and burned in flames that, being continually re-fuelled, never went completely out. A particularly malevolent species of worm ('*skolex*') was found there that fed upon the rotting flesh of the unclean carcasses that were deposited therein. The recurring nightmare of any religious Jew was that he or she might commit such a heinous crime as to be deposited there instead of receiving a proper burial, and so lose one's body to the worm and with it all hope of resurrection to life in God. For as their prophet had spoken:

'Then they will go forth and look on the corpses of the men who have transgressed against me. For their worm will not die and their fire will not be quenched; and they will be an abhorrence to all mankind' (Isaiah 66:24).

Truly, a place best to be avoided at all costs; a place, Jesus says, never intended for fallen human beings, but rather for the devil and his angels who will be the foremost of those forever burning and being perpetually devoured. Jesus, speaking metaphorically, recommends his listeners take extreme measures to avoid it.

41

31-32: 'It was said, 'Whoever sends his wife away, let him give her a certificate of divorce', but I say to you that everyone who divorces his wife, except for the reason of unchastity, makes her commit adultery; and whoever, marries a divorced woman commits adultery.'

The divorce question divided the Jewish people. There were two schools of thought; divorce for any act of perceived 'uncleanness', and divorce only for adultery. Rabbi Hillel taught the liberal view - if you want a divorce, don't bother making up a reason: just get divorced, while Rabbi Shammai espoused the stricter view. For Jesus (Rabbi Y'Shua) the issue went back to the beginning, as related in the Book of Genesis, which describes the 'leaving and cleaving' that takes place within the covenant relationship of marriage. For the Jews, covenant was sacrosanct; the concept towered over their history, going back to Abraham and beyond. God honoured covenant, and expected his people to do likewise - this was the conclusion that Jesus presented to his disciples.

The only grounds for divorce Jesus gives is '*porneia*', meaning any kind of illicit sexual activity,[52] an exception clause which is not repeated in the parallel passage as recounted in Luke's gospel. Luke's account gives no grounds for divorce whatsoever, much to the consternation of the listening disciples. Jesus uses the word '*porneia*' in direct contrast with '*moichao*', meaning 'adultery', demonstrating that there was not an exception on grounds of adultery. What kind of illicit sexual activity other than adultery are grounds for divorce? And is there one that applies mainly to the Jewish audience to which Matthew was writing? The fidelity vows of the first century Jewish custom of betrothal were binding on the parties involved. Matthew is therefore recording Jesus as stating that divorce can occur in the betrothal period (before the wedding's consummation) if one partner is sexually unfaithful to the other. Otherwise, divorce and re-marriage is depicted as being equivalent to adultery.

42

33-37: 'Again, you have heard that the ancients were told, 'You shall not make false vows, but shall fulfill your vows to the Lord.' But I say to you, make no oath at all, either by heaven, for it is the throne of God, or by the earth, for it is the footstool of his feet, or by Jerusalem, for it is the city of the great King. Nor shall you make an oath by your head, for you cannot make one hair white or black. But let your statement be, 'Yes, yes' or 'No, no'; anything beyond these is of evil.'

Jesus now compares his teaching with 'the ancients' ('*archaios*'). He addresses the vexed topic of false swearing or perjury - '*epiorkeo*'.[53] The ancients had said, 'Do not make false promises, instead, fulfill your vows, such as the Psalmist had said, 'Make vows to the Lord your God and fulfill them' (Psalm 76:11). To be as religious as possible, the Pharisees had taken this to the limit, making vows by everything that sounded holy but leaving themselves a loophole by leaving out the name of God himself and, in so doing, evading the potential issue of personal responsibility. Jesus does not tell them to stop making vows to God and in his name where appropriate (e.g. marriage). Rather, he tells them to stop using inappropriate terms, since God is in all of them anyway. If not using God's name, simply let it be 'Yes' or 'No', with nothing evasive and 'evil' (Greek: '*poneros*', meaning 'bad', 'bringing trouble, labours and annoyance' - from '*ponos*', meaning 'pain').[54]

38-39: 'You have heard that it was said, 'An eye for an eye and a tooth for a tooth'. But I say to you, do not resist an evil person; but whoever slaps you on your right cheek, turn the other to him also.'

In the violent society of Old Testament cultures, God had placed a restraining order. The Law allowed that whatever someone did to you might be returned, thus placing a maximum limit on what the revenge could be (Leviticus 24: 19-20).

When Jesus came, he brought with him a new level of grace and truth, one based on recognising and receiving God's fatherhood. He taught that God the Father is now in charge of our lives in a special way because we take up residence in his Son, and because both Father and Son have set about making their home in us. In the gospel of John, Jesus says, 'If anyone loves me, he will keep my word; and my Father will love him, and we will come to him and make our abode with him' (John 14:23).

There is no restriction placed here on the number of words of Christ that we have to obey for him to make his home in us. Simply coming to him in trust in what he has already done is enough. When God the Father is given control, he himself limits what happens to his children. Only what he wants can happen. This does not preclude responsible behaviour on our part. But God is big enough to use even (and perhaps especially) our own stupidity or mistakes for his good purposes.

He certainly controls the influence of external evil, in the same way that any responsible parent would. Evil cannot harm us when we are in Christ. Anything 'bad' that God allows to happen he does so for our good. Romans 8:28 - 'And we know that God causes all things to work together for good to those who love God, to those who are called according to his purpose'. When evil 'happens', it can be used by God to serve to strengthen us. When it does not happen, which is usually what we prefer, we carry on anyway.

However there are two points that are worth making about this saying of Jesus. He was not advocating a non-defence type of pacifism. In fact he advised his followers to carry a sword, possibly to dispel the bullying nature of their opponents. Luke 22:35-36: 'And he said to them, 'When I sent you out without money belt and bag and sandals, you did not lack anything, did you?' They said, 'No, nothing.' And he said to them, 'But now, whoever has a money belt is to take it along, likewise also a bag, and whoever has no sword is to sell his cloak and buy one.''

But when an 'evil' occasion (Jesus' arrest) arose shortly thereafter, the disciples had enough common sense to ask whether that was such a time to use the sword. Luke 22:49: 'When those who were around him saw what was going to happen, they said, 'Lord, shall we strike with the sword?'' One of the disciples did however strike without waiting for permission: 'One of them struck the slave of the High Priest and cut off his right ear' (Luke 22:50). Matthew, Mark and Luke refrain from telling us which disciple it was. John, who focuses particularly on the latter days of Jesus' life, does tell us: 'Simon Peter then, having a sword, drew it and struck the High Priest's slave, and cut off his right ear; and the slave's name was Malchus. So Jesus said to Peter, 'Put the sword into the sheath; the cup which the Father has given me, shall I not drink it?'' (John 18:10-11).

Peter was a fisherman, not a soldier. Presumably Malchus ducked, and the sword connected as a passing blow to the side of the head. But Jesus' foreknowledge and composure was up to the challenge. Luke 22:51: 'Jesus answered and said, 'Stop! No more of this.' And he touched his ear and healed him.' Jesus knew when to submit to his Father's will. He could also demonstrate complete power and control over the (evil) situation of his unjust arrest by healing the man Peter had wounded. 'While I was with you daily, in the Temple, you did not lay hands on me; but this hour and the power of darkness are yours' (Luke 22:53).

Peter's rash act was to later set him in jeopardy, contributing to the circumstances of his denial of Jesus. 'Now Simon Peter was standing and warming himself. So they said to him, 'You are not also one of his disciples, are you?' He denied it, and said, 'I am not.' One of the servants of the High Priest, being a relative of the one whose ear Peter cut off, said, 'Did I not see you in the garden with him?' Peter then denied it again, and immediately a rooster crowed' (John 18:25-27). Had Peter trusted in God the Father's care of his Son, these denials need perhaps never have occurred, because Peter would not have drawn such attention to himself by his display of swordsmanship in the Garden of Gethsemane.

But there is also another possible wrong interpretation of this saying of Jesus ('Do not resist an evil person'). That is, that injustice to others can go unchecked. Jesus is speaking here about offences against us singly as individuals. He is not commenting on what our attitude should be to others who are being unjustly oppressed. In plain fact, our attitude should be that of God, who himself is 'A father to the fatherless, a defender of widows' (Psalms 68:5 ANIV), and one who 'executes justice for the orphan and the widow' (Deuteronomy 10:18). God calls us to be like him in protecting the weak and the defenceless from evil. Had a bland pacifist attitude been adopted in the late 1930s, much of Europe might now be under Nazi rule, with many fewer Jews and other minority groups alive today.

40: 'If anyone wants to sue you and take your shirt, let him have your coat also.'

This verse literally reads, 'If anyone judging you receives from you your tunic, leave with them your cloak as well'. In other words, live in such a way that you can rely on your innocence and genuineness to be plain to all, such that you have no fear of being shown to have been in the wrong. Jewish law forbade depriving a man of his cloak, which was a necessary sleeping item. A willingness to pledge that as a sign of innocence was a strong indicator of a good testimony. The verse is not in any way teaching a repudiation of basic legal rights.

41: 'Whoever forces you to go one mile, go with him two.'

Israel was a Roman occupied country, and its inhabitants could be 'compelled' ('*angareuo*' - a term derived from Persian couriers who

46

had the power to impress men into their service) to assist, just as Simon of Cyrene was compelled to assist in carrying the cross of Christ: 'As they were coming out, they found a man of Cyrene named Simon, whom they pressed into service to bear his cross' (Matthew 27:32). Jesus is saying that if we are under an obligation to do something, we might as well do it with good grace. By extension, acting in bad grace is not good for us, or a good testimony of our lives.

42: 'Give to him who asks of you, and do not turn away from him who wants to borrow from you.'

Jesus upholds a generous spirit, one that recognizes that God has one's best interests at heart, and is not penny-pinching because we understand that it is impossible to out-give God.

43-45: 'You have heard that it was said, 'You shall love your neighbour and hate your enemy.' But I say to you, love your enemies and pray for those who persecute you, so that you may be sons of your Father who is in heaven; for he causes his sun to rise on the evil and the good, and sends rain on the righteous and the unrighteous.'

God's children should be about reflecting God's character and personality as their own. Love of enemies embodies this and is the point at which Christianity leaves all human religion behind. Being impossible to do naturally, it enters the realm of the supernatural, where God dwells, and is evidence of true spiritual change within.

46-48: 'For if you love those who love you, what reward do you have? Do not even the tax collectors do the same? If you greet only your brothers, what more are you doing than others? Do not even the Gentiles do the same? Therefore you are to be perfect, as your heavenly Father is perfect.'

Love ('*agapao*', from '*agape*') here means a deliberate commitment to put the well-being of others beyond one's own, even to the point of laying down one's own life, and so is perfectly embodied in Christ's sacrificial death. It is not to be confused with the friendship values of '*phileo*' which are practised to some degree by all towards their own, even tax gatherers (AV: 'publicans'), as Matthew well knew, having been one himself (Matthew 9:9-10), and the foreigners ('*ethnikos*') who did not embrace Judaism. Christ's goal is that we grow up into the character and likeness of his Father, into a mature son ('*telios*'- 'finished / complete / mature'),[55] as Jesus himself was, and so fulfil the Scripture: 'As he is, even so are we in this world' (1 John 4:17).

Chapter 6

1: 'Beware of practicing your righteousness before men to be noticed by them; otherwise you have no reward with your Father who is in heaven.'

The practice of using religion to show off is an old one and one which negates the future natural and spiritual blessings designed by God to follow the practices of godly spirituality. For the Jews, these acts of 'righteousness' (the passage can also be rendered as 'almsgiving') meant three things: giving, praying and fasting. Performing these from wrong motives, Jesus says, means that your reward is here and now only, and a poor one at that, being the approval of fickle men, with no reward in eternity.

2-4: 'So when you give to the poor, do not sound a trumpet before you, as the hypocrites do in the synagogues and in the streets, so that they may be honoured by men. Truly I say to you, they have their reward in full. But when you give to the poor, do not let your left hand know what your right hand is doing, so that your giving will be in secret; and your Father who sees what is done in secret will reward you.'

The Hebrew word for 'righteousness' and 'charitable giving' ('alms') is one and the same (*'tsedaqah'*), revealing the importance attached to it. The highest form of giving was held to be that where the giver gave without knowledge of the recipient, and vice versa. Ostentatious giving, for show (*'hupokrites'* here is 'hypocrite', meaning 'an actor') [56] may benefit the recipient but not, Christ tells us, the giver, who will receive no heavenly reward. God the Father is all-seeing and rewards the hidden (*'kruptos'*, meaning, 'in secret') acts of virtue because they reflect God's nature and practice of giving in hidden ways.

5-6: 'When you pray, you are not to be like the hypocrites; for they love to stand and pray in the synagogues and on the street corners so that they may be seen by men. Truly I say to you, they have their reward in full. But you, when you pray, go into your inner room, close your door and pray to your Father who is in secret, and your Father who sees what is done in secret will reward you.'

Acting as a show-off was not confined to giving. Prayer, the cornerstone of our relationship with God, can easily be aimed at impressing others and so cease to be a dialogue with a loving, heavenly Father. Jesus is emphasising here the importance of personal intimacy with God in prayer, as opposed to the importance of corporate intercession. Both play an important role in effectual prayer.

7-8: 'And when you are praying, do not use meaningless repetition as the Gentiles do, for they suppose that they will be heard for their many words. So do not be like them; for your Father knows what you need before you ask him.'

The prayers of those who lack trust in God as Father tend towards being babble prayers, a mantra of self-repetition which trusts in words rather than in relationship of love and trust. Because God the Father knows our every need, we can approach him in the knowledge that a lot of what we would otherwise have expressed, in terms of our personal needs, can be left unsaid.

9-13: 'Pray, then, in this way:
'Our Father who is in heaven,
Hallowed be your name.
Your kingdom come.
Your will be done,
On earth as it is in heaven.
Give us this day our daily bread.

50

And forgive us our debts, as we also have forgiven our debtors.
And do not lead us into temptation, but deliver us from evil.'
(For yours is the kingdom and the power and the glory forever.
Amen.)'

There can be nothing purer spiritually than the prayer of Jesus Christ. Jesus taught his followers this prayer in direct contrast with the long flowery religious prayers of the hypocrites (Matthew 5:5) and the repetitious babblings of the pagans' prayer (Matthew 6:7). His model prayer is addressed to a Father who already knows our needs before we have asked. The prayer is a series of natural 'child to father' expressions which do not stand in isolation, but are linked together, making the 'Lord's' prayer in reality a child's prayer, and it will be expanded upon here in such a way as to emphasise this.

9: 'Our Father who is in heaven '

Luke's version of the prayer (Luke 11:2) simply has 'Father'. There is no 'our' to dilute the personal, and no 'in heaven' to dilute the intimacy with distance. Jesus' will was to make the Father known: 'I have made you *(the Father)* known to them *(the disciples)*, and will continue to make you known in order that the love you have for me may be in them and that I myself may be in them' (John 17:26 - *italics mine*).

Jesus says, when we pray as his disciples (individually as well as corporately) say 'Father'. This one word sums up the essence of the relationship. Every line of this prayer is intended to be prayed as a child speaking personally to their (perfect) Father out of a secure, loving relationship. Jesus, the perfect Son, models the relationship for us.

9: 'Hallowed be your name'

'May your name be treated as holy.' Why? God the Father's name is the family's name, of which the one praying, and his or her brothers and sisters are part. Thus the prayer says: 'May your name, which is also my name and my brothers and sisters' family name, be set apart as holy and represent uniquely your essence and nature.' We have a responsibility to 'hallow' ('*hagiazo*' - 'sanctify') [57] the Lord's name. John 17:17 reads: 'Sanctify them by the truth; your word is truth'. And John 17:19: 'For them I sanctify myself, that they too may be truly sanctified.' To be set apart is to be in the world but not of the world.

God the Father is king over all, but his kingdom is not of this world. 'Jesus said, 'My kingdom is not of this world….my kingdom is from another place'' (John 18:36). The book of Revelation declares the future reality: 'The kingdom of the world has become the kingdom of our Lord and of his Christ, and he will reign forever and ever' (Revelation 11:15). As his children, we want to see our Father's rule and reign acknowledged, emphasised, recognized, responded to and submitted to as far as possible in the world we live in. We want to see our Father's rule and reign break into the chaos of our sin-filled society, and into our hectic and sometimes disoriented lives and set all things in right order. This leads directly into the next line:

10: 'Come, your kingdom. Be done, your will.'

These sayings are expressed as commands (in the imperative mood). We insist on seeing our Father's will done, not our own wills or anyone else's. Jesus said, 'I have food to eat you do not know about. My food is to do the will of him who sent me and to accomplish his work' (John 4:34). Doing the will of his Father was what really satisfied Jesus.

10: 'On earth, as it is in heaven.'

In heaven, Father's will is done. It is never thwarted or frustrated. It is simply done. As his children, we ask him to act in that way on earth. 'Simply do it, Father. Just do it. Do your will, your perfect, complete, fulfilling satisfying will for us and in us and around us.' The perfect

52

will of God begins in heaven and is then intended to be worked out on earth. In reality it is possible to miss out on God's perfect will and to settle for God's permitted will; the prayer is that the perfect be done.

11: 'Give us each day our daily bread.'

Here, '*Kata*' (Greek, meaning 'accordingly'), links this to the previous phrase ('your will be done'), hence the reference to bread / food. We ask for our 'daily bread' (AV), because Jesus taught that his 'food was to do the will of him who had sent him' (John 4:34). Jesus taught that God the Father is committed to supplying all our human needs, so the prayer carries a spiritual meaning for that which we truly need to satisfy us - his daily life-giving word to us. 'Today' ('*hemera*)' means a 24 hour day, and 'daily' is '*epiousios*', a word only ever seen three times - in Luke and Matthew's versions of the Lord's Prayer, and, much more recently, in an Egyptian accounting book, which gives us an understanding of its meaning. There are no other surviving written citations. W. E. Vine says on '*epiousios*' that some would derive the word from '*epi*', 'upon,' and '*eimi*', 'to go', as if to signify '(bread) present', i.e., 'sufficient bread', but this formation is questionable. The same objection applies to the conjecture, that it is derived from '*epi*', and '*ousia*', and signifies '(bread) for sustenance'. The more probable derivation is from '*epi*', and '*eimi*', 'to go,' '(bread) for going on', i.e., for the morrow and after, or (bread) coming (for us)'[58] - 'to be going on with'. History, in the form of an Egyptian accounting papyrus, indicates that this is correct. 'Daily bread' is therefore that which we need to be going on with in doing the will of God.

So verse 11 reads, in effect: 'Accordingly, give us today everything we need to be going on with in doing your will today.' This is exactly in line with what Jesus would go on to teach in Matthew 6:34 - 'Therefore do not worry about tomorrow, for tomorrow will worry about itself. Each day has enough trouble of its own', and in Matthew 6:32-33: 'The pagans run after all these things, and your heavenly Father knows that

53

you need them. But seek first his kingdom and his righteousness, and all these things will be given to you as well.' No child has to beg their father for their daily meals (rather, parents often have to repeatedly ask their children to come and eat what has been prepared for them!) Matthew 22:2-3 reflects this sad state of affairs. 'The kingdom of heaven is like a king who prepared a wedding banquet for his son. He sent his servants to those who had been invited to the banquet to tell them to come, but they refused to come.' We are far more reluctant to expect and receive provision than God the Father is to give it. The prayer is for everything we need to be going on with in doing the will of God, which God our Father has committed himself to provide for us at our point of need - which may not necessarily be when we would prefer to receive it!

12: 'Forgive us our sins / debts.'

'Sin' here is *'opheilema'* - another accounting term, on this occasion meaning a legal obligation or debt, in this case one accrued by our offending against God. The prayer asks that Father let us off the negative consequences of these debts. The prayer does not use the most common of the New Testament terms for sin (*'hamartia'* - 'to miss the mark'),[59] instead, it maintains an accounting theme.

12: 'As we forgive everyone who sins against us.'

'Forgive' as used here is still another accounting term, meaning to be 'let off' the negative consequences of an omission in payment or a debt. The person let off is an *'opheiletes'* - a debtor.[60] The prayer expresses the following: 'Father, we have an obligation to act towards those who have offended us (are indebted to us), in the same way that you, Father, have related to us - in free forgiveness. We can leave any unfinished business with you, knowing that your justice is perfect, and we can move on free of any resentment or bitterness, knowing that you, Father, are in complete control of our lives and can truly use everything for our good, including the sins of those who have sinned against us. We know Father, to receive your ongoing forgiveness, we must forgive others. Only through receiving your nature, as adopted members of your family, can we do this, Father. Thank you that in Christ we have received God the Father's own nature and disposition.'

13: 'And lead us not into temptation.'

Thus translated, this prayer makes nonsense of what we know about God. Jesus was led to a place of temptation and he is our example in everything. God promises to use all things for our good (Romans 8:28) and especially uses temptation and testing to strengthen us. Besides, God the Father does not tempt anyone, according to James 3:14, 'When tempted, no-one should say, 'God is tempting me.' For God cannot be tempted by evil, nor does he tempt anyone; but each one is tempted when, by his own evil desire, he is dragged away and enticed.' How can children of God the Father ask God not to do something that he does not do, and which he promises to turn to our strengthening and good when in fact it happens? The answer is found in the Greek text.

Whereas the English reads 'Lead us not into temptation', the preposition 'into' is duplicated in the Greek, literally saying, 'do not bring-into us into temptation'. The second 'into' here means a change for the person not merely of outward position, but of inward condition. 'To enter into the Kingdom of God' is much more than to stand within the Kingdom; it is to yield to its claims, to be dominated by it, to take its law as the law of one's being' (Canon A. Deane). The prayer is that we might not be brought *into* temptation, in the sense of into its power to change us so that we are mastered by it.

13: 'But deliver us from evil (the evil one)'.

One could expand the intention of this prayer as follows: 'Father, the evil one is your enemy and so is our enemy because we are a part of

55

your family. Father, we know that we can be attacked by him, and sometimes be tricked and persuaded to give in to his thoughts and plans for us instead of holding fast to your thoughts and plans for us. So, if we are ever dragged away and enticed (James 1:14), please rescue us! Father King, when he tries today to do that to us, rescue us from his influence. Do not allow temptation and evil to change us in any way, but keep us true to your nature, character and identity as our Father.' This type of situation is reflected in Luke 22:31-32, where Jesus says to Simon, 'Simon, Satan has asked to sift you as wheat. But I have prayed for you, Simon, that your faith may not fail. And when you have turned back, strengthen your brothers.'

Some later manuscripts of Matthew's Gospel add these words: 'For yours is the kingdom and the power and the glory forever. Amen' (Matthew 6:13).

This could be expressed as follows: 'Father, it's your kingdom that counts, it's your power that we need to do your will and see it coming into our lives and the lives of those around us and it is all to your praise and glory now and eternally. We agree with you and your will.'

14-15: 'For if ye forgive men their trespasses, your heavenly Father will also forgive you: But if ye forgive not men their trespasses, neither will your Father forgive your trespasses' (KJV).

This is presented as a simple statement of fact, and mirrors Jesus' teaching on forgiveness in Matthew 18:23-35. Choosing to remain in 'unforgiveness' is to choose to have our own sins remain unforgiven, and is a common trap of the enemy in keeping believers tied up and unfruitful.

16-18: 'Moreover when ye fast, be not as the hypocrites, of a sad countenance: for they disfigure their faces, that they may appear unto men to fast. Verily I say unto you, they have their reward. But thou, when thou fastest, anoint thine head, and wash thy face; that thou appear not unto men to fast, but unto thy Father which is in secret: and thy Father, which seeth in secret, shall reward thee openly' (KJV).

The principle that drawing attention to yourself and your own efforts reveals your own unworthy motives is again mentioned, this time in relation to fasting, and the practice of announcing the fact. Fasting for right motives brings a reward, as the prophet Isaiah had pointed out: 'Is it a fast like this which I choose, a day for a man to humble himself? Is it for bowing one's head like a reed, and for spreading out sackcloth and ashes as a bed? Will you call this a fast, even an acceptable day to the Lord? Is this not the fast which I choose, to loosen the bonds of wickedness, to undo the bands of the yoke, and to let the oppressed go free, and break every yoke? Is it not to divide your bread with the hungry and bring the homeless poor into the house; when you see the naked, to cover him; and not to hide yourself from your own flesh?' (Isaiah 58:5-7).

There are many spiritual benefits to fasting for the right motives, including as an extra weapon in our spiritual armouries as an adjunct to intercessory prayer.

19-21: 'Do not store up for yourselves treasures on earth, where moth and rust destroy, and where thieves break in and steal. But store up for yourselves treasures in heaven, where neither moth nor rust destroys, and where thieves do not break in or steal; for where your treasure is, there your heart will be also.'

Jesus is teaching that what is stored up and unused is effectively lost to the owner - no one derives any benefit and eventually corrosion and other forms of loss occur. 'Treasures in heaven' was a common phrase for the eternal rewards that could be obtained by putting resources to the service of God and possessing them instead of them possessing us. If the centre of the will - the heart - is focused on heaven and God's priorities, then we will use our resources in the service of heaven.

22-23: 'The eye is the lamp of the body. If your eyes are good, your whole body will be full of light. But if your eyes are bad, your whole body will be full of darkness. If then the light within you is darkness, how great is that darkness!' (ANIV).

Here Jesus utilises humour, as many Rabbis did when they were teaching, to make a point. The word for 'single' is '*haplous*', or '*haplotes*' in the noun form. These have two meanings, firstly 'single' (in the sense of a 'singleness of purpose' in performing acts of goodness) and secondly 'generous'. Jesus employs a humourous play-on-words to connect the idea that generosity reflects the attitude of God the Father and results in the spiritual blessing of inner light, if done with the right motives. The pun is concluded with a further humourous flourish - if the light-giver (in this instance, a generous attitude) is giving out darkness (because it is not working properly), how great is that person's (moral and spiritual) darkness! We might frequently be handicapped by the idea that giving generously leads to want, when in fact the opposite is true, because Jesus taught: 'Give, and it will be given to you. They will pour into your lap a good measure - pressed down, shaken together, and running over. For by your standard of measure it will be measured to you in return' (Luke 6:38). It is impossible to out-give God!

24: 'No one can serve two masters; for either he will hate the one and love the other, or he will be devoted to one and despise the other. You cannot serve God and wealth.'

Some years later, Jesus' half-brother James (who would have known him better than almost anyone) would teach that a 'double-minded man is unstable in all his ways' (James 1:8). Truly, the pursuit of wealth distracts from the pursuit of God like little else, communicating to God the Father that he cannot be trusted to provide for us, so we need to concentrate our efforts on providing for ourselves rather than seeking first his kingdom's purposes and right relationship with him.

25-26: 'For this reason I say to you, do not be worried about your life, as to what you will eat or what you will drink; nor for your body, as to what you will put on. Is not life more than food and the body more than clothing? Look at the birds of the air, that they do not sow, nor reap nor gather into barns, and yet your heavenly Father feeds them. Are you not worth much more than they?'

Worry and anxiety betray our underlying sense of lack of trust in God's care as Father. If we genuinely believe that God is more committed to providing for his children's basic needs than even the best earthly father, then we will have no trouble relaxing in the knowledge that he is in control and all we need to do is to behave responsibly (e.g. not jumping off temples, as Satan had tempted Christ to do) and trust that he will give us all we need. Hoarding too betrays a lack of trust, and actually jeopardises our possessions by exposing them to the risk of decay or bank collapse, etc. The birds seem to have no problem with stress and anxiety. Jesus reveals the fact that God the Father is an ardent bird-feeder; if that is his level of care for them, what must it be for those he says are made in his image?

27-30: 'And who of you by being worried can add a single hour to his life? And why are you worried about clothing? Observe how the lilies of the field grow; they do not toil nor do they spin, yet I say to you that not even Solomon in all his glory clothed himself like one of these. But if God so clothes the grass of the field, which is alive today and tomorrow is thrown into the furnace, will he not much more clothe you? You of little faith!'

Worrying has been medically shown to shorten lifespan, not lengthen it, nor add to our stature. In an age when clothing indicated wealth, not even the world's richest man, Solomon, could compete with the flowers of the field. Worrying over whether or not we will lack the things that God the Father himself has pledged to provide is a sad reflection on our lack of trust in him, to say nothing of it being a waste of time and bad for our health. 'Oh ye of little faith' has become a common phrase in the vernacular; however the first three words are not present in the Greek text. Jesus addresses his friends with the very affectionate term 'little faiths', knowing that one day they would be 'big faiths'.

31-34: 'Do not worry then, saying, 'What will we eat?' or 'What will we drink?' or 'What will we wear for clothing?' For the Gentiles eagerly seek all these things; for your heavenly Father knows that you need all these things. But seek first his kingdom and his righteousness, and all these things will be added to you. So do not worry about tomorrow; for tomorrow will care for itself. Each day has enough trouble of its own.'

Jesus sets out the basic needs (food, drink, clothing, shelter) that any competent father provides of his own volition without need of reminder. In fact, to keep asking for them 'as the pagans do' demonstrates a lack of trust in God the Father's competence and willingness to provide, which always greatly exceeds our willingness to receive. This attitude of trusting (faith) enables us to live daily life peacefully knowing that God watches over us to provide for us. As we go about our business of following him and seeking his rule and his ways, he promises to add to us all we need to do his will. One day at a time is all that is necessary - the challenges of each day are sufficient for that day and, while some fore-planning is necessary, it should be done prayerfully, without worry, allowing God to re-direct as required.

Chapter 7

1-5: 'Do not judge so that you will not be judged. For in the way you judge, you will be judged; and by your standard of measure, it will be measured to you. Why do you look at the speck that is in your brother's eye, but do not notice the log that is in your own eye? Or how can you say to your brother, 'Let me take the speck out of your eye,' and behold, the log is in your own eye? You hypocrite, first take the log out of your own eye, and then you will see clearly to take the speck out of your brother's eye.'

'Judge' here is '***krino***', meaning to 'pronounce a determining judicial decision',[61] often in a negative sense as opposed to an acquittal and not in the sense of making an observation that something is happening in contravention of God's word. Jesus told the Jewish crowd to 'not judge according to appearance, but judge with righteous judgement' (John 7:24). There is a place for objective assessment in line with what God has set down in his word. But if we sit in judgement over our brothers and sisters in Christ in a condemnatory manner then we take on a role contrary to that of our Heavenly Father who has said that in his Son that there is no condemnation (Romans 8:1). As Paul was to say, 'for in that which you judge another, you condemn yourself; for you who judge practice the same things' (Romans 2:1). God takes it upon himself to judge his children and he does so with loving fatherly discipline (1 Corinthians 11:32). While the elders of God's people have a role in judging problem situations (1 Corinthians 6:6) our personal role in judgement starts with ourselves and not others (what is the speck or log in our own eye? - Matthew 7:4). 'Log' here is '***dokos***', meaning a huge 'beam' [62] of the type used to support a roof, and is an example of Rabbinic hyperbole, whereby marked contrasts are used (often humourously) to make a point. Installing a roof beam would have been well within the working practice of '***tektons***' such as Jesus and his adoptive father Joseph - e.g. in the Temple sanctuary roof, 165 feet above the ground, and without the benefit of cranes for lifting.

6: 'Do not give what is holy to dogs, and do not throw your pearls before swine, or they will trample them under their feet, and turn and tear you to pieces.'

Dogs and swine were the two most unclean animals (from the Jewish perspective) found locally. Jesus' concern is that people who do not yet know him receive what they can digest, and that those who offer such spiritual food do so wisely with the benefit of both in mind.

7-11: 'Ask, and it will be given to you; seek, and you will find; knock, and it will be opened to you. For everyone who asks receives, and he who seeks finds, and to him who knocks it will be opened. Or what man is there among you who, when his son asks for a loaf, will give him a stone? Or if he asks for a fish, he will not give him a snake, will he? If you then, being evil, know how to give good gifts to your children, how much more will your Father who is in heaven give what is good to those who ask him!'

'Ask', 'seek' and 'knock' are all expressed in the present tense and the imperative mood, indicating that they are something we are commanded to continue doing, with the promise that we will succeed when we do. The promise is based on God's nature as Father, from which we derive our own desires to provide for children. 'How much more' sums up God's attitude and disposition to give - far greater even than ours is to receive. God's gifts are always 'good', yet we are often quick to believe the lie that somehow they may not be in our best interests.

12: 'In everything, therefore, treat people the same way you want them to treat you, for this is the Law and the Prophets.'

This famous 'Golden Rule' sums up and closes the Sermon on the Mount. Previously the sentiment had only been recorded in the negative form. Rabbi Hillel had said 'What is hateful to yourself, do to no other;

that is the whole Law, and the rest is commentary. Go and learn'.[63] Jesus breaks new ground spiritually by commanding a positive dimension of help which so inspired the building of hospitals and orphanages (for all people) that has marked out the Christian faith over the centuries. He uses a natural human benchmark - how would you yourself like to be treated in any situation - one in reach of us all without requiring any second guessing what others may or may not want or think about the situation. We are all able to consider what would be best for us, and that is what we are required to do and apply to others.

13-14: 'Enter through the narrow gate; for the gate is wide and the way is broad that leads to destruction, and there are many who enter through it. For the gate is small and the way is narrow that leads to life, and there are few who find it.'

The entrance to life is as narrow as the width of one man hanging from a cross, as opposed to the way to hell which is as wide as the Devil can make it. Jesus makes no comment regarding how many will enter eternal life as a direct result of the Father's mercy, only about the numbers who find eternal life following their own searching, who are indeed relatively few.

15-20: 'Beware of the false prophets, who come to you in sheep's clothing, but inwardly are ravenous wolves. You will know them by their fruits. Grapes are not gathered from thorn bushes nor figs from thistles, are they? So every good tree bears good fruit, but the bad tree bears bad fruit. A good tree cannot produce bad fruit, nor can a bad tree produce good fruit. Every tree that does not bear good fruit is cut down and thrown into the fire. So then, you will know them by their fruits.'

The image here is of those who arrive among God's people as those bringing the word of God but who are actually 'pseudo-prophets'. They can be detected by their inability to produce lasting quality in the fruit of their lives, evidenced by the wide trail of destruction that they leave behind them - the reason for their often moving on to new situations. Such people try and blend in with God's flock as a part of them but they have a taste for destructive behaviour which soon becomes evident, the negative consequences of which are difficult to hide.

21-23: 'Not everyone who says to me, 'Lord, Lord,' will enter the kingdom of heaven, but he who does the will of my Father who is in heaven will enter. Many will say to me on that day, 'Lord, Lord, did we not prophesy in your name, and in your name cast out demons, and in your name perform many miracles?' And then I will declare to them, 'I never knew you; depart from me, you who practice lawlessness.'

Jesus then looks forward to judgement day, when the wolves' (some of whom may even be able to exercise spiritual gifts) lack of relationship with the Father and his Son is made known openly. 'Practicing lawlessness' means to go about with a complete disregard for God's word, and the principles laid down therein. Only those who march to the beat of Christ's drum will enter the kingdom of heaven.

24-27: 'Therefore everyone who hears these words of mine and acts on them may be compared to a wise man who built his house on the rock. And the rain fell, and the floods came, and the winds blew and slammed against that house; and yet it did not fall, for it had been founded on the rock. Everyone who hears these words of mine and does not act on them will be like a foolish man who built his house on the sand. The rain fell, and the floods came, and the winds blew and slammed against that house; and it fell - and great was its fall.'

Jesus presents his teaching not as some sort of bolt-on addition that makes life go better, but as foundational, something requiring an action and a response in order to gain that which is essential for stability, and without which we will get found out by the trials of life.

28-29: 'When Jesus had finished these words, the crowds were amazed at his teaching; for he was teaching them as one having authority, and not as their Scribes.'

Scribes presented as faithfully as possible the reflections of the rabbis who had gone before them. They had no role in delivering new or original thought, only in re-hashing yesteryear's words and ideas. Their authority rested solely in the text they presented and the spiritual authority of the one who had delivered it: 'As Rabbi So and So said…'. Jesus came with the spiritual authority of the one who delivered the Torah to Moses and who wrote the commands of God on the stone tablets with his own finger (Exodus 31:18), as well as societal and legal authority. The contrast that Matthew is drawing is not mainly in terms of authority (both the Scribes, and Jesus as a Doctor of the Law, carried legitimate legal authority), but in terms of what was taught. Jesus deviated from the Scribes in presenting teaching that was proclaimed to be 'new' (Mark 1:27), whereas the Scribes exclusively taught what was old and had been passed down to them from previous generations of scholars.

Chapter 8

1-3: 'When Jesus came down from the mountain, large crowds followed him. And a leper came to him and bowed down before him, and said, 'Lord, if you are willing, you can make me clean.' Jesus stretched out his hand and touched him, saying, 'I am willing; be cleansed.' And immediately his leprosy was cleansed.'

Jesus' original, powerful and authoritative teaching drew huge popular interest. His ability to heal was another massive draw in a world where sickness and death were commonplace. Leprosy, a disease where the mycobacterium Leprae (which robs the nerve endings of their ability to detect the pain warnings necessary for protection against injury and disease) was commonplace and the Jewish Law provided for the segregation of all those with a priest-confirmed diagnosis. It was strictly illegal for a leper to approach within six feet of a non-leper, something the leper recklessly ignores - the Greek for bowed down being *'proskuneo'*, meaning 'to come towards and kiss',[64] in the manner of a dog licking it's master's hand. This, combined with his use of *'Kurios'*, meaning 'Master' and 'Lord',[65] indicates that he had correctly deduced Jesus' true identity, namely God in human form, and is the basis for his confident expression of trust in Christ's powers. Being ever-willing, and in line with Father's will, Jesus renders himself ritually and legally unclean by healing via a touch and not a word of command. He thereby clearly demonstrated his authority over the mycobacterium as well as the laws prohibiting contact with lepers - contact with him made them clean and healthy rather that vice-versa.

4: 'And Jesus said to him, 'See that you tell no one; but go, show yourself to the priest and present the offering that Moses commanded, as a testimony to them.'

To re-enter society and so avoid the need to return to the infectious proximity of other lepers a priest's certificate of healing (Leviticus 14)

66

was required, something that, given the then untreatable nature of leprosy had very rarely, if ever, happened - another Messianic sign for the priests to think about. Jesus' ability to move freely was already becoming limited, and further publicity is discouraged, lest the more hot-headed members of the public should seek to make him king by force, something that occurred after the 'feeding of the five thousand' described in John chapter 6.

5-9: 'And when Jesus entered Capernaum, a centurion came to him, imploring him, and saying, 'Lord, my servant is lying paralyzed at home, fearfully tormented. Jesus said to him, I will come and heal him.' But the centurion said, 'Lord, I am not worthy for you to come under my roof, but just say the word, and my servant will be healed. For I also am a man under authority, with soldiers under me; and I say to this one, 'Go!' and he goes, and to another, 'Come!' and he comes, and to my slave, 'Do this!' and he does it.'

The backbone of Rome's army, centurions did not normally have much time or inclination to look much to the needs of those servants whom the Greek philosopher Aristotle had described as 'living tools'.[66] This centurion was evidently different, given the language that he used - 'fearfully' is *deinos* meaning 'grievously' or 'terribly' [67] suffering in the centurion's own home, not tossed aside as some did with useless slaves. Luke's account (Luke 7: 1-10) records that the slave was 'highly regarded', as was the centurion himself, for the local Jewish elders came personally to entreat Jesus to perform the healing, citing the centurion's love, piety and generosity towards the Jewish community in building their synagogue. Jesus is actually on his way to becoming even further legally unclean by entering a Gentile's house when he is stopped by the centurion's words regarding the nature of authority. The centurion demonstrates amazing spiritual understanding, not only of who Jesus was but of the fact that Jesus himself was operating under his Father's authority, and so whatever was spoken in his name would be done, even at a remote distance. Luke 7:9 records, 'Now when Jesus heard this, he marvelled at him, and turned and said to the crowd that was following him, 'I say to you, not even in Israel have I found such great faith.' High praise indeed! It is because God the Father delegates his authority to his children to exercise that we may have confidence that whatever we ask in his name (i.e. on his behalf, in accordance with his wishes) will be done for us (John 14:14). This was something that the centurion appears to have had a very good working grasp of.

14-17: 'When Jesus came into Peter's home, he saw his mother-in-law lying sick in bed with a fever. He touched her hand, and the fever left her; and she got up and waited on him. When evening came, they brought to him many who were demon-possessed; and he cast out the spirits with a word, and healed all who were ill. This was to fulfill what was spoken through Isaiah the prophet: 'He himself took our infirmities and carried away our diseases."

Jesus' confidence in who he was and the fact that he was not under the ceremonial law meant that having touched a leper he is now quite willing and able to touch a mother-in-law without rendering her unclean, necessary given her role in preparing their meal! The day is likely to have been a Sabbath as the people wait until evening before bringing the more agitated and extreme stretcher-type cases to Jesus to heal. Matthew, speaking to a predominantly Jewish audience, draws out the prophetic connection to Isaiah 53:4 which heralded the merciful acts of love performed by the sacrificial Messiah-servant. 'Surely our griefs he himself bore, and our sorrows he carried; yet we ourselves esteemed him stricken, smitten of God, and afflicted. But he was pierced through for our transgressions, he was crushed for our iniquities; the chastening for our well-being fell upon him, and by his scourging we are healed.'

18-20: 'Now when Jesus saw a crowd around him, he gave orders to depart to the other side of the sea. Then a Scribe came and said to him, 'Teacher, I will follow you wherever, you go. Jesus said to him, 'The foxes have holes and the birds of the air have nests, but the Son of Man has nowhere to lay his head."

Always sure to be following God the Father's agenda and not the crowd's, Jesus leaves. But some want to join him! The Scribes were very important teachers of the Jewish Law. They occupied positions of great status in Jewish society, and were generally wealthy as though they could not be paid for the advice they gave, many gave gifts to them as signs of piety, even leaving homes and land to them. Jesus describes some of them in Luke 20:47: 'Beware of the Scribes, who like to walk around in long robes, and love respectful greetings in the market places, and chief seats in the synagogues and places of honour at banquets, who devour widows' houses, and for appearance's sake offer long prayers. These will receive greater condemnation.'

Jesus was an extremely well respected Rabbi and Doctor of the Jewish Law, hence the Scribe's offer of himself as a disciple. Wealthy people followed Jesus, as we can see from the example of Joseph of Arimathea, but it was not easy for them. Jesus travelled on a very demanding schedule, visiting the many towns and cities of Israel. Luke 10:1 records: 'Now after this the Lord appointed seventy others, and sent them in pairs ahead, of him to every city and place where he himself was going to come.'

Discipleship with Jesus would not have been easy for a Scribe to participate in as they were used to comfortable lifestyles. Jesus tells him that while the female foxes have dens for their young and to which they regularly return, as indeed do birds to their nests where their young are, the Son of Man has no such regular billet or resting place for his own head. Jesus must have slept in hundreds of homes belonging to various ones of his supporters and indeed in summer, probably in the open air too while travelling through Israel. That Jesus had a home base in Capernaum can be seen from Mark 2:1, which says, 'When he had come back to Capernaum several days afterward, it was heard that he was at home.' But he had little time to spend there, because of the travel pressures of his ministry.

21-22: 'Another of the disciples said to him, 'Lord, permit me first to go and bury my father.' But Jesus said to him, 'Follow me, and allow the dead to bury their own dead.''

'Burying your father' in that society did not mean that he had just died and was awaiting burial, because bodies in such hot climates were buried fairly immediately. It meant the duties and responsibilities of an oldest or only son in the care of his father. Jesus' response is in line with his teaching on the tension between human and spiritual relationship ties that can develop within families when people decide to follow Christ in a whole-hearted way and that were present in his own family. For example, in Mark 3:32-35: ''Behold, your mother and your brothers are outside looking for you.'' Answering them, he said, ''Who are my mother and my brothers?'' Looking about at those who were sitting around him, he said, ''Behold my mother and my brothers! For whoever, does the will of God, he is my brother and sister and mother.'' Natural family ties must never be allowed to interfere with the ties associated with God's fatherhood.

23-27: 'When he got into the boat, his disciples followed him. And behold, there arose a great storm on the sea, so that the boat was being covered with the waves; but Jesus himself was asleep. And they came to him and woke him, saying, 'Save us, Lord; we are perishing!' He said to them, 'Why are you afraid, you men of little faith?' Then he got up and rebuked the winds and the sea, and it became perfectly calm. The men were amazed, and said, 'What kind of a man is this, that even the winds and the sea obey him?''

70

In Luke's account of this event (Luke 8:22), Jesus prefixes the incident with the instruction to his disciples that they would go over to the other side of Lake Galilee. Drowning was not mentioned as being part of their itinerary. But when the strong west wind funneled through the surrounding hills creating storm conditions that Matthew, a local, describes as a '*seismos*' (normally translated as 'earthquake'), creating huge waves that covered the boat, even the experienced lake fishermen among the disciples panic and wake Jesus who is sleeping to call on him to save them. When Jesus calms the lake with a word, the disciples, Luke records, find their fear of drowning being replaced with the wonder of who exactly it was who could successfully command the wind and waves.

28-34: 'When he came to the other side into the country of the Gadarenes, two men who were demon-possessed met him as they were coming out of the tombs. They were so extremely violent that no one could pass by that way. And they cried out, saying, 'What business do we have with each other, Son of God? Have you come here to torment us before the time?' Now there was a herd of many swine feeding at a distance from them. The demons began to entreat him, saying, 'If you are going to cast us out, send us into the herd of swine.' And he said to them, 'Go!' And they came out and went into the swine, and the whole herd rushed down the steep bank into the sea and perished in the waters. The herdsmen ran away, and went to the city and reported everything, including what had happened to the demoniacs. And behold, the whole city came out to meet Jesus; and when they saw him, they implored him to leave their region.'

Jesus arrives at the Roman controlled region of the Decapolis (ten cities) in time to meet two men who evil spirits held in their power, giving them a supernaturally violent strength. Their reaction to Jesus is abrupt, bordering on the rude - they use a common Hebrew idiom, equivalent to 'what's it to you?' This is found in 2 Samuel 16:10, 'But

71

the king said, 'What have I to do with you, O sons of Zeruiah? If he curses, and if the Lord has told him, 'Curse David,' then who shall say, 'Why have you done so?'' Jesus himself used the phrase to his mother when being told about the wine shortage at the wedding in Cana (John 2: 1-11). Essentially the demons are saying, through the men, 'What's up with you, Son of God? Don't you know it's not the time yet for you to be interfering with us and tormenting us? Huh?' While they understood that hell is a place of torment for them, not just unbelievers, they had not yet become acquainted with the early, pre-final fulfillment taste of the Kingdom that the arrival of grace and truth personified in a human body was bringing. Any time was now right for demon removal.

The look on Jesus' face must have spoken volumes that Matthew has not included in this summary description. The demons quickly wise-up to their impending demise and negotiate a compromise - 'let's take out those pigs, the unclean for the unclean'. Jesus confines himself to one word of command - there is no dialoguing - 'Go!' As the pigs drown, the local Gentile pig-herding townsfolk arrive to express their reaction. They might have been grateful that the region was now safe from demonically inspired attack or indeed happy that the men are restored to their right minds, but in fact Luke records that they were 'overcome with fear' and begged Jesus to leave the region (Luke 8:37). While they were unable to cope with Jesus, and so implored him to leave, Jesus did not leave them without witnesses to his love. While they were begging him to go, the newly freed men were begging him to take them with him. But Jesus had another role in mind for them - 'Return home and tell how much God has done for you.' Jesus thereby commissioned the first Gentile evangelists to the Gentiles.

Chapter 9

1-8: 'Getting into a boat, Jesus crossed over the sea and came to his own city. And they brought to him a paralytic lying on a bed. Seeing their faith, Jesus said to the paralytic, 'Take courage, son; your sins are forgiven.' And some of the Scribes said to themselves, 'This fellow blasphemes.' And Jesus, knowing their thoughts said, 'Why are you thinking evil in your hearts? Which is easier, to say, 'Your sins are forgiven,' or to say, 'Get up, and walk'? But so that you may know that the Son of Man has authority on earth to forgive sins' - then he said to the paralytic, 'Get up, pick up your bed and go home.' And he got up and went home. But when the crowds saw this, they were awestruck, and glorified God, who had given such authority to men.'

Jesus had a home base in Capernaum (Matthew 9:33 and John 2:12). Mark's account of this miracle underlines Jesus' popularity at this stage in his ministry - the house was full to bursting (Mark 2:4). The 'paralytic' man would have been a hemi or quadriplegic who required a stretcher to move him, carried by four men, traditionally described as his friends. This passage has a special significance because whereas the word 'son' occurs ninety-nine times in the New Testament, it is only used by Jesus to an individual on one particular occasion - the healing of the paralytic. This raises a question - where was this man's family? None of the Gospel's accounts of this miracle mentions them. In Israel then, as in much of the world today, the responsibility of care for an invalid fell to the family, yet there is nothing to indicate that they were present or had even been involved in sending him.

The likelihood is that his own family had been unable (perhaps through poverty) or unwilling to care for his disability, and so had passed his care over to others. If so it was most probably to a Jewish religious order such as the Essenes, who were noted for their care of the sick, to do what the family were unable or unwilling to do, despite it being their responsibility. Josephus records of the Essenes: 'They have no one certain city, but many of them dwell in every city... there is, in every city where they live, one appointed particularly to take care of strangers...' [68] This being the case, the man is likely to have faced a painful estrangement from his family and especially his parents.

Jesus sees the faith of the friends (the Essenes would have been familiar with Jesus' ministry and shared his concerns over the corruption of the Temple worship) who had put their trust in him and his ability to heal. He rewards their trust, and makes no allusion to their having dug a hole in his roof which Mark describes but which Matthew makes no reference to. Jesus was, after all, a type of architect / builder or construction engineer, as well as being a teacher, so to fix his own roof was not a problem for him.

Jesus speaks to the man, and every word appears to have been chosen carefully. 'Son': (Greek: *'tetron'*) means 'child of a family'. The man had no natural family around him, probably because of his disability, and so Jesus meets him at the point of his deepest need, deeper even than the need of forgiveness, the need for fatherhood and sonship. This was the one word that the man had stopped hearing and stopped being addressed by, because of the painful estrangement from his family that his disability had occasioned. 'You are a son. You are a family member!' Jesus never said this in the Gospel records, to any other living person - it is only used in parables. God the Father had reserved it for this moment: this 'one' among the ninety-nine, this lost one, this lost son.

2: 'Your sins are forgiven'

Many disabled people carry a burden of guilt for the difficulties they cause others in caring for them. In Israel at this time, there was also a commonly held notion that sickness and disability was linked to sin - a punishment for some wrongdoing, or for 'being bad'. Many disabled people see themselves as being punished by God for something. All need forgiveness, but this man needed to be released from his particular burden of guilt - 'Your sins are forgiven.' The second most pressing personal issue is dealt with. Jesus could have said, straight away, 'Be healed.' He didn't, because the man had two deeper needs - to know he was a son, and to know he was forgiven, and these had to be addressed first.

Mark enlarges: 'But there were certain of the Scribes sitting there.' These men were experts in the Mosaic Law. They had come, not because they wanted to follow Jesus, but in all likelihood had been sent to look for irregularities in his teaching which they could latch onto as a means of accusing him of unorthodoxy or heresy, and so to then attack and disqualify him from the role of Doctor of the Law that he held. They were not likely to have been there all at the same time by accident; they would have been there by arrangement, something that Jesus must have been party to and was continuing to cooperate with by teaching in their presence. Jesus is quite comfortable with their presence in his home, despite their enmity towards him as one who did not uphold their own Mishnaic interpretations of the Law, which Jesus referred to as 'rules taught by men' (Mark 7:7 - NIV).

Jesus is aware of why they are there - to find out an error and disqualify or disbar him from that office as a false teacher - a heretic. Yet, they were unsuccessful. On no occasion do we find it recorded that Jesus' teaching is assailed, quite the reverse. His miraculous acts and deliverance ministry were held up for scrutiny ('some of them said, "He casts out demons by Beelzebul, the ruler of the demons"' - Luke 11:15), but never his teaching, which was always held in high honour, even by his enemies. In saying 'Your sins are forgiven', Jesus appears to score a spectacular own goal. He hands the Scribes, on a plate, a golden opportunity to disbar him from office, ruin his reputation as a teacher within the Jewish community, and even get him killed.

3: 'And some of the Scribes said to themselves, 'This fellow blasphemes.'

Their reaction would have been one of triumph - 'It's blasphemy! Now we can stone him! We've heard it - with witnesses!' This is their reasoning 'in their hearts' (verse 4). Because only God can forgive sins, and this paralytic in the care of the religious order could not have sinned against Jesus personally - Jesus was standing in the place of God, which was illegal under the Law and meant the death penalty.

4-5: 'And Jesus, knowing their thoughts said, 'Why are you thinking evil in your hearts? Which is easier, to say, 'Your sins are forgiven,' or to say, 'Get up, and walk'?'

Mark's account (2:8) states that: 'Immediately Jesus, aware in his spirit that they were reasoning that way within themselves, said to them, "Why are you reasoning about these things in your hearts?"'. 'Immediately' God the Father spoke to Jesus ('in his spirit') about their attitude, because it was crucial that the issue got addressed. Jesus asks: 'Why reason you those things in your heart?' 'Let me give you an illustration,' is the gist of Jesus' response. Matthew records: 'Which is easier to say - 'someone's sins are forgiven' (*you can't tell*) or, 'get up and walk?' (*words in italics mine*). Obviously, it's the first. Only God can say and do the second, because miraculous power is needed. Anyone can 'say' the first. It might be blasphemy, or not, if the person who says it is actually God. But only God could say, and perform, such a miracle of healing as this.

6: 'But so that you may know that the Son of Man has authority on earth to forgive sins' - then he said to the paralytic, 'Get up, pick up your bed and go home.'

'You' meaning the teachers of the Law and Scribes - Jesus' enemies, who opposed him and were trying to get him disbarred and killed. Jesus

76

is saying: 'That you may have an opportunity to receive what I have come to give - that you may be able to get beyond your own natural prejudices and into the eternal life of the kingdom of my Father.'

This would have been something equally amazing, for the man himself. Not, 'go back to the house you have come from' or 'return with your friends'. Rather, 'Go your way to your house / home' (Greek: '*oikos*', 'the place your family and father live').[69] Go to your own home, where your own father lives, to the place that you have been separated from by your disability. Jesus restores the man, not only to full health and spiritual wholeness, but to his own natural family.

7-8: 'And he got up and went home. But when the crowds saw this, they were awestruck, and glorified God, who had given such authority to men.'

The man, being healed, immediately obeys Jesus. Mark (2:12) tells us: 'And *immediately*, he rose and went forth.' No hesitation - he probably ran home to his father. The people watching 'were all amazed and glorified God' - even, and perhaps especially, his opponents. This miracle changed their personal attitudes toward Christ completely. While others of the religious leaders continued to oppose Jesus and his ministry, those present, including these men, praised God saying, 'We never saw anything like this!' (Greek: '*oida*', meaning 'to discover something' - 'to perceive something for the first time.') [70] They had discovered something about Jesus that changed their whole lives.

9-13: 'As Jesus went on from there, he saw a man called Matthew, sitting in the tax collector's booth; and he said to him, 'Follow me!' And he got up and followed him. Then it happened that as Jesus was reclining at the table in the house, behold, many tax collectors and sinners came and were dining with Jesus and his disciples. When the Pharisees saw this, they said to his disciples, 'Why is your Teacher eating with the tax collectors and sinners?' But when Jesus heard this, he said, 'It is not those who are healthy who need a physician, but those who are sick. But go and learn what this means: 'I desire compassion, and not sacrifice,' for I did not come to call the righteous, but sinners.'

Just as the film director, Hitchcock, would later do in his productions, so Matthew appears in his own gospel. Revenue collectors for the harsh Roman authorities, men like Matthew (his Jewish name was Levi) were highly unpopular with the general public. They would charge more than was strictly necessary, pocketing the difference, or overlooking certain non-payments in return for a higher fee. Jesus, instead of seeing a villain, sees a prime candidate for the love and mercy of God ('where sin abounds, there grace abounds' - Romans 5:20), and is happy to eat with him and his 'sinner' friends. 'Sinner' was the shorthand term for the many Jews who had not studied and so did not attempt to keep all the minutiae of the demands of the Oral Law on daily life. Grace almost invariably ends up being criticized by the more legalistically minded religious folk, and it was thus with Christ. He cites God the Father's job description for his ministry, affirming that he was bringing spiritual medicine mixed with a good dose of compassion for the recipients.

14-17: 'Then the disciples of John came to him, asking, 'Why do we and the Pharisees fast, but your disciples do not fast?' And Jesus said to them, 'The attendants of the bridegroom cannot mourn as long as the bridegroom is with them, can they? But the days will come when the bridegroom is taken away from them, and then they will fast. But no one puts a patch of unshrunk cloth on an old garment; for the patch pulls away from the garment, and a worse tear results. Nor do people put new wine into old wineskins; otherwise the wineskins burst, and the wine pours out and the wineskins are ruined; but they put new wine into fresh wineskins, and both are preserved.'

The Pharisees were not alone in their legalistic critique. John the Baptist's disciples are curious as to why the austerity of John (Jesus' cousin, their mothers being 'kinswomen' - Luke 1:36), had not rubbed off onto the younger of the two ministers. Jesus appeals to common sense. Reason one was that fasting was most commonly associated with mourning for sin - hard to do in the presence of a joyful Saviour - however the day for fasting as an adjunct to prayer in spiritual warfare was certainly coming. Reason two was that the day of the 'new skins' (the new natures given by trust in Christ's saving sacrifice and inhabited by his very own Spirit) had yet to arrive. The 'new wine' of the Spirit requires a new nature ('skin') to contain it. One with sufficient flexibility within itself to adapt to the new thing that God was doing.

18-26: 'While he was saying these things to them, a synagogue official came and bowed down before him, and said, 'My daughter has just died; but come and lay your hand on her, and she will live.' Jesus got up and began to follow him, and so did his disciples. And a woman who had been suffering from a hemorrhage for twelve years, came up behind him and touched the fringe of his cloak; for she was saying to herself, 'If I only touch his garment, I will get well.' But Jesus turning and seeing her said, 'Daughter, take courage; your faith has made you well.' At once, the woman was made well. When Jesus came into the official's house, and saw the flute-players and the crowd in noisy disorder, he said, 'Leave; for the girl has not died, but is asleep.' And they began laughing at him. But when the crowd had been sent out, he entered and took her by the hand, and the girl got up. This news spread throughout all that land.'

Jesus never rushed - he always moved in peaceful accordance to his Father's schedule. When answering an emergency call to the sickbed (and ultimately deathbed) of a *'thugater'* ('a pre-pubertal girl'),[71] and being interrupted by an elderly lady with a problem of the same

79

duration as the age of the girl (twelve years - Luke 8:42), he is not at all put out. Rather, he takes the opportunity to pass an underlying and almost subliminal message of faith, trust and hope to the increasingly anxious father by addressing the woman with the title 'Daughter, (*'thugater'*), your faith has healed you'. Were those words echoing in Jairus' (the father - Luke 8:41) mind when he was confronted with the fact of her death and heard Jesus repeat, almost verbatim, the exact same words again to him? Luke 8:50: 'Do not be afraid (*take courage*), only believe (*have faith*), and she (*your* '*thugater*') will be made well.' He would have needed the encouragement they gave, with the semi-professional mourners in attendance and playing for all they were worth. What fees did they miss out on when Jesus curtly dismissed them only to re-appear with a living '*thugater*', one recently fortified by a meal? (Luke 8:55).

27-31: 'As Jesus went on from there, two blind men followed him, crying out 'Have mercy on us, Son of David!' When he entered the house, the blind men came up to him, and Jesus said to them, 'Do you believe that I am able to do this?' They said to him, 'Yes, Lord.' Then he touched their eyes, saying, 'It shall be done to you according to your faith.' And their eyes were opened. And Jesus sternly warned them: 'See that no one knows about this!' But they went out and spread the news about him throughout all that land.'

Neonatal eye infections are a common cause of blindness in an antibiotic-free world. These two men deliberately call Jesus by a Messianic title, having no doubt been informed of his teaching and his miraculous powers. Jesus asks whether they trust him, using the imperative mood in the Greek, meaning he is commanding a response, which they happily give in simplicity ('Yes, Lord') and so receive their sight with no fuss and with the usual warning about no publicity. So euphoric were they that they just could not help themselves - they would have been known locally as beggars and while their new-found sight would have been hard to disguise, concealing the identity of their healer might least have been attempted. Freedom of movement was becoming harder for Jesus to maintain.

32-35: 'As they were going out, a mute, demon-possessed man was brought to him. After the demon was cast out, the mute man spoke; and the crowds were amazed, and were saying, 'Nothing like this has ever been seen in Israel.' But the Pharisees were saying, 'He casts out the demons by the ruler of the demons.' Jesus was going through all the cities and villages, teaching in their synagogues and proclaiming the gospel of the kingdom, and healing every kind of disease and every kind of sickness.'

The mute are not excluded either. This case was the work of an evil spirit, perhaps the easiest to deal with, as they were obliged to leave upon Jesus' word of command. The Pharisees are quick to counter the crowd's pleasure with their soon to become familiar argument that Jesus is playing for the wrong team - using demonic powers himself - an absurd argument that Jesus exposes as fallacious in Matthew 12:25-28. 'Any kingdom divided against itself is laid waste; and any city or house divided against itself will not stand. If Satan casts out Satan, he is divided against himself; how then will his kingdom stand? If I by Beelzebul cast out demons, by whom do your sons cast them out? For this reason, they will be your judges. But if I cast out demons by the Spirit of God, then the kingdom of God has come upon you.' The 'gospel of the Kingdom' - such as faith (trust), grace, salvation, God's Fatherly care, etc, is proclaimed accompanied by the miraculous behaviour of the One whose Kingdom is being proclaimed, resulting in healing in every instance where the Kingdom's plan for wholeness had been disrupted. Acts 10:38 records that Jesus 'went about doing good and healing all who were oppressed by the devil, for God was with him.' The range of healings undertaken had no limit, demonstrating his Father's power and authority and accompanying the 'good news' being heralded from that kingdom.

81

36-38: 'Seeing the people, he felt compassion for them, because they were distressed and dispirited like sheep without a shepherd. Then he said to his disciples, 'The harvest is plentiful, but the workers are few. Therefore beseech the Lord of the harvest to send out workers into his harvest.'

Giving up his eternal omnipresence at the point of the incarnation must have been hard for Jesus, the second Person of the Trinitarian Godhead, especially when he saw the scope of the need. The harvest was certainly plentiful. The Jewish prophets (including John the Baptist) who had come before Christ had well prepared the hearts and minds of the people. However he was only one man and his friends were of limited number as well. His solution, as with all needs, was to ask his disciples to join together in asking his Father to meet it.

Chapter 10

1: 'Jesus summoned his twelve disciples and gave them authority over unclean spirits, to cast them out, and to heal every kind of disease and every kind of sickness.'

Jesus worked most closely with three of his disciples (Peter, James and John) within his group of twelve apostles, then with a group of seventy other disciples (Luke 10:1). Because Jesus was fully submitted to God the Father's authority, he was perfectly able to exercise it, and also to pass it on to those whom his Father God directed. Authority is given for those areas God has given someone responsibility for. It is not a sort of blanket covering over whatever we have decided to do, and we cannot just summon it up as our right to use however we see fit. Jesus said that all authority had been given to him (Matthew 28:18), hence we have none without him having explicitly given it to us for things we have responsibility for as stewards - our own bodies, our work, families, homes, specific service tasks etc. The twelve's authority now extended to evil spirits, sickness and disease - before, it had not done so.

2-4: 'Now the names of the twelve apostles are these: The first, Simon, who is called Peter, and Andrew his brother; and James the son of Zebedee, and John his brother; Philip and Bartholomew; Thomas and Matthew the tax collector; James the son of Alphaeus, and Lebbaeus, whose surname was Thaddaeus; Simon the Zealot, and Judas Iscariot, the one who betrayed him.'

Jesus' choice of twelve makes for interesting reading. Made after a night spent talking to his Father in prayer (Luke 6:12), there were apparently no scholars as might have been expected in a conventional Rabbinic school of disciples. Instead we find an ex-tax collector (a former Roman appointee and quisling, the author of this Gospel). He is rubbing shoulders with a revolutionary Zealot activist named Simon, who, just a matter of months earlier, might happily have killed a tax-collector. That they could now work together is evidence of the amazing power that Jesus had to change people's lives. Many of the others were men who had in all likelihood grown up with Jesus - James and John were cousins on Jesus' mother's side; Peter and Andrew were partners in a fishing business and friends of theirs and hence, in all probability, of Jesus also from childhood. Phillip was an old friend of Peter and Andrew from Bethsaida (literally 'house of fishing'), a village on the north-east shore of Lake Galilee.

Judas (from Kerioth in Southern Judea) was a man motivated by love of his country's freedom and also by money. He seems to have wanted Jesus to take political action against the Romans; for him a dead Messiah was of no use (Mark 14: 6-10). That Jesus made him treasurer of the group contains an insight into dealing with temptation - the tree of the knowledge of good and evil was always before Adam and Eve, in the 'middle of the garden' (Genesis 2:9). The fact that it was not out of reach meant that they had a daily choice to make in terms of not eating of its fruit, in obedience to God's command.

There was another Judas too - Luke 6:16 refers to Judas the son of James, also known as Labbaeus. He is thought to have been the author of the book of Jude. Thaddaeus is a derivation of Tadda, Aramaic for 'large hearted',[72] hence a nickname for a close friend. Then there was James (son of Alphaeus) an honest man; one ready to ask for clarification (John 14:22). Thomas was a man who seems to have worn his heart on his sleeve and was so deeply affected by Jesus' betrayal and death that he could not risk being let down a second time by the other disciples' story of resurrection, which he did not at first believe.

In Matthew, Mark, Luke, and Acts, Bartholomew is mentioned as one of the twelve, but does not figure at all. Conversely, in John 21:1, Nathanael is listed, but Bartholomew is not. This has led some scholars to postulate that Bartholomew, meaning 'son of Talmai' (Aramaic for 'farmer') was his family name, with Nathaniel (from the Hebrew *'natan'* ('given') and *'El'* ('God') - meaning 'gift from God', being his given or familiar name.

5-10: 'These twelve Jesus sent out after instructing them: 'Do not go in the way of the Gentiles, and do not enter any city of the Samaritans; but rather go to the lost sheep of the house of Israel. And as you go, preach, saying, 'The kingdom of heaven is at hand.' Heal the sick, raise the dead, cleanse the lepers, cast out demons. Freely you received, freely give. Do not acquire gold, or silver, or copper for your money belts, or a bag for your journey, or even two coats, or sandals, or a staff; for the worker is worthy of his support.'

Jesus' instructions encompass their target audience (the Jews). His message was centered on making God's kingdom visible through a variety of miracles, and featured a generosity and simplicity based on freedom from unnecessary possessions, thereby demonstrating an on-going reliance on God the Father to provide for them.

11-15: 'And whatever city or village you enter, inquire who is worthy in it, and stay at his house until you leave that city. As you enter the house, give it your greeting. If the house is worthy, give it your blessing of peace. But if it is not worthy, take back your blessing of peace. Whoever does not receive you, nor heed your words, as you go out of that house or that city, shake the dust off your feet. Truly I say to you, it will be more tolerable for the land of Sodom and Gomorrah in the Day of Judgment than for that city.'

Jesus tells his disciples to lodge with like-minded people and build from there. After 'saluting' the occupants, they are to give it their *'shalom'* - their impartation of peace, wholeness and general blessing. That would be a tenable reality, one that the household would lose if they did not receive the messenger favourably. Rejection will occur, Jesus warns. Luke (9:5) adds that 'shaking off the dust' is a 'testimony against them'. The Greek here is '*marturion*' meaning 'witness' [73] and the word from which 'martyr' is derived - a witness unto death. That life is not always a bed of roses for the disciple is amply illustrated by this passage! But while life may get rough for the disciple, it will pale into insignificance compared to what is in store for those who persistently reject Christ. Sodom and Gomorrah were judged severely and they had not had the benefit of Jesus Christ's words.

16-20: 'Behold, I send you out as sheep in the midst of wolves; so be shrewd as serpents and innocent as doves. But beware of men, for they will hand you over to the courts and scourge you in their synagogues; and you will even be brought before governors and kings for my sake, as a testimony to them and to the Gentiles. But when they hand you over, do not worry about how or what you are to say; for it will be given you in that hour what you are to say. For it is not you who speak, but it is the Spirit of your Father who speaks in you.'

To be a sheep surrounded by hungry wolves is not a thought for the faint-hearted. However, these sheep have a shepherd right behind them with a big stick to protect them! The 'sheep' are also in a familial relationship with God the Father - who happens to be all powerful and have everything under his complete control. The sheep are encouraged to be wise, while maintaining a spiritual purity that the wisdom born of experiencing mistakes usually ends up tarnishing. Jesus counsels against trusting in man, warning that punishment, trial and prison will result, but that God will use these things, too. In fact he will become their voice of defence, inspiring and anointing their testimony of him.

21-23: 'Brother will betray brother to death, and a father his child; and children will rise up against parents and cause them to be put to death. You will be hated by all because of my name, but it is the one who has endured to the end who will be saved. But whenever they persecute you in one city, flee to the next; for truly I say to you, you will not finish going through the cities of Israel until the Son of Man comes.'

Truly, the life of an obedient disciple is not guaranteed to be a picnic - at least not one which has no bears seeking feeding! The sort of tribulations Jesus describes have occurred infrequently over the course of history, but did occur in the disciples' day (all but one of whom died for their faith), when the Jews and Romans tried to suppress the infant church. More recently persecution was widespread in the USSR, and still is in China and Islamic states today. 'Hated' is *'miseo'*, 'to detest',[74] and indeed genuine Christians are increasingly unpalatable in politically correct societies seeking to promote anti-God agendas. 'Endures' is *'hupomeno'* and carries the meaning 'to endure and abide'.[75] This gives a clue to surviving under persecution - abiding in the One from whom all life flows and who allows nothing to happen to us that he will not turn to our good (Romans 8:28), painful though it may be at the time. There will always be places where Father can be usefully served; watching for tribulation and avoiding it by judicious movement has served the Jewish people well over several millennia.

24-25: 'A disciple is not above his teacher, nor a slave above his master. It is enough for the disciple that he becomes like his teacher and the slave like his master. If they have called the head of the house Beelzebul, how much more will they malign the members of his household!'

Further strength and encouragement can be drawn from the example of Jesus Christ. Things were not always easy for him - why expect anything different for ourselves? Becoming like Jesus seems to be a good enough outcome, even in his persecutions. After all, household members are known by the reputation the master of the house carries, for good or ill. 'Beelzebul' is a Hebrew play-on-words around the name of a Philistine fertility god (worshipped at Ekron), but humourously altered in the Hebrew rendering of its name to mean the 'lord of the flies' (*'Ba'al Zebûb'*).

26-27: 'Therefore do not fear them, for there is nothing concealed that will not be revealed, or hidden that will not be known. What I tell you in the darkness, speak in the light; and what you hear whispered in your ear, proclaim upon the housetops.'

Why be afraid of people who can only do what a loving Father allows to happen for our good? The worst they can do is kill the body, for which we will receive an eternal crown. And God the Father will, if we listen, make their schemes known to us in just the same way he did with his servant Elisha (2 Kings 6:9) and Paul (Acts 18:9), often at night when the silence makes hearing God's still small voice easier. What he tells us can then, as he directs, be made known openly.

28-31: 'Do not fear those who kill the body but are unable to kill the soul; but rather fear him who is able to destroy both soul and body in hell. Are not two sparrows sold for a cent? And yet not one of them will fall to the ground apart from your Father. But the very hairs of your head are all numbered. So do not fear; you are more valuable than many sparrows.'

Fear (*'phobeo'*) means 'to treat with reverential obedience and respect'. We *'phobeo'* those we obey - who do we obey most? God, or secular authorities? If there is a conflict, then God should come out on top! After all, he decides the place of our eternal abode. Sparrows touch down regularly to preserve their wing-power, and God knows about it every time they do. 'Fall' (*'pipto'*) means 'to descend',[76] and Jesus uses the illustration in Matthew 6 to demonstrate God's all-knowing prowess; fortunately for those underneath, birds tumbling dead from the sky are rather rare. The Father knows everything - grains of sand, hair numbers, etc. 'More value' here is '***diaphero***',[77] which can also mean to be 'carried through' in the sense of being taken from place to place, an idea which fits well Jesus' context of fatherly protection in times of trouble. God 'values' us enough to 'carry' us.

32-33: 'Therefore everyone who confesses me before men, I will also confess him before my Father who is in heaven. But whoever denies me before men, I will also deny him before my Father who is in heaven.'

'Confess' ('***homologeo***') means 'to declare something freely and openly' [78] (no embarrassment or inhibitions here); 'deny' ('***arneomai***') means 'to refuse or reject' [79] as well as 'deny'; the oft-humourous Jesus using another of his many plays-on-words. Be careful not to be refused (denied) entry to the heavenly party to end all parties.

34-36: 'Do not think that I came to bring peace on the earth; I did not come to bring peace, but a sword. For I came to set a man against his father, and a daughter against her mother, and daughter-in-law against her mother-in-law; and a man's enemies will be the members of his household.'

One of the main functions of God's word is to divide (Hebrews 4:12), and the Gospel message carries the same function for all its life-changing properties. Sensitivity in sharing it is important. Let there be no needless offense given - but don't be surprised if it creates disagreements to the roots even of families. It was the same in Jesus' own human family too (Mark 3:21, also John 7:5), although they were eventually convinced!

37-39: 'He who loves father or mother more than me is not worthy of me; and he who loves son or daughter more than me is not worthy of me. And he who does not take his cross and follow after me is not worthy of me. He who has found his life will lose it, and he who has lost his life for my sake will find it.'

Family must take its place in relative proportion to Christian discipleship, and where there is occasionally a conflict, God must be put first. To 'take up your cross' was a something well-known to the disciples, who were familiar with the sight of condemned men carrying their cross-beam to the place of crucifixion. It meant to identity with someone to death, even a nasty, painful death. 'Finding' ('*heurisko*') means to 'find by enquiry, thought, examination, scrutiny, observation, to find out by practice and experience' [80] - very pertinent in the process of 'finding' real life in Christian discipleship, prayer and Bible study.

40-42: 'He who receives you receives me, and he who receives me receives him who sent me. He who receives a prophet in the name of a prophet shall receive a prophet's reward; and he who receives a righteous man in the name of a righteous man shall receive a righteous man's reward. And whoever, in the name of a disciple gives to one of these little ones even a cup of cold water to drink, truly I say to you, he shall not lose his reward.'

Solidarity is a helpful by-product of times of persecution, and like-for-like rewards are promised, not a bad way to win a bonus in Christian service. Prophets and 'righteous men' ('*dikaios*'- meaning 'one who keeps God's laws', and hence called 'righteous' or 'just')[81] get a special mention here. But even something as simple and basic as giving a drink to a traveller will win a reward.

Chapter 11

1: 'When Jesus had finished giving instructions to his twelve disciples, he departed from there to teach and preach in their cities.'

Jesus sets off to follow-up the work he has sent his disciples to begin, not in the 'ways of the Gentiles' (foreigners) at first but to the lost sheep of the house of Israel (chapter 10 verse 5). He was to bring not only instruction in God's word and his ways of doing things but also to preach, meaning to proclaim or announce something openly. Matthew 4:17 sums up his proclamation as 'Repent *(change your mind and way of thinking and relating towards God),* for the kingdom of heaven *(God's rule and authority experienced and submitted to in our lives)* is at hand'. God always rules; his rule is now within reach of all but we do not always submit to it!

2-3: 'Now when John, while imprisoned, heard of the works of Christ, he sent word by his disciples and said to him, 'Are you the expected One, or shall we look for someone else?'

Meanwhile, Jesus' cousin John the Baptist had been imprisoned by Herod Antipas. He had criticized Herod for taking his brother Phillip's wife Salome. This had caused severe political ructions in the region, as Antipas' original wife's father was the powerful neighbouring ruler of the Nabatean Empire based in Petra in Jordan. John, like many Jews, seems to have been expecting a quick fulfillment of the prophetic words concerning God's messianic plans for Israel. He is naturally concerned about the rather limited immediate political impact of Jesus' ministry. He wonders if somehow he and his mother Elizabeth, his Aunt Mary and her husband Joseph had somehow heard wrongly about the destiny of this most gifted of Rabbis and Doctors, that they had named Jesus at the angel's behest. So he sends some of his disciples to Jesus to receive clarification.

4-6: 'Jesus answered and said to them, 'Go and report to John what you hear and see: the blind receive sight and the lame walk, the lepers are cleansed and the deaf hear, the dead are raised up, and the poor have the gospel preached to them. And blessed is he who does not take offense at me.'

Jesus responds by sending back a report concerning the signs that the Old Testament prophet Isaiah would have recognized as introducing the Messianic era. Isaiah (29:18) had recorded that the deaf would hear and that the blind would see; Isaiah (53:5) also reported that the Messiah would heal and restore to God, and there was no disease that separated within the people of God more than leprosy. Isaiah prophesied (26:19) that the dead would live when they hear God's voice, and (61:1) that the poor would hear the good news of a better kingdom's rule. The fact that Jesus did not fully meet the expectations of any of the religious groups of his day should not have allowed John to stumble ('offense' here is, again, '*skandalizo*' - 'to cause someone to fall', from the word for the 'trigger of a trap').[82] Jesus is aware that John's days are numbered, and that the devil would love an opportunity to trip John up in any sense of self-pity that his imprisonment might have brought.

7-9: 'As these men were going away, Jesus began to speak to the crowds about John, 'What did you go out into the wilderness to see? A reed shaken by the wind? But what did you go out to see? A man dressed in soft clothing? Those who wear soft clothing are in kings' palaces! But what did you go out to see? A prophet? Yes, I tell you, and one who is more than a prophet.'

Who did the people think that John was? Before John's messengers are out of earshot, Jesus takes the opportunity to affirm John in their hearing. Reeds in Israel were units of measurement (Ezekiel 40:3). Many had gone out to John to see whether their lives measured up to God's standards and to receive a baptism that would help them in the process of turning their lives towards him. A reed that was badly blown around or caused to 'totter' (shaken) by life's storms was not of much use, and John had never been one of that type and would not be one now, certainly not once Christ's words of encouragement were received. Neither was he a man who enjoyed luxury - he wore camel skins and ate locust beans (Matthew 3:4). Perhaps most startling of all is Jesus' comparison with John's current fellow residents, not in the dungeon, but those who lived in the more comfortable parts of Herod Antipas' palace in Galilee. They differ to John in that they are dressed 'soft' (the word 'clothing' is not present in the Greek text). The Greek here is '*malakos*', meaning 'effeminate', and was used to describe young men kept by older men for immoral and pedaristic purposes. It was also a general term for men who practiced a variety of types of sexual lewdness.[83] This would appear to be a dig at Antipas' household, as well as Antipas himself, whom Jesus would later describe as a 'vixen'; the word 'fox' in Luke 13:32 being in the feminine tense. Herod was heavily influenced by Greek culture, as can be seen by the type of dancing (Greek-style) that Herodias performed at Antipas' party (Matthew 14:6 and Mark 6:22); Greek culture at that time was permeated by a variety of lewd sexual practices. So John is affirmed as being a reliable, tough, thoroughly straight-talking man who spoke God's word as a prophet would be expected to, but on an altogether greater level to previous prophets in Israel.

10-11: 'This is the one about whom it is written, 'Behold, I send my messenger ahead of you, who will prepare your way before you.' Truly I say to you, among those born of women there has not arisen anyone greater than John the Baptist!'

What set John apart was the specific mission God had given him to perform. Luke records that the angel Gabriel had given the following message to Zechariah, John's father, regarding John's mission: 'He will be great in the sight of the Lord; and he will drink no wine or liquor, and he will be filled with the Holy Spirit while yet in his mother's womb. And he will turn many of the sons of Israel back to the Lord their God. It is he who will go as a forerunner before him in the spirit and power of Elijah, to turn the hearts of the fathers back to the children, and the disobedient to the attitude of the righteous, so as to make ready a people prepared for the Lord' (Luke 1:15-17). John was the prophet about whom other prophets such as Malachi (4:6) and Isaiah (40:3) had prophesied. Matthew (11:14 and 17:12) records that Jesus identified John as fulfilling the 'pre-Messiah' role of preparation that the prophets had foretold. Some Jews believed that Elijah himself would be resurrected to do this, and that this was indeed theoretically possible can be seen from the account of his bodily appearance together with Moses in a meeting with Jesus (Matthew 17:2 and Mark 9:2). This is what John seems to be denying in his comment to the Jewish leaders (John 1:21) that he was not Elijah (bodily, at least). He quotes from Isaiah's prophecy about preparing the way, rather than from Malachi, which is the reference that the angel Gabriel had given to his father Zacharias. John, like the other theologians of his day, had not grasped the concept that the Old Testament Messianic prophecies fell into two camps: those referring to the first coming as a 'suffering servant', and those about his second coming as judge of all humanity. Consequently it was a struggle to clarify why Jesus was not going about fulfilling the second (triumphant) category.

11-15: 'Yet the one who is least in the kingdom of heaven is greater than he. From the days of John the Baptist until now the kingdom of heaven suffers violence, and violent men take it by force. For all the prophets and the Law prophesied until John. And if you are willing to accept it, John himself is Elijah who was to come. He who has ears to hear, let him hear.'

John's ministry represented a type of fulcrum between two eras; a kind of tipping-point between the dispensation of the Jewish Law and sacrificial offerings, and the coming of the grace and truth embodied in the Person of the Messiah and the greater authority of his kingdom's rulership. From now on the emphasis would be on sons and daughters

94

who served their Father-King, rather than on servants who had a rather distant, though familial, type of relationship with God. Now that Jesus' ministry is underway the kingdom is subject to '*biazo*' ('violence'), meaning that it may be 'forcibly grasped' and 'crowded into'.[84] And because every blood-bought child of God has the status of a son or daughter, they are greater even than John in their vigorous exercise ('violent' men here is '*biastes*' meaning 'strong', 'energetic' or 'forceful') [85] of the kingdom's newly revealed authority on earth. Jesus does not however say that they will be greater in their heavenly reward than John, who lived in a manner faithful to the age he was born into. 'Ears to hear' is a proverb, meaning, 'Listen up and try and understand!', or 'Pay attention!'

16-19: 'But to what shall I compare this generation? It is like children sitting in the market places, who call out to the other children, and say, 'We played the flute for you, and you did not dance; we sang a dirge, and you did not mourn.' For John came neither eating nor drinking, and they say, 'He has a demon!' The Son of Man came eating and drinking, and they say, 'Behold, a gluttonous man and a drunkard, a friend of tax collectors and sinners!' Yet wisdom is vindicated by her deeds.'

Jesus now switches track and addresses his audience, some of whom had switched their focus of popular allegiance from John to Jesus (as in John 1:37), but in many cases would remain most true to the fickleness of their own human nature. Some had rejected John as being too austere - camel skins and locust beans were not their thing. They then criticized Jesus for being too relaxed in his choice of company and hence the sort of food and drink that would get consumed in their presence. No doubt it was not all prepared in keeping with the strict Jewish oral legal traditions as recorded in the Jewish Mishnah, much of which Jesus eschewed as being 'traditions of men' (Mark 7:8). Their complaints had even taken the form of exaggerated slander (there is no evidence whatsoever that Jesus was ever guilty of their allegations). They had

95

been unable to accept that a revered Rabbi would prefer the company of social outcasts such as tax collectors to their own persons. 'Sinners' here is, again, the technical Jewish term meaning those who systematically broke the Law of God (usually the Mishnah), because they had occupations that made it impossible for them to keep it, and so made no attempt to. As well as tax-collectors (also known as 'publicans'), they included shepherds; hence it was a sign of God's grace to announce Messiah's arrival to them first. They had fewer civil rights, and they were not permitted to give evidence. The Mishnah includes in their ranks 'those who play at dice, usurers, those who breed doves, those who traffic in the fruits of the Sabbath year,[86] and also 'Shepherds, publicans and those who live off interest".[87] Consequently, religious Jews avoided contact with them (as their Oral Law taught) [88] lest they also became ritually impure. This may be seen from the reactions of the priest and Levite to the injured Jewish man in the parable of the Good Samaritan (Luke 10: 30-35). The Apostle Peter, however, was prepared to lodge with Simon the tanner (a handler of dead animals' skins - Acts 10:6), showing that he was following Christ's own example, in contradiction to the Mishnah which Christ referred to as 'rules taught by men' (Mark 7:7 NIV).

Jesus likens his religious opponents' attitude to that of spoiled children who are never satisfied. The saying 'wisdom is vindicated / justified by her deeds' has a double application - 'your actions demonstrate the nature of your 'wisdom', and so do mine'.

20-24: 'Then he began to denounce the cities in which most of his miracles were done, because they did not repent. 'Woe to you, Chorazin! Woe to you, Bethsaida! For if the miracles had occurred in Tyre and Sidon which occurred in you, they would have repented long ago in sackcloth and ashes. Nevertheless I say to you, it will be more tolerable for Tyre and Sidon in the day of judgement than for you. And you, Capernaum, will not be exalted to heaven, will you? You will descend to Hades; for if the

96

miracles had occurred in Sodom which occurred in you, it would have remained to this day. Nevertheless I say to you that it will be more tolerable for the land of Sodom in the day of judgement, than for you.'

Jesus and John had grown up together and were close humanly and psychologically speaking as well as in the purpose of their overlapping spiritual missions. Jesus was deeply moved by the suffering John was enduring, as his subsequent reaction to the news of John's execution as recorded in Matthew 14:13 shows. The reminder of John's physical and spiritual plight as guest of Herod Antipas now triggers a withering rebuke to the area of their common mission field around Lake Galilee. (Chorazin, Bethsaida and Capernaum are all just to the north of the lake). Tyre and Sidon, the sea-pirate fortress cities of the Old Testament's prophetic condemnation (e.g. Jeremiah 25:22), had not witnessed the teaching, let alone the miracles, that Jesus' ministry had bought; hence would receive a lesser judgement on the final day when all outstanding accounts are settled forever. Even notorious Sodom would do better on that day than the cities that had not responded to Jesus' ministry.

25-27: 'At that time Jesus said, 'I praise you Father, Lord of heaven and earth, that you have hidden these things from the wise and intelligent and have revealed them to infants. Yes Father, for this way was well-pleasing in your sight. All things have been handed over to me by my Father; and no one knows the Son except the Father; nor does anyone know the Father except the Son, and anyone to whom the Son wills to reveal him.'

His rebuke given, Jesus turns to a prayer of praise to God the Father, to whom belongs all truth and who reveals it to whomever he wishes, even to those without a degree in theology! If wisdom and intelligence lead to pride and self-reliance then they actually obstruct the possessor's spiritual progress. The Son has come to reveal the Father, but only to those whom Father knows are ready to respond. He is quite willing to reveal Father to all, but a personal response is needed and not all are ready to make one. God knows this and does not wish to worsen someone's spiritual condition through provoking a rejection before they are ready to respond.

28-30: 'Come to me, all who are weary and heavy-laden, and I will give you rest. Take my yoke upon you and learn from me, for I am gentle and humble in heart, and you will find rest for your souls. For my yoke is easy and my burden is light.'

That Jesus' desire is for all men to know him as he truly is becomes evident by Jesus' final saying of this section. It is an invitation to all to come to him, assuming, that is, that they can recognise that their own spiritual condition gives them need to do so. His lifestyle is one free from stress because it is lived according to God's standards and timetable, which involves him working and us following and joining in with what he is doing. His double yoke fits brilliantly and enables him to take the strain and multiply the power output enormously. 'Gentle' here (*'praus'* - 'meek') carries the meaning of strength under control (and in this case, enormous, all-powerful strength), and 'humble' (*'tapeinos'* - 'lowly') means that Jesus Christ will never force his will upon his yokemate. Jesus is a good choice of partner! But it offers a definite choice, one which can also be ignored. Jeremiah (6:16) had said: 'Thus says the Lord, 'Stand by the ways and see and ask for the ancient paths, Where the good way is, and walk in it; and you will find rest for your souls.' But they said, 'We will not walk in it.' Sadly, some things haven't changed.

Chapter 12

1-2: 'At that time Jesus went through the grain fields on the Sabbath, and his disciples became hungry and began to pick the heads of grain and eat. But when the Pharisees saw this, they said to him, 'Look, your disciples do what is not lawful to do on a Sabbath."

Most observant Jews would prepare their Sabbath food the day before, as it was forbidden to make meals on the Sabbath itself. Jesus and his disciples were probably too busy for this, and so were hungry on their way to the local synagogue for the morning service. His disciples therefore are picking ears of corn from the fields they have to pass through, rubbing the husk off in their hands and eating the grain. Gleaning in this way was quite legal and was part of the Jewish Law's provision for the poor. It was the de-husking that the Pharisaic lawyers were objecting to, on the grounds that any sort of threshing, even on this small scale, was work and so prohibited on the Sabbath. This was a minor incident perhaps, but an offence nonetheless. The Pharisees, whose job it was to teach and uphold the Law, point this out to their Rabbi-master, the respected Doctor of the Law who had such unconventional views in his regard to Mishnaic interpretation. Jesus had previously clashed with them on the issue of casting out evil spirits. He was to clash again with them over other issues such as 'Corban' - the withholding of alms giving to parents if put for a 'higher' purpose such as the support of Temple offering and sacrifice. But it was the issue of what constituted the breaking of the Sabbath that really caught the Pharisees' attention as a point about which they felt, in all good conscience, they really must oppose the Rabbi from Nazareth.

3-6: 'But he said to them, 'Have you not read what David did when he became hungry, he and his companions, how he entered the house of God, and they ate the consecrated bread, which was not lawful for him to eat nor for those with him, but for the priests alone? Or have you not read in the Law, that on the Sabbath the priests in the Temple break the Sabbath and are innocent? But I say to you that something greater than the Temple is here."

Jesus meets their challenge head-on. 'Haven't you read?' constitutes a rabbinic challenge. He is saying, 'You have read this but you haven't understood it. So now I am going to explain it to you.' David, who was not a priest, placed himself and his companions in the position of priests and ate that which it was only lawful for the priests to eat. Indeed, they were aided and abetted in this illegal act by none other than the official priest, Ahimelech, himself (1 Samuel 21:1-4). Ahimelech had discerned that David's need is a more suitable use in God's agenda for the bread than its role in sitting before the altar going gradually drier and mouldier by the day as time passed until the next Sabbath, when they were finally eaten by the priests themselves as the next batch was put out.

This 'bread of the presence' ('Shewbread' in Exodus 25:30) constituted 12 loaves, enough for a brief snack for David and the companions whom he was to meet - David only asked for five of them. This faith-filled and compassionate attitude of Ahimelech was to result in his and his family's death at the hands of King Saul, David's enemy through their betrayal by Doeg, the servant of Saul (1 Samuel 22:18) who witnessed it. Ahimelech had simply acted in charity towards others - those he genuinely thought to be in need (David and his companions), and was completely removed from any political implication (1 Samuel 22:14-15). The act of slaughter can be seen as a type of prophetic foreshadowing of the death Jesus who, along with many of his companions, was to die at the hands of the Jewish authorities of his day.

Just as David's men were acting like priests, so Jesus said that his followers too were acting like priests. To pretend to be a priest was an

100

extremely serious offence in Jewish eyes. How did that make the Pharisees feel? They must have considered that Jesus was placing himself and his followers above the dictates of the Mishnah. They were not able to see that he was indeed the promised Messiah.

Having compared himself favourably with King David, Jesus takes a step further. There was no more holy place than the Temple in Jerusalem, and the work of the priests there, much of it on the Sabbath, was exempt from the prohibitions laid down in the Mishnah. In verse 5, Jesus refers the Pharisees to this very question of work done by the Temple priests themselves in performing the necessary sacrifices and offerings every Sabbath day (Numbers 28:9). How is it they can work? The Pharisees understood that the Temple priests were exempt from their Sabbath regulations on this regard because their work was an integral part of Jewish worship. Jesus likens himself and his followers to Temple priests, something highly offensive to the Pharisees, at least in regard to Jesus' disciples, given the serious way in which they approached family lineage with regard to qualification for the role of priest.

Jesus likening himself to King David and then to a Temple priest, was bad enough, but worse was to come. Understanding their quite natural objections to his statements, Jesus ratchets up the stakes still further.

6: 'I tell you that one greater than the Temple is here.'

For the Jews, nothing except God himself was greater than the Temple. This remark of Jesus' must have absolutely infuriated them. Here was this respected Rabbi, trained (as far as it was possible to train someone who always ended up teaching the trainers) and ordained within the Temple, ordained by the Sanhedrin itself, their highest authority, taking upon himself the title of 'greater than the Temple', i.e. God. A clearer statement of his divinity, to their ears, would not have been possible. Joseph, Jesus' earthly father, would have been well known as the *'tekton'* who had, in all probability, served as architect and trainer of the priests that Herod needed to build the Temple. The Jews held that the builder of the house was greater than the house (Hebrews 3:3), and Jesus cleverly employs the use of this personally applicable double meaning to make his point that he was indeed greater than the Temple, even if his opponents would not recognise or respect his claim to divinity.

7-8: 'But if you had known what this means, 'I desire compassion, and not sacrifice', you would not have condemned the innocent. For the Son of Man is Lord of the Sabbath.'

What was God the Father's intention in all of this? Jesus quotes to them Hosea 6:6, 'God desires mercy, not sacrifice.' In fact, God had required sacrifice but that was not his highest intention. Sacrifices were only necessary because of sin. God's intention, from the beginning, was for a sin-free world. The disciples could have simply kept on being hungry, and treated the absence of food as a type of enforced fast. But Zechariah 7:3 says, speaking of fasting, 'Administer true justice, show mercy and compassion to one another', and this was his Father's higher intention.

In their concern to tie up the Law with enough ring fences to keep people from ever getting remotely close to breaking it, the Pharisees had shut people out of God's courts, preventing access to his presence (Matthew 23:13). In doing so, they were condemning the innocent. Not that anyone is truly innocent before God, but the disciples of Jesus had probably been simply following their master's example from previous non-Sabbath occasions. Jesus himself was always careful to not give unnecessary offense - he could confidently say to his detractors, 'Which one of you convicts me of sin?' (John 8:46).

In verse 8, Jesus summarises his teaching in an unequivocal fashion. 'For the Son of Man is Lord of the Sabbath.' There has been much debate about what Jesus meant by the term 'Son of Man'. Here in a few simple words recorded in Matthew's gospel, we find the definition and explanation. 'Lord of the Sabbath' and 'One greater than the Temple' were idiomatic expressions for God. The 'Son of Man' being 'Lord of the Sabbath' makes it a clear title of divinity. How furious must the Pharisees have been? Matthew does not record their response at this point, and technically, Jesus could not be tried for blaspheming here because he had not defined who the 'Son of Man' was. And he himself does not appear to have picked or de-husked any corn. But Matthew reveals their intentions in verse 10. After this they arrived at the synagogue, where Jesus might well have been invited to preach. Fortunately for the Pharisees, a more solid opportunity soon arose to accuse this Rabbi who broke so blatantly with their traditions.

9-14: 'Departing from there, he went into their synagogue. And a man was there whose hand was withered. And they questioned Jesus, asking, 'Is it lawful to heal on the Sabbath?' - so that they might accuse him. And he said to them, 'What man is there among you who has a sheep, and if it falls into a pit on the Sabbath, will he not take hold of it and lift it out? How much more valuable then is a man than a sheep! So then, it is lawful to do good on the Sabbath.' Then he said to the man, 'Stretch out your hand!' He stretched it out, and it was restored to normal, like the other. But the Pharisees went out and conspired against him, as to how they might destroy him.'

The man had a palsied hand, probably the result of a birth injury. Perhaps it was a brachial plexus nerve injury caused by pulling under the shoulder in an attempt to deliver the baby who had become stuck by means of shoulder 'dystocia' - an abnormality of labour due to a malpresentation of the baby's shoulders. In labour the head of a baby with shoulder disproportion can be delivered but with the body still inside the mother. This is potentially fatal if the baby is not speedily and often forcibly delivered, with occasional traumatic consequences.

For whatever reason, this man's hand had never developed. Could the Pharisees tempt Jesus into breaking the Law? The Law said healing on the Sabbath (medically) was illegal except in the case of an emergency where death might occur as a result of any delay. This man did not meet the emergency criteria. He had been disabled, in all probability, since birth. There was no rush to perform any healing.

So they ask Jesus if is it lawful (according to their Law) to heal on the Sabbath. In verse 11 Jesus replied in a way that they could understand. God had made provisions for sheep. A sheep left in a pit would not die if left till evening, when the setting sun signified the end of the Sabbath day. A few hours would not hurt it. But the Law [89] allowed for carrying food to it and assisting in extraditing it, because of the principle in Jewish Law of relative loss. A sheep was considered a great loss, one worthy of work during the Sabbath day. So if God was concerned about meeting the needs of natural sheep, how much more was he concerned to meet the needs of his spiritual sheep?

Jesus takes this Mishnaic principle and turns it on its head. He was saying that if it is right to do good of a certain value on the Sabbath, then it is evil to refuse to do good of a certain relative value. The man has the higher value. Therefore it is lawful (according to the principles of the Mishnaic Law) to do good on the Sabbath.

And so Jesus speaks to the man, 'Stretch out your hand.' He is intentionally very careful not to do anything that could be interpreted as being healing or work. Asking someone to stretch out their hand was not work. Stretching out your hand was not work. Jesus is being very careful not to give unnecessary grounds for offense, or any opportunity for his opponents to have grounds to criticise him on. He is also demonstrating his divine power in an ever more convincing way; in this instance by healing from a distance and re-creating human tissue by the spoken word of God alone and not with a touch.

He is also asking the man to do the impossible. God will frequently ask us to do, with him, the impossible; because anyone can do the possible but only God can do the impossible. Luke 1:37 - 'For with God nothing shall be impossible.' As we respond to his word in simple trust and obedience, so the miraculous happens. The damaged hand is made like the other hand, which would itself have been overdeveloped due to the extra use required of it, there being no other hand to call upon. His good hand would have therefore had an excessive development of musculature. Jesus restored his withered hand to be 'just as sound as the other', in other words, perfect symmetry. Many people in that synagogue (including the man's possibly impoverished family) must have praised God for this extraordinary miracle.

But the Pharisees went out and plotted how they might kill Jesus! A miracle that God has sent to them to confirm the truth about Jesus' remarks concerning his divinity had the opposite effect on them. Their hearts were so hardened that they hated Jesus even more - this Rabbi, turned Messiah-figure, who dared to undermine their religious system by pointing to the God who had designed it in the first place. Jesus was showing that the Law was not mainly a means of approaching God, (which was through trust and faith), but as a means of revealing to us our own inability to keep it. Sadly, the Law had become to them a means of pride in their own attainments.

15-21: 'But Jesus, aware of this, withdrew from there. Many followed him, and he healed them all, and warned them not to tell who he was. This was to fulfill what was spoken through Isaiah the prophet: 'Behold, my servant whom I have chosen; my beloved in whom my soul is well-pleased; I will put my spirit upon him, and he shall proclaim justice to the Gentiles. He will not quarrel, nor cry out; nor will anyone hear his voice in the streets. A battered reed he will not break off, and a smouldering wick he will not put out, until he leads justice to victory. And in his name the Gentiles will hope.''

Provocations to Jesus' spirit such as this one seem to be followed by an increase in the manifestation of the miraculous - he healed all who came to him. Perhaps they threw his sense of dependency, always rooted in Father's agenda, yet more firmly thereon. Again there is the request for silence from those healed to permit freedom of movement. Matthew wishes to ground his readers in Jesus' Messianic identity, hence his frequent quotations from Isaiah. Here it is chapter 42:1-4, in particular, which foretold much of Jesus' life and sacrificial suffering. Jesus is God the Father's servant: the Greek word is '*pais*' - 'an attendant on a King'.[90] The Hebrew of Isaiah 42: 1 indicates that the servant is a 'personal bondservant' (the word also describes an act of prophetic service). He is also specially selected for this service, perhaps due to the particular favour he enjoys from the one sending him on the mission, which Isaiah tells us, includes governing the Gentiles. He will not engage in strife (the Hebrew phrase is 'make an outcry'), hence Jesus' requests for privacy. Nor will he make a loud commotion in the street, but he will look after things that are damaged or on their last legs rather than consigning them to the rubbish tip to be utterly destroyed.

Salvation ('*soteria*') carries the meaning of preservation - a type of recycling - most notably with men's and women's lives. The rulership he has (and which the Gentile foreigners are now to be included in) is based on God's truth (in the Hebrew version of Isaiah 42:3), which the Greek of Matthew's Gospel tells us utterly vanquishes the enemy. This is illustrated in Jesus' quoting Scripture to the devil during the testing in the desert - Scriptural truth that all can confidently trust in. Isaiah also tells us that the distant regions ('isles') wait expectantly ('in hope') for his law.

22-24: 'Then a demon-possessed man who was blind and mute was brought to Jesus, and he healed him, so that the mute man spoke and saw. All the crowds were amazed, and were saying, 'This man cannot be the Son of David, can he?' But when the

Pharisees heard this, they said, 'This man casts out demons only, by Beelzebul the ruler of the demons."

Evil spirits were an aspect of Jesus' ministry that was generally considered a fringe activity for a master Rabbi such as Jesus. For Jesus it was a visible evidence of his identity and victory over all of the powers of darkness. The Gospel on this occasion does not actually say that the demon was causing the blind-mute state (c.f. Mark 9:14). Jesus performed a supernatural healing after evicting the demon, who was trespassing on property where it had no right to be. Ever ready with a slanderous comment, the Pharisees have a good reason why they do not perform such signs - they allege the need to invoke the ruler of demons in their eviction. (For more on 'Beelzebul' see Matthew 10:25).

25-29: 'And knowing their thoughts Jesus said to them, 'Any kingdom divided against itself is laid waste; and any city or house divided against itself will not stand. If Satan casts out Satan, he is divided against himself; how then will his kingdom stand? If I by Beelzebul cast out demons, by whom do your sons cast them out? For this, reason, they will be your judges. But if I cast out demons by the Spirit of God, then the kingdom of God has come upon you. Or how can anyone enter the strong man's house and carry off his property, unless he first binds the strong man? And then he will plunder his house."

Jesus, who was always in tune with what his Father was telling him about his opponents, makes short shrift of their daft retort. 'How can Satan be casting out Satan? If so, great! His evil rule is about to end. But if he is, how do your own people manage it? Are they demon-possessed, too? Conversely, my casting out evil spirits is therefore clear evidence of God's working among you and, by the way, don't forget to bind (literally, 'chain up') their power first, because they are 'mighty'.' This is a piece of advice that the sons of the Jewish priest Sceva, in Ephesus, would have done well to take note of! (See Acts 19:16).

30: 'He who is not with me is against me; and he who does not gather with me scatters.'

Jesus identifies the unhelpful influence that those not willing to be identified publicly with him can have. This is distinct from the positive efforts of those publicly identifying themselves with him and his ministry, such as occurred in Mark 9:39-40. Here, on being told of a man outside their immediate circle who was successfully casting out an evil spirit in Christ's name, Jesus defends the man by saying: 'No one who performs a miracle in my name will be able soon afterward to speak evil of me. For he who is not against us is for us.'

31-32: 'Therefore, I say to you, any sin and blasphemy shall be forgiven people, but blasphemy against the Spirit shall not be forgiven. Whoever speaks a word against the Son of Man, it shall be forgiven him; but whoever speaks against the Holy Spirit, it shall not be forgiven him, either in this age or in the age to come.'

In ascribing Jesus' power to cast out demons to the chief of the demons himself, the Pharisees were quite intentionally slandering Jesus (Greek: *'blasphemia'*). Jesus says this can be forgiven, but there is a type of slander that shall not be - that committed against the Holy Spirit (hence equivalent to the sin that leads to death of 1 John 5:16). 1 John 2:2, however, indicates that Christ's sacrifice is for the sin (without distinction) of the whole world. So it is the particular role of the Holy Spirit that must be looked at to understand when this 'unforgivable' sin occurs. The Spirit, Jesus tells us in John 16:8-11, 'will convict the world concerning sin and righteousness and judgement; concerning sin, because they do not believe in me; and concerning righteousness, because I go to the Father and you no longer see me; and concerning judgement, because the ruler of this world has been judged.' The Spirit's role involves the preparatory work of bringing someone to salvation - convincing them of their inner condition of indifference or

108

rebellion to God and their need to receive his gift of righteousness and hence avoid judgement. But that role can be resisted and refused, and to do so may involve subtle resistance ('speaking against') or even violent rejection (by 'evil speaking' or 'blasphemy'). If so, the person concerned places themselves outside the grace of repentance, and hence salvation, and so never receives forgiveness. Believers therefore can only come into this category by an active and willful rejection of their salvation, which their free will entitles them to do but is extremely rare. For them the Scripture of Hebrews 6:4-6 applies: 'For in the case of those who have once been enlightened and have tasted of the heavenly gift and have been made partakers of the Holy Spirit, and have tasted the good word of God and the powers of the age to come, and then have fallen away, it is impossible to renew them again to repentance, since they again crucify to themselves the Son of God and put him to open shame.'

33: 'Either make the tree good and its fruit good, or make the tree bad and its fruit bad; for the tree is known by its fruit.'

The tree and its fruit go together. The Pharisees made a great show of appearing holy, but Jesus, who knew their hearts, could see that they were rotten within (Matthew 23:27 - 'full of dead men's bones and all uncleanness'), as was evidenced by their lack of good fruit.

34-37: 'You brood of vipers, how can you, being evil, speak what is good? For the mouth speaks out of that which fills the heart. The good man brings out of his good treasure what is good; and the evil man brings out of his evil treasure what is evil. But I tell you that every careless word that people speak, they shall give an accounting for it in the day of judgement. For by your words you will be justified, and by your words you will be condemned.'

'Brood' or 'generation' is '*gennema*' which also means fruit in terms of offspring or natural fruit - another fine play-on-words.[91] This

109

particular fruit is poisonous, just as the snake mentioned is a generic poisonous one. Jesus is echoing his cousin John's words (Matthew 3:7), and makes the point that something can only come out of the mouth if it is first of all present in the heart. Speaking here is *'laleo'*, meaning to 'declare one's mind and disclose one's thoughts'.[92] Later, the Apostle Paul was to write that 'if you confess with your mouth Jesus as Lord, and believe in your heart that God raised him from the dead, you will be saved; for with the heart a person believes, resulting in righteousness, and with the mouth he confesses, resulting in salvation' (Romans 10:9-10).

38: 'Then some of the Scribes and Pharisees said to him, 'Teacher, we want to see a sign from you.''

Without the greatest gift of timing, the Pharisees and Scribes irritate Jesus still further with a demand for further proof of his identity. Not content with the miracles he had already performed, they want further verification of his authority to make claims about himself that deviated from the acceptable norms.

39-41: 'But he answered and said to them, 'An evil and adulterous generation craves for a sign; and yet no sign will be given to it but the sign of Jonah the prophet; for just as Jonah was three days and three nights in the belly of a sea monster, so will the Son of Man be three days and three nights in the heart of the earth. The men of Nineveh will stand up with this generation at the judgement, and will condemn it because they repented at the preaching of Jonah; and behold, something greater than Jonah is here.'

How was Jonah a sign? He appeared to the Ninevites first of all covered in whale vomit. It would have been hard to rely on your own genius with seaweed particles coating you from head to foot and yet the men of Nineveh had, against his expectation, turned to God.

Jonah had, in fact, died. Jonah 2:2, 'From the depths of Sheol I called for help, and you listened to my cry.' Sheol is the Hebrew's unseen place of the dead, which Jonah had visited, after he had sunk to the bottom of the sea. He tells us, in Jonah 2:6, that 'To the roots of the mountains I sank down'. The problem at depth is not simply the water pressure on the body itself. At around 350 feet, without any sort of protection from the water pressure or any intake of pressurised air, the relative pressures of oxygen and nitrogen in the blood reach dangerously high levels, transforming them from life essential elements to something acutely toxic.

As Jonah was dying of drowning, the Scripture tells us that 'he remembered the Lord, and his prayer came to him in his holy Temple' (Jonah 2:7). The Lord heard Jonah and commanded a whale that swallowed the (then dead) body of Jonah. Either God did a miracle in preserving Jonah's life as such pressures as the sea bed (at least 1500 meters down to the roots of the mountains - verse 6), or he did a miracle in raising him from the dead. Jesus indicates it was the second (rising from the dead) by comparing Jonah to himself, although as one who, being a very human prophet, fell far short of Jesus. A 'day and a night' is a Hebrew idiom for any part of one day - one minute of one day can be expressed as a 'day and a night'. The Jerusalem Talmud [93] quotes rabbi Eleazar ben Azariah (AD 100): 'A day and night are an onah (a portion of time) and the portion of an onah is as the whole of it'. There is a good illustration of this principle in 1 Samuel 30:12-13. 'He (a slave) had not eaten any food or drunk any water for three days and three nights. David asked him, 'To whom do you belong, and where do you come from?' He said, 'I am an Egyptian, the slave of an Amalekite. My master abandoned me when I became ill three days ago.'' 'Three days ago' can mean any time during the third day previously.

Jesus spent part of Good Friday, all of Easter Saturday and a part of Easter Sunday morning with his physical body in the tomb of Joseph of

Arimathea (Matthew 27:59-60). He was then bodily resurrected after having proclaimed his victory (1 Peter 4:6) in the unseen place of the dead, where Jonah had been. The sign of Jonah is therefore the sign of the resurrection.

42: 'The Queen of the South will rise up with this generation at the judgement and will condemn it, because she came from the ends of the earth to hear the wisdom of Solomon; and behold, something greater than Solomon is here.'

In Israel, they understood well the significance of this Queen. This Gentile woman had come to Jerusalem from Sheba (an empire comprising present-day Ethiopia, Yemen, or both). She was full of herself and her own riches (with 4.5 tons of gold), questions and ideas, and had gone away converted to the God of Israel. It was one of the great moments in Israel's nation's history. How the Jewish audience longed to see those days again, to get rid of the Romans, be 'top nation' again, just as the prophets said would happen: 'Then the survivors from all the nations that have attacked Jerusalem will go up year after year to worship the King, the Lord Almighty, and to celebrate the Feast of Tabernacles' (Zechariah 14:16). If Gentiles, like the Queen of Sheba, could see something special, from God, and respond to it, why couldn't the Jews? Was it their pride in being the nation God had chosen? Was it their reliance on the Law, substituting human regulations for divine principles, which blinded them so much that many of them did not recognise who Jesus was?

43-45: 'Now when the unclean spirit goes out of a man, it passes through waterless places seeking rest, and does not find it. Then it says, 'I will return to my house from which I came'; and when it comes, it finds it unoccupied, swept, and put in order. Then it goes and takes along with it seven other spirits more wicked than itself, and they go in and live there; and the last state of that man becomes worse than the first. That is the way it will also be with this evil generation.'

Without the person of the Messiah at the heart of it, the house of Judaism was an empty place. The spiritual forces of darkness which Christ had demonstrated his power over would quickly turn and attack the people who rejected the salvation held out to them from the hand of God the Father in the person of Jesus, whose name meant, 'salvation'.

46-50: 'While he was still speaking to the crowds, behold, his mother and brothers were standing outside, seeking to speak to him. Someone said to him, 'Behold, your mother and your brothers are standing outside seeking to speak to you.' But Jesus answered the one who was telling him and said, 'Who is my mother and who are my brothers?' And stretching out his hand toward his disciples, he said, 'Behold my mother and my brothers! For whoever, does the will of my Father who is in heaven, he is my brother and sister and mother.'

Having been rejected by the Pharisees, Jesus now receives a visit from his mother and younger step-brothers. Mark 3 records that they were anxious, owing to the changes that had occurred in him and to his schedule since his anointing with the Holy Spirit and returning from his forty days in the desert. On arriving at his house in Capernaum, they are unable to enter because of the crush of people trying to see and hear Jesus and send in word to him to come out to them. Jesus takes the opportunity to again affirm that relationships based on membership of God's family and household are of even more importance that natural human ties, because they will last through eternity.

Chapter 13

1-9: 'That day Jesus went out of the house and was sitting by the sea. And large crowds gathered to him, so he got into a boat and sat down, and the whole crowd was standing on the beach. And he spoke many things to them in parables, saying, 'Behold, the sower went out to sow; and as he sowed, some seeds fell beside the road, and the birds came and ate them up. Others fell on the rocky places, where they did not have much soil; and immediately they sprang up, because they had no depth of soil. But when the sun had risen, they were scorched; and because they had no root, they withered away. Others fell among the thorns, and the thorns came up and choked them out. And others fell on the good soil and yielded a crop, some, a hundredfold, some sixty, and some thirty. He who has ears, let him hear."

Large crowds could gather on the shores of Lake Galilee, and Jesus would use one of his friend's boats as a pulpit to avoid getting his feet wet. On the first such occasion the boat had been Simon Peter's, and Jesus had capped his message off with a demonstration of his power over nature. The resulting catch of fish had convinced Peter of his own sinful nature in the holy presence of this local man who had gone away and returned as a Doctor of the Law and a miracle worker. Jesus frequently employed parables (Greek: '*parabole*', 'placing two things [earthly and spiritual] side by side for comparison') [94] to illustrate his point, also getting around people's mental barriers to truth. A sower was a common sight and Jesus' audience would have been aware that much of the seed, lavishly thrown around, would be wasted, either because it missed the target, got eaten by birds, got scorched or got squeezed out by the local weed (thorny bramble) population. Some, however, would find its way to good soil and bring a return. Jesus tells the crowd: 'Pay attention!' ('he who has ears to hear, let him hear'). They would not have the advantage of the first-hand explanation that

Jesus' disciples received; instead, their response to the spiritual content of the parable would be reflective of their own heart's receptivity or lack thereof.

10-13: 'And the disciples came and said to him, 'Why do you speak to them in parables?' Jesus answered them, 'To you it has been granted to know the mysteries of the kingdom of heaven, but to them it has not been granted. For whoever has, to him more shall be given, and he will have an abundance; but whoever does not have, even what he has shall be taken away from him. Therefore, I speak to them in parables; because while seeing they do not see, and while hearing they do not hear, nor do they understand."

By the first century AD, mysticism had become recognized as a part of Jewish life (e.g. the writings of Philo Judaeus of Alexandria). The concept of mysteries (*'musterion'*: 'hidden spiritual truth' - revealed only to a chosen few) [95] was well understood. Parables would be understood by those whose hearts were pure enough to receive the message, but they would remain sitting in the subconscious minds of the rest. For some, eventually the penny would drop and the lights of comprehension would come on. Jesus said that if you have this quality of right standing with God ('given' means it is 'gifted' to you, unearned and undeserved), then you are in line for a whole lot more because, like the sower, God the Father is lavish in what he gives.

14-15: 'In their case the prophecy of Isaiah is being fulfilled, which says 'You will keep on hearing, but will not understand; you will keep on seeing, but will not perceive; for the heart of this people has become dull, with their ears they scarcely hear, and they have closed their eyes, otherwise they would see with their eyes, hear with their ears, and understand with their heart and return, and I would heal them."

Jesus describes the spiritual condition of the religious folk of his day as having been prophesied about in Isaiah 6: 9-10. The Hebrew language used there is very clear. It describes someone who has become so morbidly obese (Isaiah 6:9's '**shaman**' means to 'grow fat', Matthew's Greek word is '**pachuno**' which means to 'thicken with fatness'),[96] that their ears and eyes have closed over with fat to the point of causing deafness and blindness, as in fact happens in the really grossly obese. Matthew implies that the closing of eyes and ears has a voluntary element to it in addition to being a consequence of spiritual obesity. Some of Jesus' Jewish audience had become so well fed on God's word but with so little correct practical application, that they had become spiritually obese and incapable of seeing and hearing spiritually, let alone of moving much. This is pertinent to the spiritual condition of many today - overfed and under-worked. The devil is quite happy to see people fed to the point of obesity if it will prevent them from a gaining the genuine understanding of the heart that leads to a true conversion ('**epistrepho**' - 'to turn / return', as per the Hebrew '**shuwb**' of Isaiah 6:10) [97] under God's healing power of restoration.

16-17: 'But blessed are your eyes, because they see; and your ears, because they hear. For truly I say to you that many prophets and righteous men desired to see what you see, and did not see it, and to hear what you hear, and did not hear it.'

The disciples' eyes and ears, however, are not obese - they can see and hear. And they are 'happy' (fortunate), because there have been many spiritually fit men and women over the ages who could see and hear but were not so privileged to see and hear much about Jesus.

18-19: 'Hear then the parable of the sower. When anyone hears the word of the kingdom and does not understand it, the evil one comes and snatches away what has been sown in his heart. This is the one on whom seed was sown beside the road.'

Jesus now puts the spiritual alongside the natural in his explanation. The devil will do his best to rob people of the word they have heard ('snatch' is '*harpazo*', meaning to 'carry away forcibly', as used by Jesus in the 'carrying off' of the strong man's property in Matthew 12:29).[98] Such is the degree of control the devil has over those outside God's kingdom.

20-21: 'The one on whom seed was sown on the rocky places, this is the man who hears the word and immediately receives it with joy; yet he has no firm root in himself, but is only temporary, and when affliction or persecution arises because of the word, immediately he falls away.'

If he can't prevent a response, the devil has other strategies to employ. Human shallowness, if not dealt with, will not withstand the pressures to conform to the world's value systems that will arise as soon as someone dares to step outside of the various party lines in order to follow Jesus. Being birthed spiritually can be a long process and the devil is a danger to the efforts of any spiritual midwife.

22: 'And the one on whom seed was sown among the thorns, this is the man who hears the word, and the worry of the world and the deceitfulness of wealth choke the word, and it becomes unfruitful.'

If he can't kill off the process at birth, he has other demonic tactics. These include suppressing fruitfulness by distractions such as stress and love of money, or anything that will keep our attention turned away from Jesus who said 'Do not worry about your life … it is more than food or clothing' (Matthew 6:25).

23: 'And the one on whom seed was sown on the good soil, this is the man who hears the word and understands it; who indeed bears fruit and brings forth, some a hundredfold, some sixty, and some thirty.'

'Good soil' means good in the sense of as originally created by the God who looked on all that he had made and saw that 'it was very good' (Genesis 1:31). Hence there is the sense of being 'fitting to the circumstances' as well as 'moral uprightness'. In such soil the seed does what God has designed it to - it produces multiple numbers of its original quantity. God is a God of multiplication and not simply addition.

24-30: 'Jesus presented another parable to them, saying, 'The kingdom of heaven may be compared to a man who sowed good seed in his field. But while his men were sleeping, his enemy came and sowed tares among, the wheat, and went away. But when the wheat sprouted and bore grain, then the tares became evident also. The slaves of the landowner came and said to him, 'Sir, did you not sow good seed in your field? How then does it have tares?' And he said to them, 'An enemy has done this!' The slaves said to him, 'Do you want us, then, to go and gather them up?' But he said, 'No; for while you are gathering up the tares, you may uproot the wheat with them. Allow both to grow together until the harvest; and in the time of the harvest I will say to the reapers, 'First gather up the tares and bind them in bundles to burn them up; but gather the wheat into my barn.''

Jesus develops the agricultural imagery further with a parable designed to illustrate the sort of spiritual interference we might reasonably expect from a cunning adversary who has to look up to see an earthworm. The devil, Jesus said, 'comes only, to steal and kill and destroy' (John 10:10), a very limited range of options which must surely have become rather boring some time ago! Father God, however, knows his ploys in advance, and uses them to suit his own purposes. In the parable, the 'tares' are bearded darnel, a poisonous weed

118

resembling wheat, the seeds of which produce symptoms of drunkenness (trembling, inability to walk, hindered speech and vomiting). It is hard to tell them apart, and uprooting them too early will damage the wheat, so it is left until harvest time to separate out and burn the poisonous plants. Perhaps the good wheat will have had a positive effect on some of the darnel by harvest time, and so some of the efforts of the 'enemy' will have been undone and turned to good.

31-32: 'He presented another parable to them, saying, 'The kingdom of heaven is like a mustard seed, which a man took and sowed in his field; and this is smaller than all other seeds, but when it is full grown it is larger than the garden plants and becomes a tree, so that the birds of the air come and nest in its branches.'

Mustard seeds were tiny - some of the smallest known, yet they could still produce small trees, capable of housing nesting birds, and so illustrating the amazing power of the life of the kingdom of heaven to turn something apparently insignificant into something life-giving, that grows and in turn can reproduce itself, like the good seed did.

33: 'He spoke another parable to them, 'The kingdom of heaven is like leaven, which a woman took and hid in three pecks of flour until it was all leavened.'

Yeast is similarly small but has a hidden power to change the dough from within, and so cause growth and a transformation of nature and flavour that is clear for all to see and taste.

34-35: 'All these things Jesus spoke to the crowds in parables, and he did not speak to them without a parable. This was to fulfill what was spoken through the prophet: 'I will open my mouth in parables; I will utter things hidden since the foundation of the world."

Since rejecting the plainly spoken message would have resulted in condemnation upon the one doing the rejecting, Jesus was careful to administer his spiritual medicine in doses and preparations that would be absorbed. Parables worked for both the close-minded (in their subconscious) and the more open and sympathetically-minded people.

36-43: 'Then he left the crowds and went into the house. And his disciples came to him and said, 'Explain to us the parable of the tares of the field.' And he said, 'The one who sows the good seed is the Son of Man, and the field is the world; and as for the good seed, these are the sons of the kingdom; and the tares are the sons of the evil one; and the enemy who sowed them is the devil, and the harvest is the end of the age; and the reapers are angels. So just as the tares are gathered up and burned with fire, so shall it be at the end of the age. The Son of Man will send forth his angels, and they will gather out of his kingdom all stumbling blocks, and those who commit lawlessness, and will throw them into the furnace of fire; in that place there will be weeping and gnashing of teeth. Then the righteous will shine forth as the sun in the kingdom of their Father. He who has ears, let him hear.''

Jesus' explanation identifies the '*skandalon*' ('stumbling block') as being key to the devil's three-fold ministry of theft, murder and wanton destruction. This is literally the movable trigger or baited part of a trap - the little dainty designed to trigger the violent snapping shut and resulting imprisonment in a lifetime of sin and misery that the devil has so carefully mapped out for us if we fall for his ruses. These will be cleared away, along with all the law-breakers ('*anomia*' - the 'workers of iniquity' described in Matthew 7:23). Many of these are demonic spirits. As Paul was to say: 'the mystery of lawlessness ('*anomia*') is already at work - 2 Thessalonians 2:7, as are their co-workers such as the Antichrist, described as '*anomos*' - the 'man of lawlessness' of 2 Thessalonians 2:8. Hell is described, as usual, as a place where rubbish gets burned; only this time the burning is an eternal process, the rubbish never being consumed just as those in right relationship with Father never stop shining with his reflected likeness. Again, 'he who has ears to hear, let him hear' is 'Pay attention!'

44: 'The kingdom of heaven is like a treasure hidden in the field, which a man found and hid again; and from joy over it he goes and sells all that he has and buys that field.'

There is a more positive impetus to avoid hell which should be kept in mind. The kingdom is immensely valuable on all sorts of levels of human life and contentment, because it allows the benevolent rule of an all-powerful father-King to become experienced in our lives. It is worth selling everything (things that cannot be kept anyway) to gain. Treasure here is '*thesauros*', indicating the great value that the Jews placed on truly wise spiritual words and sayings, as reflected in the 'treasury' of wisdom that the Scribe of verse 52 dips in and out of. As Proverbs 2:2-4 says: 'Make your ear attentive to wisdom, incline your heart to understanding… seek her as silver, and search for her as for hidden treasure.'

45-46: 'Again, the kingdom of heaven is like a merchant seeking fine pearls, and upon finding one pearl of great value, he went and sold all that he had and bought it.'

Pearl here (Greek: '*margarites*') also means a proverb of great wisdom and value. We still use 'pearl of wisdom' in this sense today. This image therefore completes that of the valuable wisdom of verse 44.

47-50: 'Again, the kingdom of heaven is like a dragnet cast into the sea, and gathering fish of every kind; and when it was filled, they drew it up on the beach; and they sat down and gathered the good fish into containers, but the bad they threw away. So it will be at the end of the age; the angels will come forth and take out the wicked from among the righteous, and will throw them into the furnace of fire; in that place there will be weeping and gnashing of teeth.'

The image of separating good and bad on the final day is revived with that of the '*sagene*', or dragnet,[99] a large quantity of netted rope thrown into the sea and towed along, indiscriminately collecting all manner of marine life as it moves through the water. Clearly not everything will be edible, let alone kosher for the Jewish audience to partake of. Some indeed are '*kalos*' - 'beautiful', the genuine article, whereas others of them unfortunately are found to be 'rotten', 'corrupt' and 'putrid' ('*sapros*') [100], only fit to be thrown away. The rubbish, as always, gets burned.

51-52: 'Have you understood all these things?' They said to him, 'Yes.' And Jesus said to them, 'Therefore, every Scribe who has become a disciple of the kingdom of heaven is like a head of a household, who brings out of his treasure things new and old.'

Jesus has repeated himself enough that the disciples have got the message. 'Yes', they reply. Jesus then advises them to be like a Scribe (Greek: '*grammateus*'), who were the official keepers and interpreters of the scrolls of the Law of Moses. A competent Scribe that is also a disciple can be promoted to the position of 'master of the house' ('*oikodespotes*').[101] His excellence lies in his reaching into the treasury of God's word for the pearls contained therein, some of which have never seen the light of day! They are 'new' (Greek: '*kainos*' - 'previously unheard of', 'of a new and unprecedented kind'). [102]

53-56: 'When Jesus had finished these parables, he departed from there. He came to his hometown and began teaching them in their synagogue, so that they were astonished, and said, 'Where did this man get this wisdom and these miraculous powers? Is not this the carpenter's son? Is not his mother called

122

Mary, and his brothers, James and Joseph and Simon and Judas? And his sisters, are they not all with us? Where then did this man get all these things?"

Ever one to practice what he preached, Jesus heads off into Nazareth to see his family, and as was customary for a visiting Rabbi, especially a 'local boy made good', to teach, no doubt with some of the pearls he had mentioned to his disciples. His wisdom and new-found powers are widely recognized, but not without a certain jealousy and resentment. Like crabs in an open bucket (which prevent their fellow crabs from escaping), they try and pull Jesus down to their level. 'His brothers and sisters are with us' - the implication being that Jesus is not 'one of them' anymore. Jesus would have left Nazareth to join the rabbinic schools in the Temple in Jerusalem at age 13, but whereas his titles of 'Rabbi' and 'Doctor' came from there his wisdom did not. It was on a level that was unrecognizable to his hometown audience, and his miraculous powers made the change in him all the harder to swallow. The crowd struggle to reconcile the adult Jesus' gifting with those members of his family who had remained with them. Far from being pleased for him, they, like the Jewish authorities in Jerusalem (Matthew 27:18), lapse into envy and take offense.

57-58: 'And they took offense at him. But Jesus said to them, 'A prophet is not without honour except in his hometown and in his own household.' And he did not do many miracles there because of their unbelief.'

They fell against the 'trap-trigger' of their own pride and short-sightedness. Again, 'took offense' is *skandalizo* - 'a trap'. They rejected the prophetic figure and the Christ that had grown up among them, thereby limiting Jesus to 'not many' miracles!

Chapter 14

1-5: 'At that time Herod the tetrarch heard the news about Jesus, and said to his servants, 'This is John the Baptist; he has risen from the dead, and that is why miraculous powers are at work in him.' For when Herod had John arrested, he bound him and put him in prison because of Herodias, the wife of his brother Philip. For John had been saying to him, 'It is not lawful for you to have her.' Although Herod wanted to put him to death, he feared the crowd, because they regarded John as a prophet.'

The ruling house of Judea at that time was dominated by the name of Herod, which means 'the song of the hero'. Herod the Great, the father of Antipas by his fourth of ten wives, had started out as just such a figure, putting down local revolts on behalf of his Roman masters. Antipas is the Latin form of the Greek word '***antipatros***', meaning 'like the father' (not 'against the father'). 'Like father, like son', the proverb goes, and the saying is certainly true of Herod Antipas, who resembled his father Herod the Great in many ways, and very few of them good! After his father died, Antipas unsuccessfully challenged the will and testament before the Emperor Augustus in Rome on the basis that another will and testament was in existence, favouring him over his older brother Archelaus. While Antipas failed to get his own way with Augustus, he fared rather better with another of his designs, particularly his attachment to his younger half-brother Philip's wife Herodias (she was actually his niece). He persuaded her to leave Philip and move up a notch in terms of territorial rule with him, sending his first wife Phasaelis back in distress to her father King Aretas VI, in Petra in Jordan. This had not gone down well in Petra. King Aretas responded by invading Roman-occupied Judea west of the River Jordan. The adultery did not go down well in Galilee where John was ministering either - his rebuke of Antipas' immoral behaviour led to John's arrest, imprisonment in Antipas' dungeon and later execution.

6-12: 'But when Herod's birthday came, the daughter of Herodias danced before them and pleased Herod, so much that he promised with an oath to give her whatever she asked. Having been prompted by her mother, she said, 'Give me here on a platter the head of John the Baptist.' Although he was grieved, the king commanded it to be given because of his oaths, and because of his dinner guests. He sent and had John beheaded in the prison. And his head was brought on a platter and given to the girl, and she brought it to her mother. His disciples came and took away the body and buried it; and they went and reported to Jesus.'

Antipas desired to please his new wife through winning the favour of her daughter, who must have been rather put out by the precipitate loss of her natural father Philip by this show-off from Galilee. A rather athletic girl, Herodias' daughter (by Philip) could dance in the Greek style, of which there were two types, the slower 'shuffling' dances and the vigorous 'leaping' dances. The latter were traditionally male, but sometimes women danced them as well. Luke records that she 'danced' (Greek *'orceomai'* - in the traditionally male way, literally, 'to raise the feet'),[103] and his guests were 'pleased'. This was a form of dance not normally seen in Israel, and certainly not from girls. Keen to impress his friends and guests, and perhaps at the same time win the favour of his new step-daughter and the further approval of her mother, Antipas offers 'whatever you ask for, up to half my kingdom'. Like most young girls, she knew what to do - ask mum. And mum saw her opportunity to get rid of the thorn in the side of her new and more promising relationship. She asked for the head of John the Baptist. What was the servant thinking who presented such a hideous gift to the young girl for her mother? We do not know. But it may have been, 'Welcome to the family. Watch out, worse things than this have happened to members of this man's extended family.' All this was duly reported to Jesus, who would have been deeply concerned about his cousin John's well-being in Antipas' prison.

125

13-14: 'Now when Jesus heard about John, he withdrew from there in a boat to a secluded place by himself; and when the people heard of this, they followed him on foot from the cities. When he went ashore, he saw a large crowd, and felt compassion for them and healed their sick.'

Jesus was a human being with normal human emotions. He deeply felt the loss of his cousin John, whom he would have known while growing up, who had gone ahead of him into ministry and who had baptized him. He went off to be in the solitary presence of his Father to grieve the loss that he must have known for some time in his spirit was coming. However he wasn't to be left alone for long. A measure of his selflessness was to put the needs of the crowd before his own needs.

15-21: 'When it was evening, the disciples came to him and said, 'This place is desolate and the hour is already late; so send the crowds away, that they may go into the villages and buy food for themselves. But Jesus said to them, 'They do not need to go away; you give them something to eat!' They said to him, 'We have here only five loaves and two fish. And he said, 'Bring them here to me.' Ordering the people to sit down on the grass, he took the five loaves and the two fish, and looking up toward heaven, he blessed the food, and breaking the loaves he gave them to the disciples, and the disciples gave them to the crowds, and they all ate and were satisfied. They picked up what was left over of the broken pieces, twelve full baskets. There were about five thousand men who ate, besides women and children.'

Six o'clock came and went and the wilderness Jesus had retreated to was no place for a large crowd in terms of local food supplies. Jesus challenges his disciples to meet their need. This first of the two recorded instances of miraculous food multiplication seems to have overflowed from being thrown onto his Father in prayer in the pain of the news of John's murder. In 'bring them to me' there is the steely ring

126

of the imperative mood in the Greek, also found in his command to the disciples concerning the demon oppressed and epileptic boy of Matthew 17:17. "Bring the boy here to me". There was a similar degree of strength in his 'command' (Greek: *'keleuo'* - to order) [104] that the crowd be seated. Jesus appears to be greatly moved; as well he might be given the recent events concerning John. After giving the customary Jewish blessing to Father for his provision (where God, not the food, is blessed), Jesus performs a sign so in keeping with the abundance associated with the Messiah (Amos 9:13), that the crowd, John 6:15 tells us, make plans to adopt Jesus as their king without further ado.

22-23: 'Immediately he made the disciples get into the boat and go ahead of him to the other side, while he sent the crowds away. After he had sent the crowds away, he went up on the mountain by himself to pray; and when it was evening, he was there alone.'

Jesus will have none of it, however, and dismisses the crowd to continue his unfinished business in mourning John's loss in the presence of his Heavenly Father, having sent his disciples on ahead.

24-27: 'But the boat was already a long distance from the land, battered by the waves; for the wind was contrary. And in the fourth watch of the night he came to them, walking on the sea. When the disciples saw him walking on the sea, they were terrified, and said, 'It is a ghost!' And they cried out in fear. But immediately Jesus spoke to them, saying, 'Take courage, it is I; do not be afraid.'

Lake Galilee's location in proximity to the neighboring mountains made the storms on it notorious for their speed of onset and severity. Many of the disciples were experienced fisherman and their minds would have been recalling former colleagues or friends who had drowned in those days of little safety flotation aids. They were well aware of the danger they were in and would have been baling furiously, despite their tiredness from the effort of rowing against the prevailing wind. When they saw a figure obscured by spray but quite definitely approaching the boat in the ghostly moonlight, they would have had but one thought from their cultural perspective. The Jews believed that at the point of death a spirit came to accompany the deceased person to Sheol, the place of shadows; hence their cry of terror prior to recognizing him.

28-33: 'Peter said to him, 'Lord, if it is you, command me to come to you on the water.' And he said, 'Come!' And Peter got out of the boat, and walked on the water and came toward Jesus. But seeing the wind, he became frightened, and beginning to sink, he cried out, 'Lord, save me!' Immediately Jesus stretched out his hand and took hold of him, and said to him, 'You of little faith, why did you doubt?' When they got into the boat, the wind stopped. And those who were in the boat worshipped him, saying, 'You are certainly God's Son!'

Peter's mouth often worked faster than his brain. When Jesus' single word 'Come' ignited faith in Peter's spirit, (see Romans 10:17), he made good his word and stepped out of the boat to take some paces on top of the waves. Credit to him! It was the Father's hand in response to faith (trust in action) that was keeping Peter aloft until his attention was diverted from Jesus to the storm. Fear always undermines trust, but like a caring older brother Jesus is there to catch him, with the mildest of rebukes - 'Little Faith!' (*'oligopistos'* is a title of affection), 'Why did you doubt?' The wind, which was waiting for this test of Peter's faith to be concluded, ceases on his re-entering the boat and the disciples are once again confronted with Jesus' divinity. The only appropriate response is *'proskuneo'* - 'drawing near to kiss' his hand in worship and acknowledgement of the fact that God has a Son, as Proverbs 30:4 ('Who has established all the ends of the earth? What is his name or his Son's name?') makes clear.

128

34-36: 'When they had crossed over, they came to land at Gennesaret. And when the men of that place recognized him, they sent word into all that surrounding district and brought to him all who were sick; and they implored him that they might just touch the fringe of his cloak; and as many as touched it were cured.'

Part of a beautiful and fertile plain of the River Jordan, Gennesaret was a town belonging to the tribe of Naphtali, also known as 'Kinnereth' (Joshua 19:35), and was easily accessible by boat. Its residents would have been well acquainted with news of this amazing Rabbi and miracle-worker. Jesus did not disappoint them - one touch of his coat's tassels (twisted fringes which served as reminders to the Israelites to keep the commands of God) was all it needed, such was their faith and confidence in him.

Chapter 15

1-2: 'Then some Pharisees and Scribes came to Jesus from Jerusalem and said, 'Why do your disciples break the tradition of the elders? For they do not wash their hands when they eat bread.'

The Sanhedrin sent investigating parties of scribal experts and lawyers to check out any teacher's orthodoxy, as they had with John the Baptist. They are still trying to find some fault with Christ, but keep having to make do with picking on some aspect of his disciples' behaviour as there is nothing in Jesus' behaviour even to offend the minutiae of their Mishnaic interpretation and recording of the oral traditions of their rabbinic forefathers. Jesus is simply not giving them even an inch! So they take note of the absence on the part of the disciples of ceremonial hand rinsing prescribed therein. Whether Jesus himself observed this tradition is not here recorded - he may have been fasting!

3-6: 'And he answered and said to them, 'Why do you yourselves transgress the commandment of God for the sake of your tradition? For God said, 'Honour your father and mother,' and 'He who speaks evil of father and mother is to be put to death.' But you say, 'Whoever says to his father or mother, 'Whatever I have that would help you has been given to God,' he is not to honour his father or his mother.' And by this you invalidated the word of God for the sake of your tradition.'

Jesus responds to the attack on his disciples' credibility as men of God by going onto the offensive himself. The Pharisees had arrived at a number of ingenious ways of getting around requirements within the formal Torah (upon which the Mishnah was based), including one that required the support of elderly parents. All one needed to do was to declare the support that would have been available to them '*korbana*' (Mark 7:11 - literally 'treasury offering'),[105] and so devoted to God, and one was released from giving it to one's parents if one did not wish to (perhaps out of spite). Hence the oral-based Mishnah prevailed over the Torah!

7-9: 'You hypocrites, rightly did Isaiah prophesy of you: 'This people honours me with their lips, but their heart is far away from me. But in vain do they worship me, teaching as doctrines the precepts of men.'

Ever the straight talker, Jesus calls them '*hupokrites*' - 'actors',[106] or those who 'pretend' at religion for show. God is not deceived however; neither was Isaiah (29:13-14): 'Because this people draw near with their words, and honour me with their lip service, but they remove their hearts far from me, and their reverence for me consists of tradition, learned by rote. Therefore behold, I will once again deal marvellously with this people, wondrously marvellous; and the wisdom of their wise men will perish, and the discernment of their discerning men will be concealed.' Lip service is not what God is looking for and he can certainly tell when that is all he is getting! Tradition, learned by rote, is an apt summing-up of the Pharisaic methods which did nothing to engage the heart in inner change. God's 'marvellous' (Hebrew - '*pala*' - literally, 'beyond one's natural power of comprehension') [107] dealings were soon to come with the Roman suppression under General Tiberias in AD 70. The Temple-based Rabbinic schools would be destroyed along with 'the wisdom of their wise men' and the lives of many of those men as well; in a judgement 'marvellous' beyond comprehension.

10-11: 'After Jesus called the crowd to him, he said to them, 'Hear and understand. It is not what enters into the mouth that defiles the man, but what proceeds out of the mouth, this defiles the man.'

Jesus is keen that the common people understand that the purpose of God's Law is to change the hearts of men and women into God's likeness. It is what comes out of the mouth that is the best indication of what is inside the heart - what goes into the mouth is barely even relevant. This was a ground-breaking idea for an audience steeped in the many rules and regulations of Kosher food practices, that had been given to serve a purpose under the Law to point towards inner purity. This purity was soon to be an experiential reality with the outpouring on all of God's Holy Spirit of grace and mercy.

12-14: 'Then the disciples came and said to him, 'Do you know that the Pharisees were offended when they heard this statement?' But he answered and said, 'Every plant which my heavenly Father did not plant shall be uprooted. Let them alone; they are blind guides of the blind. And if a blind man guides a blind man, both will fall into a pit.'

Small wonder that the Pharisees were offended! Their social and religious standing was dependent on the role of slavish allegiance to a set of rules devised by their rabbinic fore-fathers, based upon the Law of Moses. Jesus however identifies them as 'plants that his Father did not plant'. Jesus then gives a humourous analogy, by virtue of the ridiculous nature of the image, of one blind man leading another and both consequently falling into a pit. By such insensitive means did Jesus respond to his opponents' sense of offense! Perhaps now they would think twice before picking on his friends and disciples.

15-20: 'Peter said to him, 'Explain the parable to us.' Jesus said, 'Are you still lacking in understanding also? Do you not understand that everything that goes into the mouth passes into the stomach, and is eliminated? But the things that proceed out of the mouth come from the heart, and those defile the man. For out of the heart come evil thoughts, murders, adulteries, fornications, thefts, false witness, slanders. These are the things which defile the man; but to eat with unwashed hands does not defile the man.'

Ever honest, Peter asks for clarification concerning the jaw-dropping nature of Jesus' teaching on food purity. And Jesus is happy to oblige with a brief lesson in the distinction between human digestive biology and the heart-centered spirituality that he is seeking to uphold. It is 'the heart' (Greek: *'kardia'*, meaning 'the centre of thinking / the will / human character') [108] that is the issue. When it is removed far from God it gives rise to all manner of things that are spiritually unclean and humanly unhealthy, in comparison with which eating with ceremonially unwashed (but not necessarily dirty) hands pales into insignificance.

21-24: 'Jesus went away from there, and withdrew into the district of Tyre and Sidon. And a Canaanite woman from that region came out and began to cry out, saying, 'Have mercy on me, Lord, Son of David; my daughter is cruelly demon-possessed.' But he did not answer her a word. And his disciples came and implored him, saying, 'Send her away, because she keeps shouting at us'. But he answered and said, 'I was sent only, to the lost sheep of the house of Israel.'

Many non-Jews resided in the coastal region of Tyre and Sidon (around 50 miles north-west of Gennesaret) and one had evidently heard something about this Rabbi that aroused her fervent interest. She was a Greek speaker, a descendant of the original Canaanites (Phoenicians), and the region was known as Syrian Phoenicia (hence a 'Syro-Phoenician' - Mark 7:26). Jesus was true to the mission to his lost Jewish brethren that his Father had given him to fulfil prior to their impending judgement. Having sent messengers, the Father was now sending his one and only Son (see Luke 20:13). Possibly as a test of her faith, Jesus first ignores her, perhaps concentrating on whatever 'lost sheep of the house of Israel' happened to be present. Eventually the woman's persistent noise ('shouting at us' is *'krazo'* - 'to cry out unmelodiously like a raven does') [109] gets on the disciples' nerves sufficiently that they decide to 'represent her case' to Jesus - by asking that he send her away!

133

25-28: 'But she came and began to bow down before him, saying, 'Lord, help me!' And he answered and said, 'It is not good to take the children's bread and throw it to the dogs.' But she said, 'Yes Lord; but even the dogs feed on the crumbs which fall from their masters' table.' Then Jesus said to her, 'O woman, your faith is great; it shall be done for you as you wish.' And her daughter was healed at once.'

Her attitude to Jesus so impresses him that he grants her request. She has already persisted into importunity, now she comes to *'proskuneo'* ('worship with a kiss'). The Greek word here is derived from the word *'kuon'*, meaning 'dog',[110] after the manner which a pet dog will greet his owner with a lick to the outstretched hand. Jesus, always ready with humour, responds with a remark about giving to the pet dogs (Greek: *'kunarion'* - a family's little pet 'puppy dog')[111] what is intended for the householder's children (i.e. the Jews). But his wit is outdone by the woman's - and her response of trust so impresses Jesus that she enters the annals of history as one of the two Gentiles given the term *'megas pistis'* - 'great faiths', the other being the Centurion of chapter 8. Her daughter is healed with no visit or audible word of command or prayer being uttered.

29-31: 'Departing from there, Jesus went along by the Sea of Galilee, and having gone up on the mountain, he was sitting there. And large crowds came to him, bringing with them those who were lame, crippled, blind, mute, and many others, and they laid them down at his feet; and he healed them. So the crowd marvelled as they saw the mute speaking, the crippled restored, and the lame walking, and the blind seeing; and they glorified the God of Israel.'

If Jesus has possibly thought that he might get a rest after the long journey homewards into Galilee, the crowd soon put paid to that, bringing the 'usual suspects' in huge numbers, all in need of Father's power of healing and deliverance. The needy are *'rhipto'* - 'thrown prostrate'[112] - at Jesus' feet. What could he do but overflow toward them in compassion and heal them? As a result the Father's name is *'doxazo'* - 'praised, magnified, exalted and generally held in high honour'.[113] In short, Jesus is going about his normal business of making his Father 'look good', by demonstrating openly his amazing power.

32-39: 'And Jesus called his disciples to him, and said, 'I feel compassion for the people, because they have remained with me now three days and have nothing to eat; and I do not want to send them away hungry, for they might faint on the way.' The disciples said to him, 'Where would we get so many loaves in this desolate place to satisfy such a large crowd?' And Jesus said to them, 'How many loaves do you have?' And they said, 'Seven, and a few small fish.' And he directed the people to sit down on the ground; and he took the seven loaves and the fish; and giving thanks, he broke them and started giving them to the disciples, and the disciples gave them to the people. And they all ate and were satisfied, and they picked up what was left over of the broken pieces, seven large baskets full. And those who ate were four thousand men, besides women and children. And sending away the crowds, Jesus got into the boat and came to the region of Magadan.'

The evening is drawing in and many of the people have a long journey home. Jesus is not simply concerned with deep spiritual and major physical needs; hunger is a concern of his as well. What a shame there is no food locally. Rather, what a shame that the disciples have such little faith or such short memories! After performing another public miraculous multiplication, Jesus feeds them all abundantly before dismissing them, and moving on to his next port of call in Western Galilee at Magadan, (also called Dalmanutha) three miles north of Tiberius, and the birthplace of Mary Magdalene (Matthew 27:56, 61).

Chapter 16

1-4: 'The Pharisees and Sadducees came up, and testing Jesus, they asked him to show them a sign from heaven. But he replied to them, 'When it is evening, you say, 'It will be fair weather, for the sky is red.' And in the morning, 'There will be a storm today, for the sky is red and threatening.' Do you know how to discern the appearance of the sky, but cannot discern the signs of the times? An evil and adulterous generation seeks after a sign; and a sign will not be given it, except the sign of Jonah.' And he left them and went away.'

The persistent Pharisees this time resort to joining forces with their natural opponents on the Sanhedrin, the Sadducees (the priestly division of the Jews). They come for a formal '*peirazo*' - a formal 'test' of orthodoxy, [114] as in their jealousy they are seeking to remove from Jesus his office of ordained Rabbi and Doctor of the Law amongst the people of Israel. So they ask for a sign from heaven! Not for them the answer to some knotty Jewish legal problem; that would be too easy for this mastermind from Nazareth. After all, the Lord God himself had said (to Ahaz): "Ask a sign for yourself from the Lord your God; make it deep as Sheol or high as heaven" (Isaiah 7:10-11)? Surely they were being very reasonable! If Jesus really had metamorphosed from Rabbi to Messiah, that would surely be no problem for him to oblige them with. Perhaps though they had forgotten Isaiah 7:12-13: 'But Ahaz said, "I will not ask, nor will I test the Lord." Then he said, "Listen now, O house of David! Is it too slight a thing for you to try the patience of men, that you will try the patience of my God as well?"'

Mark's account of this incident (Mark 8:12) tells us that 'Jesus sighed deeply' (the Greek here is '*anastenazo*' from '*stenazo*' - 'to groan') [115], possibly because it brought to his mind the pain of that other occasion (with the devil in the wilderness) when similar requests had been made of him. Jesus knows they will not respond even if they get such a sign, because their hearts are not right before God. So he repeats his words of chapter 12:39 - the only sign will be that of Jonah. But since they are so interested in the signs in the sky, and can even forecast rain, how is it that they cannot see what is clearly visible and happening all around them - spiritual activity that is clearly fulfilling Messianic prophecy? Truly they are 'evil', the Greek here being *'poneros'*, meaning 'in a bad way' spiritually, and also meaning 'annoying', [116] another example of a play-on-words. And like their ancestors, they *'moichalis'* - 'play the harlot' [117] of fast and loose, unfaithful and spiritually adulterous behaviour towards a holy God.

5-12: 'And the disciples came to the other side of the sea, but they had forgotten to bring any bread. And Jesus said to them, 'Watch out and beware of the leaven of the Pharisees and Sadducees.' They began to discuss this among themselves, saying, 'He said that because we did not bring any bread.' But Jesus, aware of this, said, 'You men of little faith, why do you discuss among yourselves that you have no bread? Do you not yet understand or remember the five loaves of the five thousand, and how many baskets full you picked up? Or the seven loaves of the four thousand, and how many large baskets full you picked up? How is it that you do not understand that I did not speak to you concerning bread? But beware of the leaven of the Pharisees and Sadducees.' Then they understood that he did not say to beware of the leaven of bread, but of the teaching of the Pharisees and Sadducees.'

Crossing Lake Galilee the disciple's stomachs remind them of the meal they have missed. But they have no bread! Jesus takes the opportunity to make a spiritual point, connecting yeast (which can stand for sin in Scriptural thought - see Galatians 5:9) with the teaching and especially the attitude (the play-acting hypocrisy - Luke 12:1) of the Pharisees and Sadducees. The disciples, who were perhaps slightly in awe of Jewish officialdom in all its splendour, were truly 'slow to understand'.

137

13-16: 'Now when Jesus came into the district of Caesarea Philippi, he was asking his disciples, 'Who do people say that the Son of Man is?' And they said, 'Some say John the Baptist and others, Elijah; but still others, Jeremiah, or one of the prophets.' He said to them, 'But who do you say that I am?' Simon Peter answered, 'You are the Christ, the Son of the living God.' And Jesus said to him, 'Blessed are you, Simon Barjona, because flesh and blood did not reveal this to you, but my Father who is in heaven."

Popular opinion about Jesus was divided. John records: 'Some were saying, "He is a good man"; others were saying, "No, on the contrary, he leads the people astray" (John 7:12). Certain others held him to be mad, as John (10:19-21) recounts: 'A division occurred again among the Jews because of these words. Many of them were saying, "He has a demon and is insane. Why do you listen to him?" Others were saying, "These are not the sayings of one demon-possessed. A demon cannot open the eyes of the blind, can he?"'

A substantial section of popular belief held him to be a re-embodiment of one of the prophets, just as the priests and Levites had come from Jerusalem to enquire of John the Baptist whether he was Elijah (John 1:19 - 21). But Peter, with the help of some revelation from Father, was clear - Jesus was the promised Messiah (Christ), an embodiment of God himself. 'Son' in Jewish culture means one with parity of status with the Father and worthy of equal respect from those outside. Jesus was not merely a former prophet on a repeat visit.

18: 'I also say to you that you are Peter, and upon this rock I will build my church; and the gates of Hades will not overpower it.'

These words of Jesus have been the subject of much dispute historically, but needlessly so. Jesus addresses Peter as '*Petros*' (a 'rock' or 'boulder').[118] He then switches noun in the next line and uses the word *petra* (meaning 'a layer of bedrock') [119] to describe the foundation that his church (*ekklesia* - 'an assembling of citizens') [120] would be built upon. The question is, was *petra* to indicate Peter or Jesus? The answer may be found by allowing the Bible to interpret itself. 'Petra' is used on 14 other occasions in the New Testament. 11 refer to natural bedrock, with the other 3 referring to Christ himself. In Romans 9:33 (ANIV), Paul says: 'See, I lay in Zion a stone that causes men to stumble and a rock that makes them fall, and the one who trusts in him will never be put to shame.' 1 Corinthians 10:4 says 'all drank the same spiritual drink, for they were drinking from a spiritual rock which followed them; and the rock was Christ.' And finally Peter himself says in 1 Peter 2:7-8: 'Now to you who believe, this stone is precious. But to those who do not believe, "The stone the builders rejected has become the capstone," and, "A stone that causes men to stumble and a rock that makes them fall"' (ANIV). Clearly here *petra* stands for Christ himself, something that does not however diminish the foundational role that the apostles, and especially Peter, played in establishing the church in the first century, even to laying down their lives in martyrdom (see Ephesians 2:20, where Paul describes apostles and prophets as making up the church's foundation).

19-20: 'I will give you the keys of the kingdom of heaven; and whatever you bind on earth shall have been bound in heaven, and whatever you loose on earth shall have been loosed in heaven.' Then he warned the disciples that they should tell no one that he was the Christ.'

Peter, with the other disciples (not exclusively), certainly had a major role to play - to them would be granted spiritual authority. 'Binding' was a Rabbinic function denoting that which was prohibited (e.g. on a Sabbath), whereas 'loosing' stood for what was permitted. Jesus changes tense from aorist (irrespective of time) to perfect (completed previously) when he moves between the two uses of 'bound' and 'loosed'. Hence the meaning is 'whatever you bind or loose on earth shall be, having been (*already*) bound or loosed in heaven'. What happens on earth therefore follows what has happened in heaven, as in the Lord's Prayer - 'Your will be done on earth as it is in heaven'.

21-23: 'From that time Jesus began to show his disciples that he must go to Jerusalem, and suffer many things from the elders and Chief Priests and Scribes, and be killed, and be raised up on the third day. Peter took him aside and began to rebuke him, saying, 'God forbid it, Lord! This shall never happen to you.' But he turned and said to Peter, 'Get behind me, Satan! You are a stumbling block to me; for you are not setting your mind on God's interests, but man's.'

Pride comes before a fall and perhaps Peter had taken Jesus' words to mean that he could now instruct even his Master! As Jesus makes his intentions plain, Peter, who may have had a more triumphalistic outcome in mind, decides that Jesus' words are bad for the others' morale and takes him to one side to '*epitimao*' him - 'admonish him sharply'.[121] Peter uses the Greek word '*hileos*' to Jesus, which carries the intent that God will have mercy on Jesus and deliver him from such an unhappy outcome. Perhaps Peter wanted to practice binding and loosing, but had missed the point about getting heaven's perspective first. Jesus identifies Satan's influence in the 'trap trigger' stumbling block of potentially missing God's mark through viewing events from an earth-bound human perspective rather than from God's point of view.

24-25: 'Then Jesus said to his disciples, 'If anyone wishes to come after me, he must deny himself, and take up his cross and follow me. For whoever wishes to save his life will lose it; but whoever loses his life for my sake will find it.''

Like all disciples, their lot would not differ substantially from their masters. If Jesus was to die at the hands of the Jewish authorities, the likelihood was that they would too. The sight of condemned men carrying their execution stakes to the place of their death was a well recognized one and the disciples would have been in no doubt as to Jesus' meaning. They are commanded to *'aparneomai'* - to 'forego their own interests' [122] - as a sign that they now belonged to another - one who would go before them into his Father's will in complete confidence in the resurrection and glory that would follow. To 'lose' one's life carries little of the sense of the strength of the Greek used. *'Apollumi'* means to 'utterly destroy or ruin' [123] - to cast one's human ambitions onto the rubbish heap and take on whatever Father gives instead. In the same way another great Jewish teacher, S'haul (the Apostle Paul) would say: 'I count all things to be loss in view of the surpassing value of knowing Christ Jesus my Lord, for whom I have suffered the loss of all things, and count them but rubbish so that I may gain Christ, and may be found in him' (Philippians 3:8-9).

26-27: 'For what will it profit a man if he gains the whole world and forfeits his soul? Or what will a man give in exchange for his soul? 'For the Son of Man is going to come in the glory of his Father with his angels, and will then repay every man according to his deeds.'

Jesus brings it down to brass tacks. Do you want to save your soul? Then give it over to God now, and your reward will be far greater than anything you imagine you might lose now. Early Christian martyrs were able to sing praises while dying, surely evidence that even 'worse case scenarios' can be overcome by Father's all-consuming power. 'Invest little in the kingdom, gain little for eternity' is the message. Discipleship is therefore a 'win-win' situation - a hundredfold in this life, and eternal reward in the next! (Matthew 19:29). No wonder the devil seeks to put people off with the fear that God will give something unpleasant, despite Jesus' teaching about asking for an egg and not receiving a scorpion from your father! (Luke 11:12).

141

28: 'Truly I say to you, there are some of those who are standing here who will not taste death until they see the Son of Man coming in his kingdom.'

Having mentioned his second coming, Jesus advises them that they will not wait long for the evidence of what he has told them. It will not be long in coming. 'Coming' is in the present tense and active voice - literally 'come imminently'. Very imminently!

Chapter 17

1-3: 'Six days later Jesus took with him Peter and James and John his brother, and led them up on a high mountain by themselves. And he was transfigured before them; and his face shone like the sun, and his garments became as white as light. And behold, Moses and Elijah appeared to them, talking with him.'

Jesus' closest three disciples accompany him 'up a high mountain', most probably Mount Hermon, which was fourteen miles from their last noted location of Caesarea Philippi and stands 9,400 feet high. On the uninhabited slopes near the top a sudden change occurred in Jesus' appearance. 'Transfigured' is '*metamorphoo*' - a 'transformation' [124] occurred, and Jesus literally 'changed into another form' - his true one. Years later John was to have a repeat experience of this while exiled on the Greek island of Patmos: 'In the middle of the lampstands I saw one like a son of man, clothed in a robe reaching to the feet, and girded across his chest with a golden sash. His head and his hair were white like white wool, like snow; and his eyes were like a flame of fire. His feet were like burnished bronze, when it has been made to glow in a furnace, and his voice was like the sound of many waters. In his right hand he held seven stars, and out of his mouth came a sharp two-edged sword; and his face was like the sun shining in its strength' (Revelation 1:13-16). The glorified Jesus must have been an awe inspiring sight, as must the figures of Moses and Elijah, as they dialogued with Jesus concerning his Father's plans.

4-8: 'Peter said to Jesus, 'Lord, it is good for us to be here; if you wish, I will make three tabernacles here, one for you, and one for Moses, and one for Elijah.' While he was still speaking, a bright cloud overshadowed them, and behold, a voice out of the cloud said, 'This is my beloved Son, with whom I am well-pleased; listen to him!' When the disciples heard this, they fell face down to the ground and were terrified. And Jesus came to them and touched them and said, 'Get up, and do not be afraid.' And lifting up their eyes, they saw no one except Jesus himself alone.'

Seemingly often one to engage his mouth before his brain, Peter decides a little religious action is called for, and offers to build three booths for them. It takes Father's voice emanating from a cloud of glory to bring about the more appropriate response of prostration before Jesus' manifestation of divinity that John immediately adopted on Patmos when he saw it again. Mark's account (9:6) explains that Peter (Mark's source) spoke out of abject fear, hence Jesus' gentle touch and encouragement to not succumb to terror.

9-13: 'As they were coming down from the mountain, Jesus commanded them, saying, 'Tell the vision to no one until the Son of Man has risen from the dead.' And his disciples asked him, 'Why then do the Scribes say that Elijah must come first?' And he answered and said, 'Elijah is coming and will restore all things; but I say to you that Elijah already came, and they did not recognize him, but did to him whatever they wished. So also the Son of Man is going to suffer at their hands. Then the disciples understood that he had spoken to them about John the Baptist.'

After Jesus enjoins them to silence, the disciples are sufficiently recovered to seek to clear up the theological question that the appearance of Elijah has prompted in their minds. The Scribes had questioned John the Baptist as to his fulfilling the role of Elijah. John's understanding of his own ministry appears to have been confined to the element of preparing the Messiah's way, as was described in Isaiah chapter 40, and not the element pertinent to Elijah described in Malachi chapter 4. Jesus however confirms that John fulfilled both roles, and that non-recognition and subsequent rejection, with suffering, will befall him too. This last is *'pascho'*,[125] the word Luke uses in Acts 1:3 to describe the suffering at Calvary (often rendered as Jesus' 'passion').

14-18: 'When they came to the crowd, a man came up to Jesus, falling on his knees before him and saying, 'Lord, have mercy on my son, for he is a lunatic and is very ill; for he often falls into the fire and often into the water. I brought him to your disciples, and they could not cure him.' And Jesus answered and said, 'You unbelieving and perverted generation, how long shall I be with you? How long shall I put up with you? Bring him here to me.' And Jesus rebuked him, and the demon came out of him, and the boy was cured at once.'

Demon oppression can manifest in a variety of ways including physical illness. This demon was seeking to take the boy's life through causing dangerous behaviour, and the remaining disciples had lacked the necessary trust and concomitant faith to bring about a deliverance. In fact Mark's account (9:22) indicates that the boy's father lacked faith for his recovery as well, contributing to Jesus' remark about their state of *'apistos'* ('faithlessness') and *'diastrepho'* ('turning aside from God's ways, to pervert or corrupt').[126] This strong language perhaps indicates some underlying sin in the father's life that had enabled the evil spirit to gain such a foothold in the boy in the first place. For example, anger - Ephesians 4:27 (ANIV) - 'Do not let the sun go down while you are still angry, and do not give the devil a foothold'.

19-21: 'Then the disciples came to Jesus privately, and said, 'Why could we not drive it out?' And he said to them, 'Because of the littleness of your faith; for truly I say to you, if you have faith the size of a mustard seed, you will say to this mountain, 'Move from here to there,' and it will move; and nothing will be impossible to you. But this kind does not go out except by prayer and fasting.'

Lack of trust in Father is the main hindrance of all spiritual activity, whereas humbling ourselves in prayer and fasting reduces any sense of self-dependency we may be experiencing. Because trust is an attitude

145

of dependency even a little is capable of unleashing God's mighty power to effect change.

22-23: 'And while they were gathering together in Galilee, Jesus said to them, "The Son of Man is going to be delivered into the hands of men; and they will kill him, and he will be raised on the third day." And they were deeply grieved.'

Having already briefed his closest three disciples Jesus now tells them all what Father's plans entail. The disciples seem to have focused on the dying rather than the rising again on the third day. 'Delivered' here is *'paradidomi'* from *'didomi'* meaning to 'give of one's own accord',[127] implying that while Jesus was certainly betrayed into the hands of the priests, it was of his own free will and by his offering of himself that this occurred.

24-27: 'When they came to Capernaum, those who collected the two-drachma tax came to Peter and said, 'Does your teacher not pay the two-drachma tax?' He said, 'Yes.' And when he came into the house, Jesus spoke to him first, saying, 'What do you think, Simon? From whom do the kings of the earth collect customs or poll-tax, from their sons or from strangers?' When Peter said, 'From strangers', Jesus said to him, 'Then the sons are exempt. However, so that we do not offend them, go to the sea and throw in a hook, and take the first fish that comes up; and when you open its mouth, you will find a shekel. Take that and give it to them for you and me.'

Now Jesus and his disciples are back at home base in Capernaum and a tax demand is awaiting them. The Temple tax was a controversial issue; not in terms of the principle, which was set out in Exodus 30:13, but because the Roman eagle over the main Temple gate and the immediate proximity of the Roman garrison's fortress of Antonia rendered the site impure to the most observant Jews. However, if Jesus

146

refused to pay then he could be rightfully accused of breaking the Law, hence the question may well have been framed with malicious intent. Ever quick with a retort, Peter tells them that Jesus does pay it, but on entering the house he finds that Jesus anticipates him. The ruling aristocracy did not themselves pay taxes, and Jesus states that the same principle applies to all of his Father's children. However in this instance there is a greater, more over-riding principle to be considered - not giving unnecessary offense - again the 'trap trigger' of '*skandalizo*' must be avoided. But to demonstrate the grace of the Father who exempts his children from such petty duties, Jesus performs a remarkable miracle. So both principles were beautifully satisfied!

Chapter 18

1-3: 'At that time the disciples came to Jesus and said, 'Who then is greatest in the kingdom of heaven?' And he called a child to himself and set him before them, and said, 'Truly I say to you, unless you are converted and become like children, you will not enter the kingdom of heaven."

It may have been that the additional domestic attentions of their home base brought about a sense of a need to establish a pecking-order, but it would be a recurring issue for the disciples who had yet to grasp the principle of the first being last. Jesus' common visual aid in such scenarios was a child. In those days children had no legal rights of their own and occupied a lowly place within society equivalent to a servant. As the Apostle Paul would later put it: 'As long as the heir is a child, he does not differ at all from a slave although he is owner of everything' (Galatians 4:1). Hence Jesus' lesson is that the disciples need to 'turn' (literally: 'be converted'), expressed in the aorist tense (an action without indication of completion), implying that this requires a continuing process. 'Becoming like children' is best understood in parallel with Jesus teaching in Matthew 19:14, where parents are bringing 'little children' (the Greek is '*paidon*', as here, meaning 'infants' or 'young children'), and where Jesus says 'the kingdom of heaven belongs to such as these', a similar idea to 'entering' it. Small children personify trust in their parents, and trust forms the basis of faith - the attribute that allows participation in the life of the kingdom.

4-6: 'Whoever then humbles himself as this child, he is the greatest in the kingdom of heaven. And whoever receives one such child in my name receives me; but whoever causes one of these little ones who believe in me to stumble, it would be better for him to have a heavy millstone hung around his neck, and to be drowned in the depth of the sea.'

A sense of complete dependency on another (in this case God), and not on oneself (however capable and gifted one may be), is the essence of the attribute of *'tapeinoo'* or 'lowliness / humility'. Jesus says this is a sign of true spiritual greatness, because it throws oneself on Father to be exalted rather than trying to advance oneself. As Peter, who must have been listening closely, would later say: 'Humble yourselves under the mighty hand of God, that he may exalt you at the proper time, casting all your anxiety on him, because he cares for you' (1 Peter 5:6-7). Jesus' concern for their spiritual wellbeing is such that terrible things are forecast for any who would seek to 'offend' or cause such a one to 'stumble' (once again, *'skandalizo'* - 'stumbling block', derived from 'a trap').

7-9: 'Woe to the world because of its stumbling blocks! For it is inevitable that stumbling blocks come; but woe to that man through whom the stumbling block comes! If your hand or your foot causes you to stumble, cut it off and throw it from you; it is better for you to enter life crippled or lame, than to have two hands or two feet and be cast into the eternal fire. If your eye causes you to stumble, pluck it out and throw it from you. It is better for you to enter life with one eye, than to have two eyes and be cast into the fiery hell.'

The world is all the poorer for ineffective Christians, who are unable to be the salt and light that Father intends them to be, thereby depriving the world of the blessing of their witness. Jesus identifies 'trap triggers' of 'stumbling' (*'skandalon'*) as the main means of snaring them into a spiritually disadvantageous position. Radical steps are necessary to avoid them, rather than risk Gehenna, a place where, as Mark 9:46 says, 'the fire never goes out and the worm is never satisfied'. Jesus is speaking of the Jerusalem rubbish dump of Hinnom, a deep and narrow ravine to the southwest of Jerusalem where the residents dumped their rubbish and also the bodies of dead unclean animals such as stray dogs, as well as the occasional human corpse. There was never any shortage of domestic refuse as fuel for the continually burning flames - definitely a place to avoid at any personal cost.

10: 'See that you do not despise one of these little ones, for I say to you that their angels in heaven continually see the face of my Father who is in heaven.'

The 'little ones' ('*mikros*') referred to here are any (not just children) who occupy a lowly place before God. They know that whatever chance they have of spiritual success is based on their sense of dependency upon God and not on their own strengths and abilities, good as they may be. Father can always tell self-dependency (pride) and does not reward it, whereas he is quick to bestow his grace and favour on the humble because they have taken a lowly position before him. Jesus clearly says that there are personally assigned angels, and that this is reflected in heaven itself.

11-14: 'For the Son of Man has come to save that which was lost. What do you think? If any man has a hundred sheep, and one of them has gone astray, does he not leave the ninety-nine on the mountains and go and search for the one that is straying? If it turns out that he finds it, truly I say to you, he rejoices over it more than over the ninety-nine, which have not gone astray. So it is not the will of your Father who is in heaven that one of these little ones perish.'

Having advised on the disciples' correct spiritual posture (lowliness), Jesus reminds them of his own job description - to seek and to save the lost. (This saying is also found in Luke 19:10). Jesus' main concern is for the lost, not the found. He does not want any of his creation to end up in Gehenna. Shepherds had a responsibility to the whole community for the communal flock, and would spend days looking for a lost sheep while their colleagues remained with the rest of the flock. As well as the sheep's intrinsic value, his reputation as a shepherd was at stake.

Jesus, the 'good shepherd' (John 10:11), is no less concerned for members of the spiritual flock, wanting none to 'perish'. The Greek here (*'apollumi'*) means to be 'rendered useless',[128] in this case, eternally, having been rendered unfit for purpose by the power of sin.

15-17: 'If your brother sins, go and show him his fault in private; if he listens to you, you have won your brother. But if he does not listen to you, take one or two more with you, so that by the mouth of two or three witnesses every fact may be confirmed. If he refuses to listen to them, tell it to the church; and if he refuses to listen even to the church, let him be to you as a Gentile and a tax collector.'

Sin is a fact of life and Jesus wanted his disciples to deal with it effectively. Sin here is *'hamartano'*, meaning to 'miss the mark' and to 'wander off the right path and trespass'.[129] The first step is to communicate privately why he is at fault, then if unsuccessful to try again with two witnesses, and then to make the issue known widely within the 'assembly' of faith - the Church. After these three strikes they are out - only 'out' means they are still to be treated as one would a foreigner or someone doing a despised job, i.e. still reached out to, as Jesus himself did towards tax collectors and other 'sinners'.

18-20: 'Truly I say to you, whatever you bind on earth shall have been bound in heaven; and whatever you loose on earth shall have been loosed in heaven. Again I say to you, that if two of you agree on earth about anything, that they may ask, it shall be done for them by my Father who is in heaven. For where two or three have gathered together in my name, I am there in their midst.'

Jesus now deals with prayer, and repeats to all the disciples the words he spoke to Peter in the previous chapter. Again the tense switches from the aorist ('loose' on earth) to the perfect ('loosed' in heaven),

151

indicating the action has already occurred in heaven. Again, this fits with the pattern Jesus taught in his own prayer (Matthew 6), when God's will is done on earth as it is (already) in heaven. Unity of agreement is important, for, as Psalm 133:3 says, 'there the Lord commands the blessing, even eternal life'. The blessing of unity includes the promise of God hearing and answering favourably, not least because Jesus himself promised to be present personally!

21-22: 'Then Peter came and said to him, "Lord, how often shall my brother sin against me and I forgive him? Up to seven times?" Jesus said to him, "I do not say to you, up to seven times, but up to seventy times seven."

It would seem that Peter's mind was still on what Jesus had said about a brother who had sinned against someone, and quite reasonably wants to know what to do if the brother owns up to the wrong-doing but then repeats the offense. Is seven times enough to forgive him? The rabbis taught up to three times, but seven was considered to be the number of God, so it was a good choice! But not good enough for Jesus, who sets a number so high that keeping tabs to that point would be difficult indeed, indicating that forgiveness is intended to be an on-going attitude of heart. Until that is achieved it may perhaps be wiser to simply keep away from the brother in question!

23-30: 'For this reason the kingdom of heaven may be compared to a king who wished to settle accounts with his slaves. 'When he had begun to settle them, one who owed him ten thousand talents was brought to him. 'But since he did not have the means to repay, his lord commanded him to be sold, along with his wife and children and all that he had, and repayment to be made. 'So the slave fell to the ground and prostrated himself before him, saying, 'Have patience with me and I will repay you everything. And the lord of that slave felt compassion and released him and forgave him the debt. But that slave went out and found one of

152

his fellow slaves who owed him a hundred denarii; and he seized him and began to choke him, saying, 'Pay back what you owe.' So his fellow slave fell to the ground and began to plead with him, saying, 'Have patience with me and I will repay you.' But he was unwilling, and went and threw him in prison until he should pay back what was owed.'

Jesus takes the opportunity to teach about the importance of forgiveness, in a parable that shows that not to offer forgiveness leads to a type of spiritual imprisonment and torment for the one who will not offer forgiveness (not the one who sinned in the first place). A king would commonly extend loans to his stewards, but might call them in at any time. An unwise business transaction might lead the steward to be out of pocket and so unable to repay, whereupon both he and his family could be literally reduced to slavery. The first steward has incurred an absolutely massive debt (equivalent to several million pounds sterling if silver talents are used, and many times more if gold talents are meant), one far beyond his ability to repay. On this occasion however the king responds to the request for mercy and 'forgives' ('**aphiemi**' means 'to let off a debt' [130] - an accounting term - as used in the Lord's Prayer in Matthew 6:12). Far from bringing a sense of relief and gratitude, the embarrassment and loss of face that his exposure had caused led him to demand repayment from a fellow steward of a comparatively very trifling sum (equivalent to about ten pounds sterling), and go to extraordinary lengths to obtain it, oblivious to the pleas for mercy.

31-35: 'So when his fellow slaves saw what had happened, they were deeply grieved and came and reported to their lord all that had happened. Then summoning him, his lord said to him, 'You wicked slave, I forgave you all that debt because you pleaded with me. Should you not also have had mercy on your fellow slave, in the same way that I had mercy on you?' And his lord, moved with anger, handed him over to the torturers until he should repay all that was owed him. 'My heavenly Father will also do the same to you, if each of you does not forgive his brother from your heart.'

When the king hears about it, retribution comes swiftly, and the unforgiving servant is not merely imprisoned, but 'tormented' (*'basanistes'* - 'tortured') [131] in punishment as well. It has rightly been said that harbouring unforgiveness is like wishing your offender dead through poisoning, and so making some poison - but then drinking it yourself and waiting in vain for the offender to die. The main person hurt by not extending forgiveness is the person who has been offended and hurt. Usually the one who has caused the offense in the first place will either be unaware of the bitterness caused, or be quite uncaring about it. Jesus clearly taught (Matthew 6:12) that offering forgiveness to those who sin against us is necessary to receive God's forgiveness for our own sins - something of vital importance for one's own spiritual well-being, as well as our physical health. If we wish to receive God's forgiveness then we have to forgive others who sin against us. How much better to offer forgiveness, release oneself from bitterness and so escape the accompanying self-torment and loss of forgiveness for oneself.

Chapter 19

1-3: 'When Jesus had finished these words, he departed from Galilee and came into the region of Judea beyond the Jordan; and large crowds followed him, and he healed them there. Some Pharisees came to Jesus, testing him and asking, 'Is it lawful for a man to divorce his wife for any reason at all?'

Having finished his teaching round in Galilee, Jesus reverts back to the territory under the direct oversight of the Sanhedrin, where he continues to attract a large following by exercising his power to heal. Now back in their own jurisdiction, the Pharisees revert to their ploy of asking hard questions, in the hope of putting Jesus out of favour with at least one group of Jewish society. They chose the question of divorce probably because it was a divisive one. They perhaps thought that Jesus would surely have to offend someone no matter how he answered them! The rabbinic view was broadly divided into two schools of thought, based on the various interpretations of what 'indecency' (Deuteronomy 24:1) actually meant. Rabbi Shammai's school took the stricter view that divorce was only legal on grounds of sexual sin, whereas Rabbi Hillel took a much more liberal line (even a spoiled dinner was held by his school to be grounds for divorce). It is this view that the Pharisees ask Jesus if he subscribes to.

4-8: 'And he answered and said, "Have you not read that he who created them from the beginning made them male and female, and said, 'For this reason a man shall leave his father and mother and be joined to his wife, and the two shall become one flesh'? So they are no longer two, but one flesh. What therefore God has joined together, let no man separate." They said to him, "Why then did Moses command to give her a certificate of divorce and send her away?" He said to them, "Because of your hardness of heart Moses permitted you to divorce your wives; but from the beginning it has not been this way."'

Jesus tackles the issue in a typically rabbinic manner - with a question. 'Have you not read' is rabbinic language for 'You have read but have not correctly interpreted; so now I will explain the meaning to you.' Jesus' approach to the issue is to go to God's expressed intention in 'the beginning', when God lays out his blueprint for marriage. He says that what God has joined together should not be separated, which is another way of stating Malachi 2:16 - 'I hate divorce'. God's intention is that marriage is for life, which actually concurs with the intentions of the vast majority of people entering that state of life. People do not marry in order to get divorced, and it is usually sin and hardness of their hearts ('*sklerokardia*' - a spiritual 'hardening of the arteries') [132] that gives rise to divorce. Far from taking sides in the Jewish debate, Jesus takes a much more radical view than that of Rabbi Shammai.

9: 'And I say to you, whoever, divorces his wife, except for immorality, and marries another woman commits adultery.'

As he had previously taught in Chapter 5, the only grounds for divorce Jesus gives is '*porneia*', meaning 'sexual wrongdoing', but used in distinction to '*moicaw*', which always means adultery.[133] The clause 'except for marital unfaithfulness' (Greek: '*porneia*') appears to apply to the Jewish custom of betrothal, because sexual infidelity after that point would be adultery. To the Jews, the betrothal was the point at which the marriage became legally binding and the couple were regarded as legally married, even though the actual wedding ceremony would not normally take place until one year later. The punishment for sexual unfaithfulness at this stage was even more severe than for adultery. So Matthew records a quite different word ('*porneia*' - 'immorality') for sexual unfaithfulness during the betrothal state than for after the wedding itself ('*moicaw*' - adultery). Hence Jesus said that unfaithfulness during the betrothal stage was grounds for divorce; the marriage ceremony not having been completed. Jesus himself gave no grounds for divorce after the wedding, though Paul gives desertion as grounds in 1 Corinthians 7:15.

156

10-12: 'The disciples said to him, 'If the relationship of the man with his wife is like this, it is better not to marry.' But he said to them, 'Not all men can accept this statement, but only those to whom it has been given. For there are eunuchs who were born that way from their mother's womb; and there are eunuchs who were made eunuchs by men; and there are also eunuchs who made themselves eunuchs for the sake of the kingdom of heaven. He who is able to accept this, let him accept it.'

The radical nature of Jesus' teaching can be seen from the astonished reaction of his disciples, who concluded that under such stringent conditions it would surely be 'better not to marry'. Perhaps a more level-headed reaction would be that it is better to have effective marriage preparation! Jesus agrees with their sentiment that for some it is indeed better not to marry, because as Paul would later say in 1 Corinthians 7:7 - 'I wish that all men were even as I myself am (*i.e. single*). However, each man has his own gift from God, one, in this manner, and another, in that.' (*Italics mine*). Paul upheld single status as a 'good' means of being undivided in the attention that one is able to give to serving God (1 Corinthians 7:8 and 32-35), if it is the state of life that God intends for that individual. This is something that clearly requires prayer and personal spiritual discernment, with adequate preparation for either state of life - married or single.

13-15: 'Then some children were brought to him so that he might lay his hands on them and pray; and the disciples rebuked them. But Jesus said, 'Let the children alone, and do not hinder them from coming to me; for the kingdom of heaven belongs to such as these.' After laying his hands on them, he departed from there.'

Matthew's account now recalls a further instance where Jesus upholds the place of the little ones, be they naturally or spiritually so. 'Little children' is, again, '*paidion*' meaning infants, and the manner of their

157

coming (*'prosphero'* - 'offered') [134] implies that they are being carried. This perfectly sums up the state of dependency on Father that the spiritual new birth is supposed to give, a state that is not supposed to be lost when they grow up! Mark (10:14) describes Jesus 'severe indignation' at his disciples attempts to prevent their coming to him. Jesus act of 'laying his hands on them' denotes a prayer of blessing. What a privilege those children received!

17-20: 'As he was setting out on a journey, a man ran up to him and knelt before him, and asked him, 'Good Teacher, what shall I do to inherit eternal life?' And Jesus said to him, 'Why do you call me good? No one is good except God alone. You know the commandments, 'Do not murder, do not commit adultery, do not steal, do not bear false witness, do not defraud, honour your father and mother.' And he said to him, 'Teacher, I have kept all these things from my youth up.'"

The young man addresses Jesus as *'agathos didaskalos'* - 'Good Doctor'.[135] 'Doctor' or 'Master' here is a title, but the young man is clearly not one of Jesus' disciples. He is addressing Jesus formally, as one asking a serious question of a Law Master, and the term 'Master' is the same word used to describe the 'Doctors of the Law' whom the twelve year old Jesus had debated with and taught in the Temple courts. Luke (2:47) had recorded that 'All who heard him were amazed at his understanding and his answers'. The twelve year old Jesus was teaching the teachers and doing so very effectively ('asking them questions' being rabbinic language for teaching - Luke 2:46). Jesus held this title of highest honour, which could only be awarded by the Sanhedrin and only to the most expert of the Jewish scribal lawyers. The Gospels record on 46 occasions that Jesus is addressed formally with this title, and 18 of these are in formal teaching sessions, many with the antagonistic Jewish hierarchy, which he would be expected, as a Doctor of the Law, to participate in. This was no itinerant carpenter-teacher! Jesus accepts the 'Doctor' ('Master') element of the title, but

158

takes issue with the 'good' aspect. Is the young man calling him God? Jesus knows that he is not doing so, but is challenging him to consider this possibility! Jesus then helps him review the second 'table of the Law' - those commandments which pertained to human relationships, and takes no issue with the young man's claim that those have been adhered to faithfully. The issue for Jesus is the first table of the Law - how has the young man measured up to God's commandments in terms of relating to God himself?

21-22: 'Jesus said to him, 'If you wish to be complete, go and sell your possessions and give to the poor, and you will have treasure in heaven; and come, follow me.' But when the young man heard this statement, he went away grieving; for he was one who owned much property.'

Luke (18:18) describes the young man as a 'ruler' ('*archon*'), meaning 'chief' [136] or 'prince'. As well as seeing his evidently wealthy dress, Jesus can see that there is an idol taking up God's rightful place in his heart. Jesus lovingly wants him to be set free of its hold on him, so advises him to get rid of the obstruction to his love for God by selling his possessions and achieving an eternal reward in their place. Jesus himself had done this in stepping out of a place of wealth and privilege in the Temple schools to travel and proclaim the Gospel. Unfortunately, at this point at least, the man's possessions possess him too strongly for this to be possible. We are not told what happened later, when the effect of Jesus' look of '*agapao*' love (Mark 10:21) was fully felt, but it would be surprising indeed if a response was not eventually made.

23-26: 'And Jesus said to his disciples, 'Truly I say to you, it is hard for a rich man to enter the kingdom of heaven. Again I say to you, it is easier for a camel to go through the eye of a needle, than for a rich man to enter the kingdom of God.' When the disciples heard this, they were very astonished and said, 'Then who can be saved?' And looking at them Jesus said to them,

'With people this is impossible, but with God all things are possible.'

Jesus contradicts the commonly held view that riches were a sign of God's blessing by making the point that they hinder a spiritual response to God (in part by fostering a sense of self-reliance), and uses witty hyperbole, where an exaggerated example (a big animal being threaded into a surgeon's needle) of impossibility is used to make a point. Fortunately, Father has things as important as people's eternal destiny well in hand! There has never been any good evidence for the small gate in the wall of Jerusalem said to have been called 'The Eye of the Needle', and a similar proverb was in use elsewhere.

27-30: 'Then Peter said to him, 'Behold, we have left everything and followed you; what then will there be for us?' And Jesus said to them, 'Truly I say to you, that you who have followed me, in the regeneration when the Son of Man will sit on his glorious throne, you also shall sit upon twelve thrones, judging the twelve tribes of Israel. And everyone who has left houses or brothers or sisters or father or mother or children or farms for my name's sake, will receive many times as much, and will inherit eternal life. But many who are first will be last; and the last, first.'

The issue of eternal reward is one that Peter wishes to explore further, from a personal perspective. What will he and his colleagues receive? He was probably not imagining anything as lofty as the role of judge within the people of Israel. But then God the Father is someone who has always been 'able to do immeasurably more than all we ask or imagine, according to his power that is at work within us!' (Ephesians 3:20 ANIV). The 'first' refers to those of Jesus' Jewish rabbinic colleagues who should have filled that role themselves but who relinquished it by their failure to discern the heart of the Torah, (mercy and justice rather than offering and sacrifice), and secondly through their rejection of the Messiah himself.

160

1-16: 'For the kingdom of heaven is like a landowner who went out early in the morning to hire labourers for his vineyard. 'When he had agreed with the labourers for a denarius for the day, he sent them into his vineyard. And he went out about the third hour and saw others standing idle in the market place; and to those he said, 'You also go into the vineyard, and whatever is right I will give you.' And so they went. Again he went out about the sixth and the ninth hour, and did the same thing. And about the eleventh hour he went out and found others standing around; and he said to them, 'Why have you been standing here idle all day long?' They said to him, 'Because no one hired us.' He said to them, 'You go into the vineyard too.' When evening came, the owner of the vineyard said to his foreman, 'Call the labourers and pay them their wages, beginning with the last group to the first.' When those hired about the eleventh hour came, each one received a denarius. When those hired first came, they thought that they would receive more; but each of them also received a denarius. When they received it, they grumbled at the landowner, saying, 'These last men have worked only one hour, and you have made them equal to us who have borne the burden and the scorching heat of the day.' But he answered and said to one of them, 'Friend, I am doing you no wrong; did you not agree with me for a denarius? Take what is yours and go, but I wish to give to this last man the same as to you. Is it not lawful for me to do what I wish with what is my own? Or is your eye envious because I am generous?' So the last shall be first, and the first last.'

The chapter division at this point should not be allowed to disconnect this parable of the ungrateful labourers with Jesus' teaching in the previous chapter about the first being last and the last first (19:30).

Parables make a point and this one is no exception - those labourers who have just arrived in God's vineyard (the Gentiles who were soon to enter, and also the uneducated disciples who have now had the rank of judge promised to them), are about to be given equal status with those who have 'worked all day' (the Jews and their leaders) in God's vineyard. A radical shift is about to be manifested in God's economy. The last shall be treated the same way as the first.

17-19: 'As Jesus was about to go up to Jerusalem, he took the twelve disciples aside by themselves, and on the way he said to them, 'Behold, we are going up to Jerusalem; and the Son of Man will be delivered to the Chief Priests and Scribes, and they will condemn him to death, and will hand him over to the Gentiles to mock and scourge and crucify him, and on the third day he will be raised up.'

Lest the disciples get ahead of themselves and start to imagine an imminent earthly rule of prestige and religious glory, Jesus brings them down to earth with a bump, with a prophetic self-disclosure that would have made grim listening. Mocking, scourging and crucifixion were not quite what they would probably have had in mind in the light of Jesus' promise of a throne and the title of judge! It was important though for there to be a reality check and to understand that Jesus was speaking of an eternal heavenly kingdom that had as yet not fully come.

20-23: 'Then the mother of the sons of Zebedee came to Jesus with her sons, bowing down and making a request of him. And he said to her, 'What do you wish?' She said to him, 'Command that in your kingdom these two sons of mine may sit one on your right and one on your left.' But Jesus answered, 'You do not know what you are asking. Are you able to drink the cup that I am about to drink?' They said to him, 'We are able.' He said to them, 'My cup you shall drink; but to sit on my right and on my left, this is not mine to give, but it is for those for whom it has been prepared by my Father.'

Some of Jesus' entourage had clearly not yet grasped the important point of servanthood! James and John's mother is recorded as Salome (Mark 15:40) and by John (19:25) as 'his mother's sister', hence Salome was Jesus' aunt. She was therefore a good person to broach the subject of the most important positions in respect of the thrones her sons had undoubtedly told her about. Like any good Jewish mother, she was keen to see her sons advance, and Jesus does not rebuke her, but rather asks whether she, as a good Jewish mother, has grasped the rather painful cost that such a role would have. Her boys are however still keen on it. Jesus makes the point that such positions are for his Father to bestow.

24-28: 'And hearing this, the ten became indignant with the two brothers. But Jesus called them to himself and said, 'You know that the rulers of the Gentiles lord it over them, and their great men exercise authority over them. It is not this way among you, but whoever, wishes to become great among you shall be your servant, and whoever, wishes to be first among you shall be your slave; just as the Son of Man did not come to be served, but to serve, and to give his life a ransom for many.'

On hearing about this initiative of Salome's, the insecurities of the others regarding their own positions and sense of self-importance come to the fore. This prompts Jesus to give yet another exhortation to servanthood (through the lowliness of which true spiritual greatness is attained). He asks them whether they wish to be like Gentile kings - notorious for their depravity. Jesus' recommended approach was the one he modeled himself - serving others and giving of himself in sacrificial love to bring about release from the power of sin and death that so motivated those despised Gentile rulers such as the family of King Herod the Great and his son Herod Antipas.

163

29-34: 'As they were leaving Jericho, a large crowd followed him. And two blind men sitting by the road, hearing that Jesus was passing by, cried out, 'Lord, have mercy on us, Son of David!' The crowd sternly told them to be quiet, but they cried out all the more, 'Lord, Son of David, have mercy on us!' And Jesus stopped and called them, and said, 'What do you want me to do for you?' They said to him, 'Lord, we want our eyes to be opened.' Moved with compassion, Jesus touched their eyes; and immediately they regained their sight and followed him.'

Jesus is headed to Jerusalem on his last and fateful journey there from Jericho. He has warned his friends and disciples of the dreadful suffering that awaited, but self-pity and Jesus were not even on a nodding acquaintance. Little wonder then that he happily overrules the bossy crowd and 'has mercy' ('*eleeo*' - 'compassion') [137] on the blind men, being 'moved with compassion' - '*splagchnizomai*' - an emotion that is literally, 'from the bowels'.[138] Thus he responds both to their need, their importunity and to the clear faith expressed in the Messianic title they bestowed on him. Their response is that of a disciple - to follow him.

Chapter 21

1-3: 'When they had approached Jerusalem and had come to Bethphage, at the Mount of Olives, then Jesus sent two disciples, saying to them, 'Go into the village opposite you, and immediately you will find a donkey tied there and a colt with her; untie them and bring them to me. 'If anyone says anything to you, you shall say, 'The Lord has need of them,' and immediately he will send them.'

Jesus is about to enter Jerusalem for his last Passover visit. He is going to give those religious leaders who had tempted him a sign after all, though not of the type they had been wanting. His would be a reply to those Jews who 'gathered around him, and were saying to him, "How long, will you keep us in suspense? If you are the Messiah, tell us plainly"' (John 10:24). This would be a prophetic sign of the type everyone would plainly understand.

A conquering king would enter an occupied city on a horse, whereas a king coming in peace would ride on a donkey. The fact that the animal had never been ridden added to the sense of the sacred, in the same way that the red heifers used in sacrifice had never worn a yoke (Numbers 19:2). It also makes the act of riding it a further sign of Jesus' command over nature, as it would have strenuously resisted being ridden, especially in close proximity to crowds shouting and waving palm branches. Jesus appears to have had foreknowledge of the animal's readiness, and the disposition of the owner to lend it to 'the Master'.

4-11: 'This took place to fulfill what was spoken through the prophet: 'Say to the Daughter of Zion, 'See, your king comes to you, gentle and riding on a donkey, on a colt, the foal of a donkey.' The disciples went and did just as Jesus had instructed them, and brought the donkey and the colt, and laid their coats on them; and he sat on the coats. Most of the crowd spread their coats in the road, and others were cutting branches from the trees and spreading them in the road. The crowds going ahead of him, and those who followed, were shouting, 'Hosanna to the Son of David; Blessed is he who comes in the name of the Lord! Hosanna in the highest! Hosanna in the highest!' When he had entered Jerusalem, all the city was stirred, saying, 'Who is this?' And the crowds were saying, 'This is the prophet Jesus, from Nazareth in Galilee.'

Jesus very deliberately sets out to fulfill Zechariah 9:9 - 'Rejoice greatly, O daughter of Zion! Shout in triumph, O daughter of Jerusalem! Behold, your king is coming to you; he is just and endowed with salvation, humble, and mounted on a donkey, even on a colt, the foal of a donkey.' He is declaring that he is indeed the promised Messiah-King, to a city packed with around 2.5 million Jews and God-fearing Gentiles, both visitors and residents, most of whom would have heard of and even seen him at his previous festival visits. In so doing he lays down a challenge to the Sanhedrin and the Chief Priests, and forces their hand to intervene. He knew that this was the time appointed by his Father for the ultimate eternal Passover sacrifice to occur.

But Jesus was also fulfilling another prophetic mission on behalf of his Father. In around 175 BC, the Syro-Macedonian King Antiochus Epiphanes, son of the Syrian King Antiochus, had conquered and attempted to hellenise the Jews and so mimic his predecessor Alexander the Great in attempting to maintain his empire through local cultural infiltration. A rather more extreme man that Alexander, Antiochus had deliberately profaned the Temple by offering pigs on the altar in sacrifice to his god Zeus, and had even used the Temple as a brothel. After the successful revolt led by Judas Maccabaeus, the son of Mattathias, a priest of the family of Joarib, the Temple had been cleansed and rededicated to Yahweh. The Jewish book of 2 Maccabees (10:7) records that the Jewish populace had, on that occasion, celebrated by 'carrying ivy-wreathed wands and beautiful branches and also fronds of palm - they offered hymns of thanksgiving to him who had given success to the purifying of his own holy place.' The public react to Jesus as a type of second Judas Maccabaeus, whom, they may have hoped, would similarly rid them of the occupying Roman army.

Mark's Gospel (11:11) records that Jesus actually led them all the way to the Temple, where he 'looked around at everything' before going back out to Bethany to return the following day and once again drive out the money changers and those selling sacrificial animals. There must have been a tremendous sense of anticipation, and apprehension among the authorities, fearful that some uprising similar to the Maccabean one was about to take place. The Romans would have been watching closely, aware that any attempted overthrow of their rule would take place at the time of one of the festivals when numbers of radical Jews would be swollen by those on tri-annual pilgrimage. The fort of Antonia garrisoned the Roman army immediately next to the Temple Courts and their soldiers would have been aware of the disturbance and so been monitoring the situation closely. When Jesus led the crowd into the Temple rather than to Antonia there must have been a palpable sense of relief on both the Jewish and Roman sides.

But his brief visit was enough to spur the Jewish leaders on to further action. Jesus' standing among the people had risen to new heights following his recent miracle in raising his friend Lazarus to life after four days in the grave (John 11:39). No wonder the people celebrated his arrival in Jerusalem with Messianic fervour! John's Gospel (12:17-19) records, 'The people, who were with him when he called Lazarus out of the tomb and raised him from the dead, continued to testify about him. For this reason also the people went and met him, because they heard that he had performed this sign.'

The Jewish authorities quickly read this shift in popular opinion (John 12:19). 'So the Pharisees said to one another, "You see that you are not doing any good; look, the world has gone after him." This appears to have been a defining shift in the balance of their opinion. As a 'Doctor of the Law', Jesus would have been philosophically closest to the Pharisaic side of the ruling Sanhedrin council. Nicodemus, a Sanhedrin member, had told Jesus that his colleagues 'knew that Jesus was a Doctor come from God' (John 3:2). Now it appears that many of them were having second thoughts. Jesus' claims such as to be able to forgive sin and to pre-date their patriarch Abraham had pushed things too far.

But still public opinion was divided. The crowds address Jesus sometimes in a Messianic fashion 'Hosanna ('Lord save us') to the 'Son of David', and also as a prophet. The concept of being a perfect offering for their and other's sins had not yet entered their consciousness.

12-13: 'And Jesus entered the Temple and drove out all those who were buying and selling in the Temple, and overturned the tables of the money changers and the seats of those who were selling doves. And he said to them, 'It is written: 'My house will be called a house of prayer,' but you are making it a 'den of robbers'.'

Jesus repeats the actions at the start of his public ministry of stamping his spiritual authority, as an ordained Doctor of the Law, on the activities within the Temple. Having once again separated the money changers from their money, he quotes Isaiah 56:6-7. 'Also the foreigners, who join themselves to the Lord, to minister to him, and to love the name of the Lord, to be his servants, everyone who keeps from profaning the Sabbath, and holds fast my covenant; even those I will bring to my holy mountain, and make them joyful in my house of prayer. Their burnt offerings and their sacrifices will be acceptable on my altar; for my house will be called a house of prayer for all the peoples.'

Jesus' concern is for 'the foreigners' about which Isaiah is prophesying. The outermost court of the Temple was the only part of the sacred site where it was permitted for non-Jews to enter. It was in this 'Court of the Gentiles' that the money changing and sale of sacrificial animals known as the 'Bazaars of Annas' occurred, turning the only place of prayer open to foreigners into a noisy market making profits for the families of the High Priests (Annas was the father-in-law of Caiaphas, the incumbent High Priest - John 18:13).

Jesus then quotes from Jeremiah 7:8-11 - 'Behold, you are trusting in deceptive words to no avail. Will you steal, murder, and commit adultery and swear falsely, and offer sacrifices to Baal and walk after other gods that you have not known, then come and stand before me in this house, which is called by my name, and say, "We are delivered!" - that you may do all these abominations? Has this house, which is called by my name, become a den of robbers in your sight? Behold I, even I, have seen it, declares the Lord.'

Jesus' comparing them to 'a den of robbers' ('*lêstês*' here means 'violent brigands') [139] would have been a major challenge to the Jewish Priesthood who ran the market and who would have had this reported to them. Jesus is making himself very clear, within a Jewish historic context. Jeremiah had preached repentance to the Jews from the very place Jesus was standing. Jeremiah 7:1-7 reads: 'The word that came to Jeremiah from the Lord, saying, 'Stand in the gate of the Lord's house and proclaim there this word and say, "Hear the word of the Lord, all you of Judah, who enter by these gates to worship the Lord!" Thus says the Lord of hosts, the God of Israel, Amend your ways and your deeds, and I will let you dwell in this place. Do not trust in deceptive words, saying, "This is the Temple of the Lord, the Temple of the Lord, the Temple of the Lord." For if you truly amend your ways and your deeds, if you truly practice justice between a man and his neighbour, if you do not oppress the alien, the orphan, or the widow, and do not shed innocent blood in this place, nor walk after other gods to your own ruin,

169

then I will let you dwell in this place, in the land that I gave to your fathers forever, and ever'. In addition to the charge made for changing money, the monopoly that the Priests had on the sale of ritually acceptable animals for sacrifice meant that they were able to charge markedly inflated prices. Not long after Jesus' death the Mishnah records that two doves (one of the cheapest offerings) were being sold there for one gold coin, before rabbinic intervention reduced their cost to one-quarter of a silver coin.[140]

The Priests and Jewish leaders of Jeremiah's day put their trust in their religious practices and in the imposing edifice that was the Temple of Solomon rather than in a living personal faith in the God of Abraham, and this was manifest in their behaviour. They had begun to oppress the vulnerable members of their community in exactly the same way that the leaders of Jesus' day had done (e.g. 'devouring widows' houses' - Matthew 23:14). Jesus is warning them that their time is running out. If they did not change their ways then they would not be allowed to 'dwell in this place' of the Temple that they took such pride in. 'Den of robbers' served both as a description of their behaviour in grossly inflating the prices for sacrificial animals and as a warning of what was to come if they refused to listen to the prophetic word that Jesus was bringing.

Jesus was also fulfilling a third Old Testament prophecy. Zechariah (14:21) had spoken of the day when: 'Every cooking pot in Jerusalem and in Judah will be holy to the Lord of hosts; and all who sacrifice will come and take of them and boil in them. And there will no longer be a Canaanite in the house of the Lord of hosts in that day.' The Hebrew word '**kenaani**' used here has a double meaning - it can be translated as 'Canaanite' or as 'merchant'.[141] In the Temple cleansing episode of John chapter 2, Jesus rebukes the Priests for creating a 'house of merchandise'. Hence Jesus is fulfilling prophecy by expelling the traders of the 'Bazaars of Annas' who made large profits for the family of the Chief Priest, and likening those most pious of Jewish figures, the

Priests, with the unclean Canaanites in their commercial pursuits. This would have been a very offensive comparison. John's account also has Jesus referring to the Temple as his 'Father's house'; a probable dual meaning to Joseph's role in training the priest-builders as *'tektons'*.[142]

14-17: 'And the blind and the lame came to him in the Temple, and he healed them. But when the Chief Priests and the Scribes saw the wonderful things that he had done, and the children who were shouting in the Temple, 'Hosanna to the Son of David,' they became indignant and said to him, 'Do you hear what these children are saying?' And Jesus said to them, 'Yes; have you never read, 'Out of the mouth of infants and nursing babies you have prepared praise for yourself?' And he left them and went out of the city to Bethany, and spent the night there.'

Having received the shouts of 'Hosanna' from the Jewish crowd, who would actually have been shouting *'yasha'* in Hebrew, meaning 'deliver us', with a very real political overtone, Jesus then proceeds to give a further demonstration of his Messianic status by healing the blind and the lame. This is a direct fulfilment of Isaiah 35:4-6. 'Say to those with anxious heart, "Take courage, fear not. Behold, your God will come with vengeance; the recompense of God will come, but he will save (*deliver*) you (*'yasha'*)." Then the eyes of the blind will be opened, and the ears of the deaf will be unstopped. Then the lame will leap like a deer, and the tongue of the mute will shout for joy.' These miraculous signs must have caused pandemonium in the Temple Courts. The Chief Priests and the scribal teachers had a different response to the children's however. Rather than give praise to God they nitpicked at the extravagance of the praise that the excited children were giving Jesus, and expect that Jesus will disclaim the Messianic status being afforded him. On the contrary, with another Rabbinic challenge ('Haven't you read...?') Jesus points them to Psalm 8:2, which states that young children are an integral part of God's purposes. Again it is clear that the Chief Priests have no legal charges that they

171

can bring against Jesus, despite the great disturbance caused by his clearing of the Temple Courts. Jesus' status and authority as a Doctor of their Law was proof against arrest, and his miraculous signs filled those who saw them with either a sense of awe or a sense of fear about what might be yet to come.

18-22: 'Now in the morning, when he was returning to the city, he became hungry. Seeing a lone fig tree by the road, he came to it and found nothing on it except leaves only; and he said to it, 'No longer shall there ever be any fruit from you.' And at once the fig tree withered. Seeing this, the disciples were amazed and asked, 'How did the fig tree wither all at once?' And Jesus answered and said to them, 'Truly I say to you, if you have faith and do not doubt, you will not only do what was done to the fig tree, but even if you say to this mountain, 'Be taken up and cast into the sea,' it will happen. And all things you ask in prayer, believing, you will receive.'

Mark's account of this incident (11:13) makes it clear that it was not the season for figs hence it is clear that Jesus is using the tree as a type of picture to make a spiritual point. Israel was noted for figs. Deuteronomy 8:8 describes it as a 'land of wheat and barley, of vines and fig trees and pomegranates, a land of olive oil and honey.' The men sent to spy out the land following the Exodus had brought back figs as a sign of the land's fruitfulness (Numbers 13:23). This fig tree had an abundance of leaves, but no fruit, and so in some ways represented the nation of Israel at the time of Jesus - much show of religion on the part of the Priests and Pharisees, but no fruit and no heart, at least in so far as their attitude to the widows and oppressed was concerned. Soon the life of the nation would be withered in accordance with Jesus' predictions in Matthew chapter 24.

Mark (11:20) makes it clear that the conversation that Jesus had with the disciples about faith occurred the next day. Withering a fig tree is simply the accelerating of the natural process of decay. Jesus promised his followers would do 'greater works' (John 14:12), if they were following their heavenly Father's lead in trust in him. 'Moving a mountain' is Hebrew proverbial language for doing the impossible, which is what God, for whom 'nothing is impossible' (Luke 1:37), does in what for him is the natural course of things. Our faith (trust and dependent obedience) is what allows us to participate in the impossible.

23-27: 'When he entered the Temple, the Chief Priests and the elders of the people came to him while he was teaching, and said, 'By what authority are you doing these things, and who gave you this authority?' Jesus said to them, 'I will also ask you one thing, which if you tell me, I will also tell you by what authority I do these things. The baptism of John was from what source, from heaven or from men?' And they began reasoning among themselves, saying, 'If we say, 'From heaven,' he will say to us, 'Then why, did you not believe him?' But if we say, 'From men,' we fear the people; for they all regard John as a prophet.' And answering Jesus, they said, 'We do not know.' He also said to them, 'Neither will I tell you by what authority I do these things.'

Having just performed many amazing miracles in the Temple, the authenticity of which could not be denied, the Jewish authorities seek to pin Jesus down on exactly who he was claiming to be. It is the same point of issue that they were pursuing in John 10:24: 'If you are the Christ, tell us plainly.' They ask, 'By what authority (*'exousia'*) are you doing these things?' *Exousia* is translated as 'authority' 29 times in the King James Bible, but as 'power' 69 times, meaning 'the ability or strength with which one is endued'.[143] The 'things' that the Jews are addressing are not Jesus' teachings, which he regularly gave using the authority that been invested in him at his ordination as both a Rabbi and as a Doctor of the Law. The 'things' the leaders want to question were the Messianic signs of healing and the cleansing of the Temple.

The Jewish leaders want to know whether Jesus is claiming to directly represent God in what he is doing. As always with this type of question from the religious authorities, Jesus knew that they would not believe him even if he told them directly who he really was. The evidence of the miracles themselves was not enough to change their hard hearts, and as Jesus taught in the parable of the rich man, neither would they be 'persuaded even if someone rose from the dead' (Luke 16:31). So Jesus tests their sincerity with a question about his cousin John - where had John's spiritual authority come from? Their unwillingness to answer such a straight question revealed that they were not sincere in asking Jesus where his power came from. Their comment about 'fearing the people' is a further sorry reflection upon their ability to govern well - they did not have sufficient fear of God, being more concerned about maintaining their own privileged societal positions.

28-32: 'But what do you think? A man had two sons, and he came to the first and said, 'Son, go work today in the vineyard.' And he answered, 'I will not'; but afterward he regretted it and went. 'The man came to the second and said the same thing; and he answered, 'I will, Sir'; but he did not go. Which of the two did the will of his father?' They said, 'The first.' Jesus said to them, 'Truly I say to you that the tax collectors and prostitutes will get into the kingdom of God before you. For John came to you in the way of righteousness and you did not believe him; but the tax collectors and prostitutes did believe him; and you, seeing this, did not even feel remorse afterward so as to believe him.'

Jesus is unwilling, however insincere they might be, to leave them in their unbelief. So he tells them a parable that points out the ability we all have to reflect and change our minds in order to go a better way. This is the essence of the concept of repentance. What counts is not the initial reaction, but the eventual outcome - obedience or disobedience to what God is saying. Jesus points out that even notorious sinners

174

changed their ways based on the ministry of John. The authorities had witnessed this but it had not been enough for them to get down from their high horse of pride and admit that perhaps God was choosing to represent himself by someone other than themselves. They remained unchanged.

33-41: 'Listen to another parable. There was a landowner who planted a vineyard and put a wall around it and dug a winepress in it and built a tower, and rented it out to vine-growers and went on a journey. When the harvest time approached, he sent his slaves to the vine-growers to receive his produce. The vine-growers took his slaves and beat one, and killed another, and stoned a third. Again he sent another group of slaves larger than the first; and they did the same thing to them. But afterward he sent his son to them, saying, 'They will respect my son.' But when the vine-growers saw the son, they said among themselves, 'This is the heir; come, let us kill him and seize his inheritance.' They took him, and threw him out of the vineyard and killed him. Therefore when the owner of the vineyard comes, what will he do to those vine-growers?' They said to him, 'He will bring those wretches to a wretched end, and will rent out the vineyard to other vine-growers who will pay him the proceeds at the proper seasons.'

Parables were a useful way to get around intellectual defences. The story could filter through the hearers' conscious and subconscious thoughts allowing the truth contained within to slowly but steadily permeate the mind. Jesus gives the authorities yet another chance to consider what is happening from a spiritual perspective. In this case the analogies were plain, given the description of Israel in Isaiah 5:7 - 'For the vineyard of the Lord of Hosts is the house of Israel.' Absentee landlords were a common feature in Israel, and the political turbulence of the region lent itself to scenarios such as the one Jesus depicts. What is extreme is the stubborn obduracy of the tenants (who stood for the

Jewish authorities who had ignored and persecuted God's messengers down the ages). There is also the amazing patience of the landlord, who is willing to send even his own son into what was clearly a hostile and dangerous situation. The analogy to Jesus' own mission, in which he regularly claimed to represent his 'Father'; was plain (his adoptive father Joseph being long since dead). The Jewish leaders are in no doubt as to the outcome for the tenants - retribution will come.

42: 'Jesus said to them, 'Did you never read in the Scriptures, 'The stone the builders rejected, this became the chief cornerstone, this came about from the Lord and it is marvellous in our eyes?'

Jesus is quoting from Psalm 118:22-23. 'The stone which the builders rejected has become the chief corner stone. This is the Lord's doing; it is marvellous in our eyes'. The Hebrew for 'chief' here is *'ro'sh'* meaning 'head' or 'top',[144] and the Psalm had been interpreted as indicating God's desire to make Israel the head among the nations, in keeping with the promise for obedience to God's ways that Moses had given them. 'The Lord will make you the head and not the tail, and you only will be above, and you will not be underneath, if you listen to the commandments of the Lord your God, which I charge you today, to observe them carefully' (Deuteronomy 28:13).

The Psalm is the same one that the crowds were quoting from when they were shouting: "Blessed is he who comes in the name of the Lord!" (Psalm 118:26). When Jesus quoted Scripture he was usually referring to the whole passage, not a single verse. The passage reads: 'Open to me the gates of righteousness; I shall enter through them, I shall give thanks to the Lord. This is the gate of the Lord; the righteous will enter through it. I shall give thanks to you, for you have answered me, and you have become my salvation. The stone which the builders rejected has become the chief corner stone. This is the Lord's doing; it is marvellous in our eyes. This is the day which the Lord has made; let

176

us rejoice and be glad in it. O Lord, do save, we beseech you; O Lord, we beseech you, do send prosperity! Blessed is the one who comes in the name of the Lord; we have blessed you from the house of the Lord.' (Psalms 118:19-26).

The Jews regarded the rejected 'stone' as representing the nation of Israel - a small and despised people had been elevated to greatness by Almighty God. Jesus however is telling them that it stands for him, and the fact that he was going to be further rejected by the Jewish leaders ('the builders', for it was the Priests who had been trained to build Herod's Temple).[145] Jesus had spoken openly (John 10:7) that he was the 'gate for the sheep', and 'I am the gate; whoever enters through me will be saved' (John 10:9 NIV). The prayer 'you have answered me, and you have become my salvation' (Psalm 118:21) was fulfilled in his own person; 'salvation' being in Hebrew '*yeshuah*',[146] that being his own name, Jesus. He is telling them that *he* is actually the 'top stone'; that their God has done it and the consequences are marvellous - at least in the eyes of unbiased children who can tell a miracle when they see several happen in front of them.

43-46: 'Therefore, I say to you, the kingdom of God will be taken away from you and given to a people, producing the fruit of it. And he who falls on this stone will be broken to pieces; but on whomever, it falls, it will scatter him like dust.' When the Chief Priests and the Pharisees heard his parables, they understood that he was speaking about them. When they sought to seize him, they feared the people, because they considered him to be a prophet.'

Jesus concludes the parable by warning them that the same fate that befell the unrighteous vineyard tenants was about to happen to them. Just as had happened in Jeremiah's day, the cycles of discipline and consequences of the disobedience described in Deuteronomy 28 would be repeated. The final and terrible judgement of verses 63-65 was about

177

to come to pass: 'It shall come about that as the Lord delighted over you to prosper you, and multiply you, so the Lord will delight over you to make you perish and destroy you; and you will be torn from the land where, you are entering to possess it. Moreover, the Lord will scatter you among all peoples, from one end of the earth to the other end of the earth; and there you shall serve other gods, wood and stone, which you or your fathers have not known. Among those nations you shall find no rest, and there will be no resting place for the sole of your foot; but there the Lord will give you a trembling heart, failing of eyes, and despair of soul.'

In AD 70 the destruction of Jerusalem and with it Herod's Temple would lead to devastation and a scattering of the people, and the owner of the vineyard would look elsewhere (to the Gentiles) for spiritual fruit. Jesus offers them a choice; fall on him and his mercy and be broken in humble repentance, or be scattered like dust in judgement upon their unbelief. Isaiah 8: 13-15 speaks of the Lord as being 'a rock of offence to the House of Israel': 'It is the Lord of hosts whom you should regard as holy. And he shall be your fear, and he shall be your dread. Then he shall become a sanctuary; but to both the houses of Israel, a stone to strike and a rock to stumble over, and a snare and a trap for the inhabitants of Jerusalem. Many will stumble over them, then they will fall and be broken; they will even be snared and caught.' Daniel (2:45) had predicted a 'stone cut without hands' (i.e. by God) which would break kingdoms to pieces, but the word used by Jesus here is of much smaller particles. 'Scattered like dust' is '*likmaô*', which also means 'to winnow',[147] in the sense of separating chaff from wheat using a winnowing fork, as in Matthew 3:12 - an image commonly used to describe God's judgement. The response of the authorities is one of an impotent fury. They know Jesus is speaking about them, but his status as a Doctor of the Law permits him to teach in this way. And just as they feared the crowd's response to anything negative that they said about John the Baptist, so now they have the same problem with opposing Jesus. It would have to be done in secret.

Chapter 22

1-7: 'Jesus spoke to them again in parables, saying, 'The kingdom of heaven may be compared to a king, who gave a wedding feast for his son. And he sent out his servants to call those who had been invited to the wedding feast, and they were unwilling to come. Again he sent out other servants saying, 'Tell those who have been invited, 'Behold, I have prepared my dinner; my oxen and my fattened livestock are all butchered and everything is ready; come to the wedding feast.' But they paid no attention and went their way, one to his own farm, another, to his business, and the rest seized his servants and mistreated them and killed them. But the king was enraged, and he sent his armies and destroyed those murderers and set their city on fire.'

The Priests' fury does not put Jesus off his task of warning them solemnly of their need to turn back to God and accept the rulership of the kingdom of one who is even at that moment still inviting them to celebrate with him. Like the story of the vineyard, the scenario was one with which Jesus' audience would have been familiar. Occupied territories such as Palestine were governed by client-kings appointed by the ruling empire. Herod's family would have sprung to mind, making the reluctance to celebrate with a notorious despot understandable from the Jews' standpoint. Indeed, the ruling family's behaviour might well inspire the violent rebellion that the story describes. By this time Jesus' audience had got the message - they were the people invited to the feast, Jesus was the son and the 'servants' sent out with the invitations were the prophets who preceded Jesus. Their violent rejection of God's messengers would result in the same judgement that befell the wicked tenants of the vineyard - an army would come and destroy them.

8-10: 'Then he said to his servants, 'The wedding is ready, but those who were invited were not worthy. 'Go therefore to the main highways, and as many as you find there, invite to the wedding feast.' Those servants went out into the streets and gathered together all they found, both evil and good; and the wedding hall was filled with dinner guests.'

Jesus now presents the other part of God's agenda - the inclusion of the marginalized and disadvantaged. Jesus had already told the Jewish authorities that 'the tax collectors and prostitutes enter before you' (Matthew 21:31). These were people whom they would not have expected God to want to include in his Kingdom. Jesus tells them that 'sinners' would share in God's feast instead of them, if they refused to turn to him and be changed by the power of his grace. The unlikely characters ('both evil and good') responded to the invitation and so are included in the wedding celebration.

11-14: 'But when the king came in to look over the dinner guests, he saw a man there who was not dressed in wedding clothes, and he said to him, 'Friend, how did you come in here without wedding clothes?' And the man was speechless. Then the king said to the servants, 'Bind him hand and foot, and throw him into the outer darkness; in that place there will be weeping and gnashing of teeth.' For many are called, but few are chosen.'

The basis of inclusion is what is being addressed here. When a great king sent out his preliminary round of invitations notifying of an impending important occasion such as a marriage feast, it was customary to provide those invited with a suit of new clothes to wear at the function. This is what Samson had been unwilling to do at his wedding, as described in Judges 14:10-12. 'Samson made a feast there, as was customary for bridegrooms. When he appeared, he was given thirty companions. 'Let me tell you a riddle,' Samson said to them. 'If you can give you the answer within the seven days of the feast, I will give you thirty linen garments and thirty sets of clothes' (ANIV). Homer's 'Odyssey' relates how Polycaste, the daughter of Nestor, clothed Telemachus (the son of Odysseus and Penelope), before a sacrificial feast: 'Meantime the youngest of the daughters fair, of Nestor, beauteous Polycaste, laved, anointed, and in vest and tunic clothed Telemachus, who, so refreshed, stepped forth from the bright laver graceful as a god, and took his seat at ancient Nestor's side.' [148]

The man with no wedding garment has either not been invited or has chosen to try and enter the feast on his own terms, rather than on those of the king, and so is ejected. Jesus is telling the Jews that they must approach God on the basis of trust in his provision, and not on the basis of their own status, heritage or religious position. They have all been called, but will only be chosen if they respond in trust and obedience to the call God has given. This double parable concludes the third of Jesus' warnings and calls to repent - calls that fell on deaf ears.

15-22: 'Then the Pharisees went and plotted together how they might trap him in what he said. And they sent their disciples to him, along with the Herodians, saying, 'Teacher, we know that you are truthful and teach the way of God in truth, and defer to no one; for you are not partial to any. Tell us then, what do you think? Is it lawful to give a poll-tax to Caesar, or not?' But Jesus perceived their malice, and said, 'Why are you testing me, you hypocrites? Show me the coin used for the poll-tax.' And they brought him a denarius. And he said to them, 'Whose likeness and inscription is this?' They said to him, 'Caesar's.' Then he said to them, 'Then render to Caesar the things that are Caesar's; and to God the things that are God's.' And hearing this, they were amazed, and leaving him, they went away.'

Angry and frustrated by their inability to make any progress against Jesus, the Pharisees show how desperate their position was becoming by joining forces with their natural enemies the Herodians - those Jews who had sided with their despised Roman and very pagan enemies. The Pharisees were willing to put aside their religious and political differences for the common purpose of bringing Jesus down. Between them they devised a very loaded legal question to try and trap Jesus. It is a lose-lose question: "Is it right to pay taxes to Caesar, or not?" If Jesus had answered, 'Yes', he could have been discredited as a collaborator. If he said, 'No', (the 'correct' answer from a Jewish perspective because the Romans were idolaters), he could have been arrested for inciting rebellion against the ruling power. Jesus' answer astonished them: "Render to Caesar what is Caesar's and to God what is God's." To say 'do what is right by both secular authority and by God' was the perfect answer - one that neither the Pharisees or the Herodians could find fault with.

23-33: 'On that day some Sadducees (who say there is no resurrection) came to Jesus and questioned him, asking, 'Teacher, Moses said, 'if a man dies having no children, his brother as next of kin must marry the widow and have children for him.' Now there were seven brothers with us; and the first married and died, and having no children left his wife to his brother; so also the second, and the third, down to the seventh. Last of all, the woman died. In the resurrection, therefore, whose wife of the seven will she be? For they all had married her.' But Jesus answered and said to them, 'You are mistaken, not understanding the Scriptures nor the power of God. For in the resurrection they neither marry nor are given in marriage, but are like angels in heaven. But regarding the resurrection of the dead, have you not read what was spoken to you by God: 'I am the God of Abraham, the God of Isaac, and the God of Jacob'? He is not the God of the dead but of the living.' When the crowds heard this, they were astonished at his teaching.'

It is now the Priests' turn to try and bring Jesus into theological disrepute. The Sadducees held that only the Pentateuch formed God's written word, believing that any Scripture other than these 5 books of Moses was not inspired. They did not believe either in angels or in the resurrection (Acts 23:8). So they attempt to discredit the concept of a

182

resurrected body with an impossibly ridiculous theoretical example of a woman who out-lived her seven related husbands in their attempts to keep the eldest brother's family name alive (Deuteronomy 25:5-6). The issue of whether the resurrection was taught in the Pentateuch had long been hotly debated between the Pharisees and the Sadducees. With one statement Jesus settled the matter. God was the God of the living; hence his commonly accepted title meant that those patriarchs mentioned therein had therefore to be alive spiritually.

34-40: 'But when the Pharisees heard that Jesus had silenced the Sadducees, they gathered themselves together. One of them, a lawyer, asked him a question, testing him, 'Teacher, which is the great commandment in the Law?' And he said to him, 'You shall love the Lord your God with all your heart and with all your soul and with all your mind. This is the great and foremost commandment. The second is like it, 'You shall love your neighbour as yourself.'

As a Doctor of the Law, Jesus would have most naturally been aligned with the Pharisees, who would have been delighted that he had 'rendered speechless' their opponents, the Sadducees. 'Silenced' here is *'phimoô'* (from *'phimos'* - a muzzle).[149] In public debates, it was common for individual teachers to be asked a question as a means of initiating an exposition upon a particular subject. This happened regularly to Jesus (e.g. the divorce question, the taxes question, etc). 'Testing' literally means an 'examination', in these instances public ones. On this occasion the lawyer concerned asks Jesus an easy question, to which the answer was obvious - the first commandment, related plainly in Deuteronomy 6:5, and contained in the Shema, the Jewish creed. The nature of the question appears to indicate that Jesus was still on relatively friendly terms with at least some of his theological legal colleagues, and also probably indicates how pleased the lawyer was to see the loss of face that the Sadducees had undergone. Mark's account relates that he 'perceived that Jesus had answered well' (Mark 12:28). The Jewish Sanhedrin leader Hillel, whose life (110BC - 10AD) overlapped with that of Jesus, had famously taught (Shabbat 31a) 'That which is hateful to you, do not do to your fellow'. Jesus pulled out of their Scripture a more positive and user-friendly text from Leviticus 19:18 - 'Love your neighbour as you love yourself.'

41-46: 'Now while the Pharisees were gathered together, Jesus asked them a question: 'What do you think about the Christ, whose son is he?' They said to him, 'The son of David.' He said to them, 'Then how does David in the Spirit call him 'Lord,' saying, 'The Lord said to my Lord: 'Sit at my right hand until I put your enemies beneath your feet.' If David then calls him 'Lord,' how is he his son?' No one was able to answer him a word, nor did anyone dare from that day on to ask him another question.'

Jesus now takes the initiative. The question on the Sanhedrin's lips was 'Are you the Christ?' (John 10:24). Jesus responds by revealing a fundamental misunderstanding in their theology. The Christ, while being a descendant of David's, and hence his 'son', was actually God, which was why David addresses him as his 'Lord'. Psalm 110:1 reads 'The Lord ('*Yahweh*') said to my Lord ('*adon*'). '*Adon*' is used as a formal term for God in Exodus 23:17 and '*adonay*', a Hebrew name for God, is derived from it. This is a revelation that put the Pharisees in the same place as the Sadducees - lost for words. Clearly any attempt to discredit Jesus intellectually was unlikely to be successful. If they wished to silence him, the authorities would have to try another method.

Chapter 23

1-7: 'Then Jesus spoke to the crowds and to his disciples, saying: 'The Scribes and the Pharisees have seated themselves in the chair of Moses; therefore all that they tell you, do and observe, but do not do according to their deeds; for they say things and do not do them. They tie up heavy burdens and lay them on men's shoulders, but they themselves are unwilling to move them with so much as a finger. But they do all their deeds to be noticed by men; for they broaden their phylacteries and lengthen the tassels of their garments. They love the place of honour at banquets and the chief seats in the synagogues, and respectful greetings in the market places, and being called Rabbi by men.'

Jesus seems determined to provoke a reaction from the authorities. Having easily won their contests of intellectual sparring, he now goes onto the offensive. Jesus is speaking here in his formal role as a Doctor of the Law, one authorized to teach publically in the Temple Courts. As such he shared the duty of expounding the Torah with the Scribes and the Pharisees, following the example of Moses himself. But Jesus' manner of so doing was completely different to theirs. They had taken the Torah and added layers of religious obligation to it, originally to fence it off so that people would not get even close to breaking any of it. This 'Oral Law' now dominated Jewish life, to the point that it had become so burdensome that many had given up trying to keep it and were given the label of 'sinners' by the religious leaders. To comply with the Rabbinic demands was a full-time job, something that Peter would later comment that even its proponents were 'unable to bear' (Acts 15:10). Pride had crept in, expressed in ostentation in clothing - phylacteries were leather containers for small rolls of Scripture worn over the forehead in response to Exodus 13:16 ('frontlet markings between your eyes'). In addition, tassels were worn in response to Numbers 15:38-40 ('to look upon it and remember all the commandments of the Lord and do them'). With them had come the enjoyment of a sense of elevated social position and special titles, including Rabbi (showing that the title was in general use at that time). All of this served to work against the spiritual changes that the Torah was intended to promote, such as love of God and one's fellow man.

8-12: 'But do not be called Rabbi; for one is your Teacher, and you are all brothers. Do not call anyone on earth your father; for one is your Father, he who is in heaven. Do not be called leaders; for one is your leader, that is, Christ. But the greatest among you shall be your servant. Whoever exalts himself shall be humbled; and whoever humbles himself shall be exalted.'

Jesus is teaching that the gap between them and himself, who as David's 'Lord' is equal with God, is so great that they should not employ spiritual titles that distinguish themselves one from another in terms of greatness. Compared to him they are all equal as 'brothers'. These verses clearly show that the title of 'Rabbi' was in common use in Jesus' day, despite some scholars' claims to the contrary. If his followers wish to be great from a spiritual perspective they must lower themselves in the humble service of others, just as Jesus himself did.

13-14: 'But woe to you, Scribes and Pharisees, hypocrites, because you shut off the kingdom of heaven from people; for you do not enter in yourselves, nor do you allow those who are entering to go in. Woe to you, Scribes and Pharisees, hypocrites, because you devour widows' houses, and for a pretense you make long prayers; therefore, you will receive greater condemnation.'

Jesus now really gets into his stride in denouncing the ungodly practices of those who were supposed to be Israel's spiritual leaders, a role he says they are 'play-acting' ('*hupokritês*' - an actor). While making it extremely difficult for people by raising the demands above

186

what God required, they themselves were not entering God's kingdom either. Jesus was not the only person to criticize the Pharisees for this type of behaviour. The historian Josephus records that the Pharisees were a 'Jewish sect that appeared more pious than the rest and stricter in the interpretation of the Law', so that Alexandra (who ruled following the death of her Maccabean husband Alexander Jannaeus in 76 BC) 'hearkened to them to an extraordinary degree, as being herself a woman of great piety towards God'.[150]

Josephus also recorded that the Pharisees have so great a power over the multitude, that when they say anything against the king, or against the High Priest, they are presently believed'.[151] They were noted for their supposed piety, and were fond of making long prayers in public (c.f. Matthew 5:5). They also acted as legal executors for widows who had no known surviving family, and could so buy their houses at a low price. If such houses were located within a walled city the dwellings would then become their own property even after the Year of Jubilee; whereas otherwise the house might have been redeemed had a surviving relative been found.

15: 'Woe to you, Scribes and Pharisees, hypocrites, because you travel around on sea and land to make one proselyte; and when he becomes one, you make him twice as much a son of hell as yourselves.'

The majority of foreigners attracted to Judaism became 'God-fearers', or 'proselytes of the Gate', who sought to follow the Jewish moral laws but not the more inconvenient ceremonial laws including circumcision. There was however a further category known as 'proselytes of the righteous', who were noted for their fanatical devotion to every aspect of the Law. To 'travel around sea and land' is a proverb meaning to leave no stone unturned. 'Twice as much a son of hell' is very strong language indeed to describe the religious perversion that some at least of the Pharisees displayed. Jesus is seeking to provoke a response.

187

16-22: 'Woe to you, blind guides, who say, 'Whoever swears by the Temple, that is nothing; but whoever swears by the gold of the Temple is obligated.' You fools and blind men! Which is more important, the gold or the Temple that sanctified the gold? And, 'Whoever swears by the altar, that is nothing, but whoever swears by the offering on it, he is obligated.' You blind men, which is more important, the offering, or the altar that sanctifies the offering? Therefore, whoever swears by the altar, swears both by the altar and by everything on it. And whoever swears by the Temple, swears both by the Temple and by him who dwells within it. And whoever swears by heaven, swears both by the throne of God and by him who sits upon it.'

Jesus returns to their practice of falsely swearing oaths. While sounding very religious in making vows by everything that sounded holy, they left a loophole by leaving out the name of God himself. By so doing they evaded the potential issue of personal responsibility should what was being promised not be delivered. Jesus insists that all such oaths are binding upon them whether they include one of the names of God or not. He also repeats the image of the 'blind guide' (Matthew 15:14), ridiculing the Pharisees' pride in being self-regulated representatives of the God of Israel who had said that he would 'lead the blind by a way they do not know, in paths they do not know I will guide them' (Isaiah 42:16). A guide who is blind is unreliable indeed.

23-24: 'Woe to you, Scribes and Pharisees, hypocrites! For you tithe mint and dill and cumin, and have neglected the weightier provisions of the law: justice and mercy and faithfulness; but these are the things you should have done without neglecting the others. You blind guides, who strain out a gnat and swallow a camel!'

The Pharisees made ostentatious shows of their piety, even tithing to the Levitical priesthood the small quantities that their herb gardens

188

produced, in an effort to abide by Deuteronomy 14:22: 'You shall surely tithe all the produce from what you sow, which comes out of the field every year.' Jesus supports the principle of tithing as a means of supporting God's people, but upbraids them for their neglect of what concerns God more. As lawyers representing the demands of the Jewish Law, they should have devoted themselves to making right judgements, in a spirit of kindness and with a fidelity that can be relied upon. As it was, they were making bad errors that were keeping people away from God's rule, the exact opposite of what their role was supposed to mean.

Even though clearly worked up, Jesus is still able to employ humour - he follows up 'blind guides' with a visual image of striking vividness. Those who drew their water from shallower pools had to strain out larvae as well as insects from it using a muslin sieve. The Greek word used for 'gnat' here ('*kônôps*') has also been used to denote an insect that was found to breed in wine.[152] Leviticus 11:23 commanded the Israelites to 'detest' winged insects, hence the straining. The image of a swallowed camel, going down someone's throat one split-hoof at a time stands in stark, and deliberately ridiculous, contrast to this sensible practice.

25-26: 'Woe to you, Scribes and Pharisees, hypocrites! For you clean the outside of the cup and of the dish, but inside they are full of robbery and self-indulgence. You blind Pharisees, first clean the inside of the cup and of the dish, so that the outside of it may become clean also.'

The Pharisees were extremely concerned with appearances, but had lost sight of inner moral purity. The 'cleansing' Jesus is speaking of here is a ceremonial one for religious purposes, not a hygiene matter. They applied rigidly the many oral traditions about ritual purity concerning household utensils, but were unchanged on the inside. 'Robbery' here ('*harpagê*') means 'to plunder',[153] in the manner that Jesus is referring to in their treatment of widows' property; whereas 'self-indulgence'

189

('*akrasia*') points to their lack of self-control. Jesus says that moral change has to start with an inner change, something that only God is able to effect.

27-28: 'Woe to you, the Scribes and Pharisees, hypocrites! For you are like whitewashed tombs which on the outside appear beautiful, but inside they are full of dead men's bones and all uncleanness. So you, too, outwardly appear righteous to men, but inwardly you are full of hypocrisy and lawlessness.'

The road to Jerusalem had many tombs by it, which were annually painted white to serve as a warning to pilgrims going to worship at the Temple. They had to avoid contact with them and so maintain the ceremonial purity necessary to participate in the Temple services. The tombs would gleam brightly in the sunshine, and so were attractive to look at in a way that belied their inner uncleanness. Again, this is a very offensive image to use to describe the guardians of the Jewish Law, who were in fact, Jesus says, '*anomia*' - 'lawless' in their wrongdoing, based on their inner spiritual condition of being cut off from God despite their correct outward appearance.

29-33: 'Woe to you, Scribes and Pharisees, hypocrites! For you build the tombs of the prophets and adorn the monuments of the righteous, and say, 'If we had been living in the days of our fathers, we would not have been partners with them in shedding the blood of the prophets.' So you testify against yourselves, that you are sons of those who murdered the prophets. Fill up, then, the measure of the guilt of your fathers. You serpents, you brood of vipers, how will you escape the sentence of hell?'

Jesus continues to use the most severe language in his exposure of the Pharisees' and Scribes' guilt. While they were happy to honour the prophets after their death, they were actually no different to their forefathers in their hostile attitude towards John the Baptist and

190

towards Jesus himself. Jesus invites them to complete the work their ancestors have begun (*'plêroô'* - 'to fulfil') and so complete their guilt by treating him in the same way. Again, no quarter is given - snakes and vipers being highly offensive terms, which Jesus alone could use, as he alone knew their hearts. 'Hell' again is *'Gehenna'*, the rubbish dump of never ending burning prepared for the devil and his demonic angels.

34-36: 'Therefore, behold, I am sending you prophets and wise men and Scribes; some of them you will kill and crucify, and some of them you will scourge in your synagogues, and persecute from city to city, so that upon you may fall the guilt of all the righteous blood shed on earth, from the blood of righteous Abel to the blood of Zechariah, the son of Berechiah, whom you murdered between the Temple and the altar. Truly I say to you, all these things will come upon this generation.'

Jesus indicates the apostolic witness that is to come from his disciples using the Jews own terms for their spiritual instructors ('prophets and wise men and Scribes'). His prophetic words were certainly fulfilled in the lives of his followers. Abel (Genesis 4:8) represents the first person murdered for following God's instructions regarding sacrifice and offering. Cain chose to offer in his own way, and this, combined with a wrong attitude of heart towards God meant that his offering was rejected - Pharisees take note! Zechariah may be the prophet of that name (Zechariah 1:2), although there is no surviving account of his murder. Jesus may also have been referring to Zechariah the son of Jehoiada the priest (Berechiah may have been the name of his grandfather). Jehoiada was stoned to death in the Temple at the command of King Joash (2 Chronicles 24:20-22). This would be particularly fitting as the death is avenged by God immediately using a foreign military force, as was to be the case soon after the rejection of Jesus. 'This generation' was about to be judged in the most severe terms.

191

37-39: 'Jerusalem, Jerusalem, who kills the prophets and stones those who are sent to her! How often I wanted to gather your children together, the way a hen gathers her chicks under her wings, and you were unwilling. Behold, your house is being left to you desolate! For I say to you, from now on you will not see me until you say, 'Blessed is he who comes in the name of the Lord."

Jesus' 'woes' now become a full lament for the city and her 'children'. A picture of tender intimacy is presented, which the Jewish leaders have rejected in favour of man-made legalism. The 'house' of the Temple, built by priests probably trained by Jesus' step-father Joseph, was to be left to those very leaders who had missed the coming of the promised Messiah. In less than forty years' time it would be destroyed by the Roman army under Vespasian. Many of the men to whom Jesus spoke would be trapped in the Temple building by the encircled army, who would systematically pull down the walls and slaughter them, even as the priests desperately carried on with their offerings and prayers. Psalm 118, from which Jesus is quoting in verse 26, would certainly have been amongst the Psalms frantically prayed with ever increasing panic as the Priests heard the walls around them coming down. Psalm 118:10-11 describes an encircling army: 'All nations surrounded me; in the name of the Lord I will surely cut them off.' The Hebrew of verses 13-14 contains the name of Y'shua: 'You pushed me violently so that I was falling, but the Lord helped me. The Lord is my strength and song, and he has become my salvation' (*Y'shua*). So do verses 20-21: 'This is the gate of the Lord; the righteous will enter through it. I shall give thanks to you, for you have answered me, and you have become my salvation' (*Y'shua*). It is possible that in praying the Psalm, these words of Jesus' may have come to their minds, and that they would have seen in his name the 'gate for the sheep' (John 10:7), that is, the way to enter the kingdom of God. They might then have called on his name and finished the Psalm in the presence of God himself, and so in fact 'see' the one that they had themselves crucified - Y'shua of Nazareth.

Chapter 24

1-2: 'Jesus came out from the Temple and was going away when his disciples came up to point out the Temple buildings to him. And he said to them, 'Do you not see all these things? Truly I say to you, not one stone here will be left upon another, which will not be torn down."

Jesus' disciples appear to be suffering from acute embarrassment after the denunciation of the Pharisees, and as they leave they attempt to change the subject by drawing Jesus' attention to the magnificence of the scale of Herod's construction. The largest stone found to date weighs ~ 400 tons.[154] Jesus, as the son of the '*tekton*' in all probability responsible for training the Priests that Herod needed to do the building on the inner sanctuary part of the Temple site, is not impressed. With awesome accuracy he gives a remarkable prediction that was fulfilled in AD 70. The Romans destroyed the Temple, setting fire to it causing some of the gold interior to melt away into the crevices. Later, people would turn the stones over to recover the lost gold.

3-8: 'As he was sitting on the Mount of Olives, the disciples came to him privately, saying, 'Tell us, when will these things happen, and what will be the sign of your coming, and of the end of the age?' And Jesus answered and said to them, 'See to it that no one misleads you. For many will come in my name, saying, 'I am the Christ,' and will mislead many. You will be hearing of wars and rumours of wars. See that you are not frightened, for those things must take place, but that is not yet the end. For nation will rise against nation, and kingdom against kingdom, and in various places there will be famines and earthquakes. But all these things are merely the beginning of birth pangs.'

The disciples ask two questions: when the destruction of the Temple will occur ('when will these things happen'), and what will precede

Christ's return at the end of the '*aiôn*' - the 'age' in relation to eternity, in other words, the end of the world. The upheavals described are likened to the labour pains of childbirth - the start of a long, slow and painful process, in which spiritual deception will be rife. The process can be traced to shortly after Jesus' death. Josephus records that at the time of Felix (appointed Roman procurator of Judea by Claudius in AD 53), 'there was an Egyptian false prophet that did the Jews more mischief than the former; for he was a cheat, and pretended to be a prophet also, and got together thirty thousand men that were deluded by him; these he led roundabout from the wilderness to the mount which was called the Mount of Olives.' [155] Jesus' answer encompasses both of the disciples' questions; the two strands are interwoven, however. With the benefit of the hindsight of history, it is possible to separate them into those that occurred around the time of the destruction of Jerusalem and those that have yet to be fulfilled.

9-14: 'Then they will deliver you to tribulation, and will kill you, and you will be hated by all nations because of my name. At that time many will fall away and will betray one another and hate one another. Many false prophets will arise and will mislead many. Because lawlessness is increased, most people's love will grow cold. But the one who endures to the end, he will be saved. This gospel of the kingdom shall be preached in the whole world as a testimony to all the nations, and then the end will come.'

It is difficult to pin this description down to any specific moment in time. Christians have been persecuted widely in many periods of history subsequently, and false voices have spoken with the results that Jesus describes. The 'tribulation' described happened under Nero (who ruled from 54-68 AD), more recently under the Soviet communists and is still happening under the Chinese communists and in many Islamic countries today. Lawlessness is again, as with the Pharisees, '*anomia*' - the wickedness that comes from discarding God's word as a guide for living. There will be a need to hold fast to Jesus himself and to his

194

testimony, so that the 'good news' of the Gospel can continue to be made known to all people.

15-20: 'Therefore when you see the 'the abomination of desolation' which was spoken of through Daniel the prophet, standing in the holy place (let the reader understand), then those who are in Judea must flee to the mountains. Whoever is on the housetop must not go down to get the things out that are in his house. Whoever is in the field must not turn back, to get his cloak. But woe to those who are pregnant and to those who are nursing babies in those days! But pray that your flight will not be in the winter, or on a Sabbath.'

Jesus now appears to switch back to the near future and the disciples' first question regarding the destruction of the Temple. Daniel (9:27) had predicted the abomination that Antiochus Epiphanes, the king of Syria would introduce by sacrificing a pig on the Temple altar, which provoked the Maccabean revolt of 166-162 BC. A similar 'abomination' would occur again when, as Josephus records, [156] 'the Romans, upon the flight of the seditious into the city, and upon the burning of the holy house itself, and of all the buildings round about it, brought their ensigns to the Temple and set them over against its eastern gate; and there did they offer sacrifices to them.' Jesus prophesies the flight from Jerusalem that must necessarily occur if his followers were to survive the onslaught of the Roman army. Eusebius (c. 263 - c. 339 AD, Bishop of Caesarea) later recorded the actions of the Christians when they saw the Roman army under the command of Vespasian preparing to besiege the city of Jerusalem: 'The whole body, however, of the church at Jerusalem, having been commanded by a divine revelation, given to men of approved piety there before the war, removed from the city, and dwelt at a certain town beyond the Jordan, called Pella. Here those that believed in Jesus, having removed from Jerusalem, as if holy men had entirely abandoned the royal city itself, and the whole land of Judea; the divine justice, for their crimes against

Jesus and his apostles finally overtook them, totally destroying the whole generation of these evildoers from the earth' (Eusebius, 3:5). The reference to the Sabbath locates the prophecy to the first part of the question (the destruction of the Temple), when the Jewish regulations would still be applied to Jews who were followers of Jesus.

21-28: 'For then there will be a great tribulation, such as has not occurred since the beginning of the world until now, nor ever, will. Unless those days had been cut short, no life would have been saved; but for the sake of the elect those days will be cut short. Then if anyone says to you, 'Behold, here is the Christ,' or 'There he is,' do not believe him. For false Christs and false prophets will arise and will show great signs and wonders, so as to mislead, if possible, even the elect. Behold, I have told you in advance. So if they say to you, 'Behold, he is in the wilderness,' do not go out, or, 'Behold, he is in the inner rooms', do not believe them. For just as the lightning comes from the east and flashes even to the west, so will the coming of the Son of Man be. Wherever the corpse is, there the vultures will gather.'

This 'great tribulation' may apply to the destruction of Jerusalem (AD 70), or to the return of Christ, or both. One certainly happened during the siege of Jerusalem. Josephus records: 'Then did the famine widen its progress, and devoured the people by whole houses and families; the upper rooms were full of women and children that were dying by famine, and the lanes of the city were full of the dead bodies of the aged; the children also and the young men wandered about the market-places like shadows, all swelled with the famine, and fell down dead, wheresoever their misery seized them... the famine confounded all natural passions; for those who were just going to die looked upon those that were gone to rest before them with dry eyes and open mouths. A deep silence also, and a kind of deadly night, had seized upon the city; while yet the robbers were still more terrible than these miseries were themselves; for they broke open those houses which

196

were no other than graves of dead bodies, and plundered them of what they had; and carrying off the coverings of their bodies, went out laughing, and tried the points of their swords in their dead bodies; and, in order to prove what metal they were made of they thrust some of those through that still lay alive upon the ground; but for those that entreated them to lend them their right hand and their sword to despatch them, they were too proud to grant their requests, and left them to be consumed by the famine.' [157]

Jesus then appears to address the second part of their question, to do with the end of the age. It is possible that Jesus' remarks were made separately but recorded together as a mixture, in part because some of his disciples later clearly thought that the destruction of Jerusalem would coincide with the end of the world: 'Do not become easily unsettled or alarmed by some prophecy, report or letter supposed to have come from us, saying that the day of the Lord has already come' (2 Thessalonians 2:2 ANIV). Christ's second coming will be sudden, unlike the destruction of Jerusalem, which took place over a 4 year period. As mentioned earlier, there will be spiritual deception of the various types described. Jesus then quotes a well-known proverb, but with a twist. 'Vulture' ('*aetos*') is also translated 'eagle', the symbol the Roman army carried on their standards.

29-31 'But immediately after the tribulation of those days the sun will be darkened, and the moon will not give its light; and the stars will fall from the sky, and the powers of the heavens will be shaken. And then the sign of the Son of Man will appear in the sky, and then all the tribes of the earth will mourn, and they will see the Son of Man coming on the clouds of the sky with power and great glory. And he will send forth his angels with a great trumpet and they will gather together his elect from the four winds, from one end of the sky to the other.'

197

Jesus continues to focus on his second coming, and particularly the 'signs' that his disciples are interested in. Just as Jesus' first coming was heralded by an astronomic event in the form of a star, so too his second coming will be accompanied by warnings that do not appear to have any current scientific basis. Having gained people's attention, Jesus will return in the same way his disciples saw him go into heaven (Acts 1:11) and then the angelic gathering and separating that Jesus taught in Matthew 13:30 will occur.

32-35: 'Now learn the parable from the fig tree: when its branch has already become tender and puts forth its leaves, you know that summer is near; so, you too, when you see all these things, recognize that he is near, right at the door. Truly I say to you, this generation will not pass away until all these things take place. Heaven and earth will pass away, but my words will not pass away.'

Jesus now reverts to the first question concerning Jerusalem. The current generation of Jews would indeed live to see the arrival of the Roman army under command of Vespasian in 66 AD. The fig tree of Israel was almost ripe for judgement.

36-41: 'But of that day and hour no one knows, not even the angels of heaven, nor the Son, but the Father alone. For the coming of the Son of Man will be just like the days of Noah. For as in those days before the flood they were eating and drinking, marrying and giving in marriage, until the day that Noah entered the ark, and they did not understand until the flood came and took them all away; so will the coming of the Son of Man be. Then there will be two men in the field; one will be taken and one will be left. Two women will be grinding at the mill; one will be taken and one will be left.'

198

'That day' appears to apply to the day of Christ's return, which at that point Jesus, in his humanity and having laid aside his omniscience, was not aware. The day of his return will, he says, be characterized by normal life being lived in supreme indifference to God. Only those in relationship with him will be taken.

42-44: 'Therefore be on the alert, for you do not know which day your Lord is coming. But be sure of this, that if the head of the house had known at what time of the night the thief was coming, he would have been on the alert and would not have allowed his house to be broken into. For this reason you also must be ready; for the Son of Man is coming at an hour when you do not think he will.'

To be 'alert' is '*grêgoreuô*', meaning 'a state of watchful wakefulness and vigilance'.[158] Jesus has given indicators of when his return is imminent (including signs in the heavens), but stresses that his return will still be a surprise, hence the need to be alert.

45-51: 'Who then is the faithful and sensible slave whom his master put in charge of his household to give them their food at the proper time? Blessed is that slave whom his master finds so doing when he comes. Truly I say to you that he will put him in charge of all his possessions. But if that evil slave says in his heart, 'My master is not coming for a long time,' and begins to beat his fellow slaves and eat and drink with drunkards; the master of that slave will come on a day when he does not expect him and at an hour which he does not know, and will cut him in pieces and assign him a place with the hypocrites; in that place there will be weeping and gnashing of teeth.'

The alertness Jesus commands is a practical one - to be carrying out one's duties faithfully and fairly. That is presented as a test of true discipleship; Jesus using the same word as that with which he upbraids the Pharisees - 'hypocrite', or 'play-actor'. The punishment for the 'evil servant' is severe. Cutting in two was a form of capital punishment practiced in the near and Middle-East, and is recorded also in Hebrews 11:37: 'They (*the prophets*) were stoned, they were sawn in two.' After physical death comes a spiritual separation from God, in a place marked by profound expressions of regret. This can be seen in Luke 16:37, where the rich man in torment asks Abraham to send a message to his still-living brothers, thus demonstrating that experience of emotion does not end with physical life. This has been testified to by the accounts of near or after death experiences of patients who have undergone cardiac arrest resuscitation. Far from down-playing hell or writing it out of God's agenda completely as some modern scholars try and do, Jesus warns his audience of its reality and the crucial need to avoid entering it.

Chapter 25

1-13: 'Then the kingdom of heaven will be comparable to ten virgins, who took their lamps and went out to meet the bridegroom. Five of them were foolish, and five were prudent. For when the foolish took their lamps, they took no oil with them, but the prudent took oil in flasks along with their lamps. Now while the bridegroom was delaying, they all got drowsy and began to sleep. But at midnight, there was a shout, 'Behold, the bridegroom! Come out to meet him.' Then all those virgins rose and trimmed their lamps. The foolish said to the prudent, 'Give us some of your oil, for our lamps are going out.' But the prudent answered, 'No, there will not be enough for us and you too; go instead to the dealers and buy some for yourselves.' And while they were going away to make the purchase, the bridegroom came, and those who were ready went in with him to the wedding feast; and the door was shut. Later the other virgins also came, saying, 'Lord, lord, open up for us.' But he answered, 'Truly I say to you, I do not know you.' Be on the alert then, for you do not know the day nor the hour.'

Jesus follows up his point regarding the need for alertness with the parable of the ten bridesmaids (Greek: *'parthenos'* - 'virgins').[159] The custom of the day was for the bridegroom to collect the bride from her father's house and take her to his own, but at an unspecified time; and sometimes with the jocular view of arriving before she was fully ready to receive him. Hence unmarried friends of the bride would place themselves on the watch for the arrival of the groom and his friends, to give advance warning to the bride-to-be. Frequently the groom would delay until the last moment, necessitating the use of lamps (often torches dipped in oil and set on fire) for keeping watch by, and hence a 'wise' (i.e. provident) bridesmaid would bring a supply of oil. Unwise (foolish) bridesmaids might be ill prepared for a delay - the Greek here is *'môros'*, which can have a deficient moral connotation as well as one of low intelligence. The immoral aspect is probably what is meant by the Lord of the feast answering, 'I do not know you.' 'Know' here is '*eidô*', which means 'perceive', or 'I cannot turn my eyes to you',[160] implying that is their (as yet unforgiven) sin that excludes them. These are the ones who end up being shut out of the marriage feast, and so Jesus repeats his exhortation regarding watchful alertness.

14-30: 'For it is just like a man about to go on a journey, who called his own slaves and entrusted his possessions to them. To one he gave five talents, to another, two, and to another, one, each according to his own ability; and he went on his journey. Immediately the one who had received the five talents went and traded with them, and gained five more talents. In the same manner the one who had received the two talents gained two more. But he who received the one talent went away, and dug a hole in the ground and hid his master's money. Now after a long time the master of those slaves came and settled accounts with them. The one who had received the five talents came up and brought five more talents, saying, 'Master, you entrusted five talents to me. See, I have gained five more talents.' His master said to him, 'Well done, good and faithful slave. You were faithful with a few things, I will put you in charge of many things; enter into the joy of your master.' Also the one who had received the two talents came up and said, 'Master, you entrusted two talents to me. See, I have gained two more talents.' His master said to him, 'Well done, good and faithful slave. You were faithful with a few things, I will put you in charge of many things; enter into the joy of your master.' And the one also who had received the one talent came up and said, 'Master, I knew you to be a hard man, reaping where you did not sow and gathering where you scattered no seed. And I was afraid, and went away and hid your talent in the ground. See, you have what is yours.' But his master answered and said to him, 'You wicked, lazy slave, you knew that I reap where I did not sow and gather where I scattered no seed. Then you ought to have put my money in the bank, and on my arrival I would have received my money back with interest. Therefore take away the talent from him, and give it to the one who has the ten talents.' For to everyone who has, more shall be given, and he will have an abundance; but from the one who does not have, even what he does have shall be taken away. Throw out the worthless slave into the outer darkness; in that place there will be weeping and gnashing of teeth.'

A 'talent' was a unit weight of precious metal, usually silver. The master of the parable gave them according to what he knew the individual's abilities to be. He represents God in some ways but not in others, thus illustrating the danger of relying on parables alone as a basis for understanding the nature of God. God does not 'go away' and leave us on our own to get on with things as best we can. Jesus later said, 'I am with you always, even to the end of the age' (Matthew 28:20), and gave his Holy Spirit 'to be with you forever' (John 14:16). God is also not 'hard', i.e. harsh; he is patient and merciful, although there are clearly limits to his patience based on his fatherly discipline, punishment and eventual eternal judgement.

Parables have an over-riding message, and the message of this one is that we should use diligently and responsibly all that God has given us. The other main character in the parable is the lazy servant who simply buries what he was given instead of using it wisely, and is described as 'worthless', i.e. unprofitable. True servants are diligent in applying themselves to the master's service.

31-40: 'But when the Son of Man comes in his glory, and all the angels with him, then he will sit on his glorious throne. All the nations will be gathered before him; and he will separate them from one another, as the shepherd separates the sheep from the goats; and he will put the sheep on his right, and the goats on the left. Then the King will say to those on his right, 'Come, you who are blessed of my Father, inherit the kingdom prepared for you from the foundation of the world. For I was hungry, and you gave me something to eat; I was thirsty, and you gave me something to drink; I was a stranger, and you invited me in; naked, and you clothed me; I was sick, and you visited me; I was in prison, and you came to me.' Then the righteous will answer him, 'Lord, when did we see you hungry, and feed you, or thirsty, and give you something to drink? And when did we see you a stranger, and invite you in, or naked, and clothe you? When did we see you sick, or in prison, and come to you?' The King will answer and say to them, 'Truly I say to you, to the extent, that you did it to one of these brothers of mine, even the least of them, you did it to me.'

Christ's return will be with the accompaniment of angelic armies, and his judgement will be of the nations, out of which will be taken those who have shown compassion to the 'least of Christ's brothers', i.e. those who have become members of his heavenly Father's family. God has foreknowledge of all who will put their trust in Christ and has had a place of blessedness in mind for them from before the whole created order was conceived (the foundation of the world). Jesus identifies himself bodily with his people, to such an extent that he could say to Saul on the road to Damascus (Acts 9:4), 'Why are you persecuting me?' Hence what is done for a Christian in need is done as though to Christ himself.

41-46: 'Then he will also say to those on his left, 'Depart from me, accursed ones, into the eternal fire which has been prepared for the devil and his angels; for I was hungry, and you gave me nothing to eat; I was thirsty, and you gave me nothing to drink; I was a stranger, and you did not invite me in; naked, and you did not clothe me; sick, and in prison, and you did not visit me.' Then they themselves also will answer, 'Lord, when did we see you

204

hungry, or thirsty, or a stranger, or naked, or sick, or in prison, and did not take care of you?' Then he will answer them, 'Truly I say to you, to the extent, that you did not do it to one of the least of these, you did not do it to me.' These will go away into eternal punishment, but the righteous into eternal life.'

Jesus states that the everlasting fire, which he earlier likened to the rubbish burning in the valley of Gehenna, was not originally prepared for mankind. It was for the devil and the demonic angels aligned with him, where they will be tormented, as opposed to the popular view of their being the tormentors. That they are cursed in this way has been evidenced by their behaviour, notably their lack of concern for human suffering and especially that of those who belong to the family of God. Their punishment is eternal in the same way that the kingdom of heaven is eternal; Christ's teaching here lends no support for the modern notion of eternal annihilation.

Chapter 26

1-2: 'When Jesus had finished all these words, he said to his disciples, 'You know that after two days the Passover is coming, and the Son of Man is to be handed over for crucifixion.'

Jesus is in perfect touch with his heavenly Father and so is in total mastery of his destiny. He knew that he was to be an offering for sin in a complete way, one that the offering of the Passover lambs could never achieve.

3-5: 'Then the Chief Priests and the elders of the people were gathered together in the court of the High Priest, named Caiaphas; and they plotted together to seize Jesus by stealth and kill him. But they were saying, 'Not during the festival, otherwise, a riot might occur among the people.'

The Mishnah [161] laid down that for a capital case, 23 of the 71 members of the Sanhedrin council were required to meet in place of the usual 3 people needed for non-capital cases. John (11:47) records that the council was convened after Jesus had raised Lazarus from the dead, because of fears that Jesus might trigger a popular uprising. This would endanger not only possibly the nation but perhaps more especially their tenure as leaders in a Temple that provided the priests with a very comfortable and prestigious standard of living. John (12:42) records that many of the ruling council actually believed in him (including Nicodemus), but Caiaphas, as ruling High Priest, would have known which Sanhedrin members it was safe to call on to get a vote to take action against Jesus. It was his family that had most to lose from Jesus' disruption of the Temple's lucrative activities, and it was he who pushed the motion through. In doing so he found himself inadvertently speaking in a prophetic way about Jesus' death on behalf of the people - 'It is expedient for you that one man die for the people, and that the whole nation not perish' (John 11:50). While they would need the authority of the Roman procurator (Pontius Pilate) to execute a sentence of death, they were keen to keep it as quiet as possible, as a riot might also jeopardise their positions if the Romans deemed them incapable of keeping order.

6-13: 'Now when Jesus was in Bethany, at the home of Simon the leper, a woman came to him with an alabaster vial of very costly perfume, and she poured it on his head as he reclined at the table. But the disciples were indignant when they saw this, and said, 'Why this waste? For this perfume might have been sold for a high price and the money given to the poor.' But Jesus, aware of this, said to them, 'Why do you bother the woman? For she has done a good deed to me. For you always have the poor with you; but you do not always have me. For when she poured this perfume on my body, she did it to prepare me for burial. Truly I say to you, wherever, this gospel is preached in the whole world, what this woman has done will also be spoken of in memory of her."

After three years of healing and performing miracles, Jesus had many devoted followers in Israel, including many lepers who were now restored to society. Simon would appear to be one such person. John's account (12:1-3) tells us that Jesus' friends were there - Lazarus (also from Bethany) was eating with them; that his sister Martha was serving the meal and her sister Mary was there sitting at Jesus' feet listening to him teach - Luke 10:39. It was Mary who poured the vial of nard over Jesus' feet as well as his head, wiping his feet with her hair. Nard (essential oils from a herb of the Valerianaceae family) was very expensive. John (12:3-5) records that she poured out about one pint which was worth three hundred denarii - a year's wages for a working man. John also tells us that it was Judas who led the protests about the terrible waste of resources that this represented. This was not because he was concerned about the poor, but because he was in charge of Jesus' money and used to help himself to the donations that Jesus received from benefactors (John 12:6). Jesus however receives the offering as appropriate of one for burial. When he hung on the cross a few days later he would still be carrying the intense musky fragrance on his head and body, truly a 'freewill offering …in your appointed feasts, to make a sweet aroma to the Lord' (Numbers 15:3 NKJV). He would carry the fragrance to his grave. His prophecy about Mary's sacrificial act of worship being remembered has certainly been fulfilled.

14-16: 'Then one of the twelve, named Judas Iscariot, went to the Chief Priests and said, 'What are you willing to give me to betray him to you?' And they weighed out thirty pieces of silver to him. From then on he began looking for a good opportunity to betray Jesus.'

This event appears to have been the last straw for Judas. Love of money is the 'root of all kinds of evil' (1 Timothy 6:10), and Luke (22:3) records that it was at about this point that 'Satan entered Judas'. Aside from being an instrument of the devil to bring about Jesus betrayal, he may have been motivated by Jesus words about burial, deciding to cash in on his privileged position as a disciple while there was still opportunity. He would also betray Jesus because he had now lost all confidence in him as a liberator from the Roman occupation. Or he may have been seeking to provoke a confrontation that he felt sure that Jesus would win. For someone motivated by love of money he made a poor bargain with the priests - thirty silver pieces being the price of a common slave (Exodus 21:32). Matthew (27:6) indicates that the priests took the coins from the Temple treasury; hence they were the special Tyrian shekels minted solely for Temple use.

17-19: 'Now on the first day of Unleavened Bread the disciples came to Jesus and asked, 'Where do you want us to prepare for you to eat the Passover?' And he said, 'Go into the city to a certain man, and say to him, 'The Teacher says, 'My time is near; I am to keep the Passover at your house with my disciples." The disciples did as Jesus had directed them; and they prepared the Passover.'

The festival lasted eight days from the fourteenth day of the first month (Abib), and the Passover meal was celebrated by Jesus at the start of the day (the evening of the fourteenth), rather than at the end (before the evening of the fifteenth) in anticipation of his arrest that night. Mark (14:3) gives us some detail about the 'certain man', who would be carrying a jug of water on his head, thereby indicating in all probability that he was an Essene from a celibate household, as water was normally carried by women. The Essenes were a highly devout section of Jewish society, who shared Jesus' views regarding the corruption inherent in the priestly families.

20-25: 'Now when evening came, Jesus was reclining at the table with the twelve disciples. As they were eating, he said, 'Truly I say to you that one of you will betray me.' Being deeply grieved, they each one began to say to him, 'Surely not I, Lord?' And he answered, 'He who dipped his hand with me in the bowl is the one who will betray me. The Son of Man is to go, just as it is written of him; but woe to that man by whom the Son of Man is betrayed! It would have been good for that man if he had not been born.' And Judas, who was betraying him, said, 'Surely it is not I, Rabbi?' Jesus said to him, 'You have said it yourself.'

The meal was eaten 'reclining' in the Roman style, probably on a triclinium of three couches arranged in a 'U-shape'. Jesus is conversing with John (who was lying next to him) regarding who it was who would betray him. This was at the request of Peter who was lying on the couch opposite (John 13:24-26). Jesus dips the first piece of bread, and after the custom of honouring a special guest, gives it to Judas. This indicates that Judas was lying on the other side of him from John, in the place of honour at the head of the table, on Jesus' right, with

209

John on his left. They would have been dipping their pieces of unleavened bread in the same bowl of bitter herbs as Jesus. Jesus appears to have situated Judas there to specifically warn him about the course of action he had set himself on and the consequences. Judas' response was to mimic the words that the other disciples were speaking in sadness - 'Surely not I?', only with the title 'Rabbi' rather than the more respectful 'Lord' that the others use. This seating arrangement explains why John was party to the conversation while the other disciples were unaware of it and therefore make no attempt to stop Judas from leaving or understand what Jesus was telling him to do - 'Jesus said to him, 'What you do, do quickly.' Now no one of those reclining at the table knew for what purpose he had said this to him. For some were supposing, because Judas had the money box, that Jesus was saying to him, 'Buy the things we have need of for the feast'; or else, that he should give something to the poor. So after receiving the morsel he went out immediately; and it was night' (John 13:27-30). Judas does not appear to have had much of an appetite for the rest of the meal and he makes no response to Jesus' appeal; 'night' was present to him in ways other than simply the setting of the sun.

26-30: 'While they were eating, Jesus took some bread, and after a blessing, he broke it and gave it to the disciples, and said, 'Take, eat; this is my body.' And when he had taken a cup and given thanks, he gave it to them, saying, 'Drink from it, all of you; for this is my blood of the covenant, which is poured out for many for forgiveness of sins. But I say to you, I will not drink of this fruit of the vine from now on until that day when I drink it new with you in my Father's kingdom.' After singing a hymn, they went out to the Mount of Olives.'

After Judas leaves, Jesus takes the opportunity to change the Passover service to incorporate its fulfillment. The broken 'bread of affliction' of the Passover meal becomes his body, which was to be afflicted and given up for them. The Passover meal (the 'Seder') has 4 common cups

210

of wine, drunk at different points in the order of service. The third is the 'cup of blessing', symbolizing redemption, and this becomes the cup of the new covenant for the forgiveness of sins. As the Apostle Paul would later write - 'Is not the cup of blessing which we bless a sharing in the blood of Christ?' (1 Corinthians 10:16).

Jesus then points his disciples towards the fulfillment of the service in the kingdom of heaven. As was customary, Psalm 113 was sung after the meal, after which Jesus went to the Mount of Olives to prepare himself for his arrest.

31-35: 'Then Jesus said to them, 'You will all fall away because of me this night, for it is written, 'I will strike down the shepherd, and the sheep of the flock shall be scattered.' But after I have been raised, I will go ahead of you to Galilee.' But Peter said to him, 'Even though all may fall away because of you, I will never fall away.' Jesus said to him, 'Truly I say to you that this very night, before a rooster crows, you will deny me three times.' Peter said to him, 'Even if I have to die with you, I will not deny you.' All the disciples said the same thing too.'

'Fall' here is, once again, *'skandalizô'*, meaning to stumble, from *'skandalon'* ('a trap', or 'trap trigger'). The disciples are going to be so afraid after the arrest that their faith in Jesus will take a temporary knock. However the promise of Jesus is that like any good Israelite shepherd, he will go ahead of the sheep on the next stage of their journey, after his resurrection. Jesus quotes from Zechariah (13:7) - 'Awake, O sword, against my shepherd, and against the man that is my fellow, says the Lord of hosts: smite the shepherd, and the sheep shall be scattered: and I will turn mine hand upon the little ones' (KJV). The good shepherd will be struck down, but in strict accordance with his Father's plan and purpose. After that Father's hand will be turned (*'al'*) - meaning 'upon, above, or over' the 'little ones' (*'tsaar'*) - those 'brought low', or 'insignificant', i.e. those 'little faiths' so often the

211

subject of Jesus' concern for them (Matthew 6:30, 8:26, 14:31, and 16:8).

Even though Father has to place the punishment for the sin of the world on the good Shepherd, Jesus is still committed to the care of the flock. In accordance with Psalm 145:14 he promises to lift up those brought low. 'The Lord sustains all who fall, and raises up all who are bowed down.' Jesus prophesied to Peter that before 'cock crow' (the last watch of the night, from 3 am to 6 am), he would deny three times that he even knew Jesus. Peter responds by repeating that he is certainly ready to share his master's fate, and the other disciples say the same, despite having heard Jesus' prophetic warning regarding their future unfaithful behaviour and their 'falling away'.

36-41: 'Then Jesus came with them to a place called Gethsemane, and said to his disciples, 'Sit here while I go over there and pray.' And he took with him Peter and the two sons of Zebedee, and began to be grieved and distressed. Then he said to them, 'My soul is deeply grieved, to the point of death; remain here and keep watch with me.' And he went a little beyond them, and fell on his face and prayed, saying, 'My Father, if it is possible, let this cup pass from me; yet not as I will, but as you will.' And he came to the disciples and found them sleeping, and said to Peter, 'So, you men could not keep watch with me for one hour? Keep watching and praying that you may not enter into temptation; the spirit is willing, but the flesh is weak.''

Gethsemane is the Hebrew for olive press,[162] a fitting name for the pressure that Jesus was under as he sought to place his human will under the will of his heavenly Father, praying that his Father's will would take precedence. Taking his closest three disciples, his struggle to reconcile himself with the approaching agony of his death manifests itself in his emotions. 'Distressed' (the Greek is '*adêmoneô*' [163] - AV: 'heavy'), is the strongest word for depression and anguish of mind in

212

the New Testament. 'Deeply grieved' is *'perilupos'*, meaning so overcome with sorrow so much as to cause one's death. [164]

Luke's account (22:44) records that Jesus sweat was mixed with blood, a sign of the most acute human stress. This is known as haematidrosis, where the constriction to the blood vessels supplying the sweat glands causes bleeding into the glands themselves and out through the skin's pores. From John's (19:34) description of the Roman spear draining blood followed by water (serum) from Jesus' side following his death on the cross it appears that Jesus had undergone a haemopericardium. This a condition where the heart's muscle ruptures into the pericardial sac around the heart causing heart compression and eventual death. That being the case it is likely that the process began during the agony Jesus experienced in the garden, as he lay prostrate in prayer before his Father God reconciling himself to and preparing himself for doing his Father's will at Calvary. The disciples, having recently drunk the four cups of wine which were a part of the Passover meal, succumbed to sleep.

42-46: 'He went away again a second time and prayed, saying, 'My Father, if this cannot pass away unless I drink it, your will be done.' Again he came and found them sleeping, for their eyes were heavy. And he left them again, and went away and prayed a third time, saying the same thing once more. Then he came to the disciples and said to them, 'Are you still sleeping and resting? Behold, the hour is at hand and the Son of Man is being betrayed into the hands of sinners. 'Get up, let us be going; behold, the one who betrays me is at hand!''

The cup of suffering that Jesus had warned James and John about (Matthew 20:22) had to be drunk, and again Jesus places himself under his Father's will, without any support from his sleepy disciples. Jesus prepares himself for the ordeal ahead by submitting himself prostrate before his Father on three occasions. Jesus had ample opportunity to

213

escape beyond the judicial reach of the Sanhedrin who at that moment were approaching to arrest him. Instead he chose to submit himself willingly to his Father's plans, using the time in Gethsemane to steel and ready himself in prayer against the suffering he knew would follow. He won the decisive battle of the will in prayer in the Garden of Gethsemane.

47-50: 'While he was still speaking, behold, Judas, one of the twelve, came up accompanied by a large crowd with swords and clubs, who came from the Chief Priests and elders of the people. Now he who was betraying him gave them a sign, saying, 'Whomever I kiss, he is the one; seize him.' Immediately Judas went to Jesus and said, 'Hail, Rabbi!' and kissed him. And Jesus said to him, 'Friend, do what you have come for.' Then they came and laid hands on Jesus and seized him.'

The Temple had extra security forces at Passover to cope with the larger numbers in Jerusalem and a detachment arrive at the garden with Judas. John describes the company of soldiers as a '*speira*'- 'a cohort', which could be anything between 200 and 600 men. The Priests were taking no chances. The garden was in darkness, apart from the torches and lanterns that John (18:3) tells us that the party of soldiers was carrying. To avoid any confusion in the dark, Judas had arranged to identify Jesus as the one to arrest by means of a kiss of greeting. Jesus' response is to address him as '*hetairos*', meaning 'friend' and 'partner',[165] perhaps an expression of his understanding of the part Judas was unwittingly playing in the greater purposes of his Father God.

51-54: 'And behold, one of those who were with Jesus reached and drew out his sword, and struck the slave of the High Priest and cut off his ear. Then Jesus said to him, 'Put your sword back into its place; for all those who take up the sword shall perish by the sword. Or do you think that I cannot appeal to my Father,

214

and he will at once put at my disposal more than twelve legions of angels? How then will the Scriptures be fulfilled, which say that it must happen this way?'

John's account (18:10) tells us that it was Peter who struck out, perhaps wanting to make good on his claim to be willing to die for Jesus. John also says that the slave's name was Malchus (who presumably ducked such that Peter only caught his ear and not his neck). Luke (22:51) records that Jesus responded by commanding an end to the violence and by healing the man's ear, thus demonstrating his total command over the situation. When told who it is that they are looking for, Jesus responds in Hebrew with the name of Yahweh - 'I am', causing the arresting party to fall to the ground in awe (John 18:6). Jesus can match their single cohort with twelve legions (each ten cohorts) of angels, i.e. twelve lots of 6000, or 72,000 angelic soldiers, should he wish to ask his Father to supply them to defend him. There was no need for a display of swordsmanship from Peter; what was important was that his Father's will was being done.

55-58: 'At that time Jesus said to the crowds, 'Have you come out with swords and clubs to arrest me as you would against a robber? Every day I used to sit in the Temple teaching and you did not seize me. But all this has taken place to fulfil the Scriptures of the prophets.' Then all the disciples left him and fled. Those who had seized Jesus led him away to Caiaphas, the High Priest, where the Scribes and the elders were gathered together. But Peter was following him at a distance as far as the courtyard of the High Priest, and entered in, and sat down with the officers to see the outcome.'

Jesus was authorised as an ordained Rabbi and Doctor of the Law to teach in the Temple, however the Priests had not dared to arrest him there for fear of the crowds and his popular support. When the Temple Guard had tried to bring him in for questioning they had not been able to, such was his authority. In the seclusion of Gethsemane Jesus suffered the ignominy of a criminal's arrest - he 'was numbered with the transgressors' (Isaiah 53:12). John records that Jesus went to Caiaphas' house having first been taken to Annas, Caiaphas' father-in-law (John 18:12-24) and an earlier High Priest. Peter bravely followed after, and was eventually admitted to the courtyard, it appears, by John himself, as John was someone who was known to the household of the High Priest (John 18:15-16), and did not seem to fear arrest.

59-64: 'Now the Chief Priests and the whole council kept trying to obtain false testimony against Jesus, so that they might put him to death. They did not find any, even though many false witnesses came forward. But later on two came forward, and said, 'This man stated, 'I am able to destroy the Temple of God and to rebuild it in three days.' The High Priest stood up and said to him, 'Do you not answer? What is it that these men are testifying against you?' But Jesus kept silent. And the High Priest said to him, 'I adjure you by the living God, that you tell us whether you are the Christ, the Son of God.' Jesus said to him, 'You have said it yourself; nevertheless I tell you, hereafter, you will see the Son of Man sitting at the right hand of power and coming on the clouds of heaven.''

The Sanhedrin convened a council of the necessary twenty-three representatives for a capital case, but the hearing was illegal for several reasons. Capital cases could not meet at night - the Talmud [166] states that criminal processes for capital charges must be held in the daytime, and the verdict left until the next day. For a verdict to be valid the hearing had to be in the Temple judgement hall, not in a private house such as Caiaphas'. Witnesses had to be examined separately and without any prior contact between them, and to give false witness was punishable by death. Eventually two witnesses can be found to attempt to repeat Jesus' statement recorded by John (2:19): 'Destroy this temple, and in three days I will raise it up.' They do so differently

216

however, not withstanding that Jesus had been speaking of his own bodily resurrection. Mark (14:59) records that even their testimonies did not agree with each other. The trial is clearly an illegal farce, and Jesus maintains a dignified silence until he is put on solemn oath by the High Priest to declare whether he is the Christ, the Son of God. 'You have said it' is a strong form of assent, and Jesus follows it up with a statement based upon the prophecy of Daniel (7:13) indicating that he has an equality of authority ('sitting at the right hand') with God: 'Behold, with the clouds of heaven, one like a Son of Man was coming, and he came up to the Ancient of Days, and was presented before him.'

65-68: 'Then the High Priest tore his robes and said, 'He has blasphemed! What further need do we have of witnesses? Behold, you have now heard the blasphemy; what do you think?' They answered, 'He deserves death!' Then they spat in his face and beat him with their fists; and others slapped him, and said, 'Prophesy to us, you Christ; who is the one who hit you?''

Rending of garments was a response to blasphemy, for which the punishment was death. The trial now descends into violence, with the pent up frustration of the Priests and Pharisees spilling over into common assault, humiliation and mockery. The huge swing of behaviour from having been previously respectful, to outrightly abusive, points to the deep sense of personal betrayal they must have felt. This gifted Rabbi and Doctor whom they had ordained and held such high hopes had moved into what seemed to them to be blasphemous statements, something that betrayed the core of what they stood for. An uneducated itinerant would not have warranted such strong emotion; neither would he have been afforded the degree of respect that Jesus was consistently shown right up to the point of his conviction on the charge of blasphemy.

69-75: 'Now Peter was sitting outside in the courtyard, and a servant-girl came to him and said, 'You too were with Jesus the

Galilean.' But he denied it before them all, saying, 'I do not know what you are talking about.' When he had gone out to the gateway, another servant-girl saw him and said to those who were there, 'This man was with Jesus of Nazareth.' And again he denied it with an oath, 'I do not know the man.' A little later the bystanders came up and said to Peter, 'Surely you too are one of them; for even the way you talk gives you away.' Then he began to curse and swear, 'I do not know the man!' And immediately a rooster crowed. And Peter remembered the word which Jesus had said, 'Before a rooster crows, you will deny me three times.' And he went out and wept bitterly.'

Peter's Galilean accent gave him away, yet he was brave enough to have entered the courtyard and to be speaking with the officers there, one of whom was a relative of Malchus whom Peter had struck (John 18:26), and whom was probably present at the time of the arrest. This final challenge tipped Peter from bravado to cursing and uttering false oaths. Luke (22:61) records that at that precise moment, Jesus was led through the courtyard, in time to strengthen Peter with a look while not giving him away. Peter is overcome with remorse. 'Rooster crowed / crows' in the Greek can also be translated as 'Cock-crow', the hour of the 3AM watch-call trumpet sound which accompanied the changing of the Roman guard at the Palace of Antonia, and is a more likely explanation than the presence of poultry in the High Priest's courtyard.

Chapter 27

1-2: 'Now when morning came, all the Chief Priests and the elders of the people conferred together against Jesus to put him to death; and they bound him, and led him away and delivered him to Pilate the governor.'

Pronouncing a sentence of death was one thing, having it carried out was quite another. The Romans controlled the right of execution, hence the conference to agree the strategy that some of the Priests would have had planned out in advance. Pilate was not likely to be swayed by protests of blasphemy.

3-10: 'Then when Judas, who had betrayed him, saw that he had been condemned, he felt remorse and returned the thirty pieces of silver to the Chief Priests and elders, saying, 'I have sinned by betraying innocent blood.' But they said, 'What is that to us? See to that yourself!' And he threw the pieces of silver into the Temple sanctuary and departed; and he went away and hanged himself. The Chief Priests took the pieces of silver and said, 'It is not lawful to put them into the Temple treasury, since it is the price of blood.' And they conferred, together and with the money bought the Potter's Field as a burial place for strangers. For this reason that field has been called the Field of Blood to this day. Then that which was spoken through Jeremiah the prophet was fulfilled: 'And they took the thirty pieces of silver, the price of the one whose price had been set by the sons of Israel, and they gave them for the Potter's Field, as the Lord directed me.'

Judas' remorse (rather than repentance) leads him to confront the Priests who maintain an attitude of supreme indifference towards him. Acts 1:8 records that Judas hanged himself over the very field ('Hakeldama', that is, 'Field of Blood') that the Priests purchased with the money he returned. Their religious scruples prevented their

219

returning the money to the treasury, so they used it to buy a burial site for those pilgrims who died while visiting Jerusalem. In returning the money Judas was unwittingly fulfilling the prophecy recorded by Zechariah (11:12-13): 'They weighed out thirty shekels of silver as my wages. Then the Lord said to me, "Throw it to the potter, that magnificent price at which I was valued by them." So I took the thirty shekels of silver and threw them to the potter in the house of the Lord.' Jeremiah is cited because the Jewish Bible entitled this section of prophetic books 'Jeremiah' after the main book therein. Zechariah's prophecy is very remarkable in that 1) the amount and type of coin is exact, 2) the amount is that which the Lord is 'valued at' by the sons of Israel, 3) the coins were thrown, 4) they were used to buy the potter's field and 5) the place they were thrown in was the 'house of the Lord' - the Temple. Judas was not a Priest and so could not enter into the Court of the Priests beyond the barrier after the Court of the Israelites. He had to settle for throwing the money back at them. The Hebrew for 'potter' (in 'throw it to the potter') is '*yatsar*', which also means 'one who forms or fashions',[167] and is frequently used of God, e.g. in its first use in Genesis (2:7) - 'Then the Lord God **formed** man of dust from the ground, and breathed into his nostrils the breath of life; and man became a living being.' So there was a double fulfilment - the money was thrown to God (the Potter) in the house of God - the Temple, and then used to purchase 'the Potter's Field'.

11-14: 'Now Jesus stood before the governor, and the governor questioned him, saying, 'Are you the King of the Jews?' And Jesus said to him, 'It is as you say.' And while he was being accused by the Chief Priests and elders, he did not answer. Then Pilate said to him, 'Do you not hear how many things they testify against you?' And he did not answer him with regard to even a single charge, so the governor was quite amazed.'

Jesus is prepared to recognise Pilate's authority as Roman procurator, and to acknowledge that he, Jesus, is indeed the King of the Jews. This had been Herod the Great's title from the Roman Senate under the influence of Marc Antony, [168] but Augustus would not allow any of Herod's sons to lay claim to the title. Pilate would probably have found it amusing that someone else whom the authorities so disliked would claim it. Jesus does not recognize the authority of the corrupt Priests and elders who had broken their own Law in having him tried illegally, and declines to acknowledge their false charges against him, causing Pilate to marvel at his composure.

15-19: 'Now at the feast the governor was accustomed to release for the people any one prisoner whom they wanted. At that time they were holding a notorious prisoner, called Barabbas. So when the people gathered together, Pilate said to them, 'Whom do you want me to release for you? Barabbas, or Jesus who is called Christ?' For he knew that because of envy they had handed him over. While he was sitting on the judgement seat, his wife sent him a message, saying, 'Have nothing to do with that righteous man; for last night I suffered greatly in a dream because of him."

The Romans were accustomed to please the festival crowds by releasing a prisoner of their choice. Mark (15:7) identifies Barabbas as an insurrectionist and a murderer, while John records (18:40) that he was a robber. Pilate appears to have been looking for a way to free Jesus, and so offers a notably wicked person for the crowd to choose between. He would have been in possession of a good deal of intelligence about Jesus and was aware of the conflict between him and the religious Jewish authorities and their envy of Jesus. Pilate was not on the best of terms with the Jewish leaders, and frequently acted in such a way to annoy them, as he later did with the sign that was placed over Jesus' cross. When he was newly appointed as procurator (a sign that Judea was considered a lesser territory than one such as Syria which warranted a proconsul to rule it), he had provoked the Jews by maintaining the Imperial standard's image (idolatrous to Jews) of

Caesar on the entry of his troops into Jerusalem.[169] He relented only after the Jews had shown that they were willing to die rather than permit the idolatry. On another occasion the Jewish historian Philo (20 BC - AD 50), records ('Legatio ad Gaium' 38, 299) that, in accordance with Roman custom, Pilate displayed some shields in his palace bearing the inscription 'DIVI AUGUSTI FILIUS' [170] in honour of Caesar's supposed divinity. Philo states that Pilate did this to 'annoy the multitude'; it worked - the Jews reported him to Rome.

Pilate, as a Roman, would have been susceptible to omens, and his wife's dream would have unsettled him. She clearly knew who Jesus was, and describes him as a 'just' (the word 'man' has been added to the English text). The Greek here is *'dikaios'*, the same description that Matthew (1:19) gives of Joseph, Jesus' earthly father, and was also used of Jesus' half-brother James ('the Just'). This meant one who had been schooled in the Torah and Mishnah sufficiently well to be said to be 'just' (or 'righteous') in terms of keeping their requirements. This is further evidence of Jesus' educational status within the Jewish community. Pilate would have been well aware of who Jesus was, and knew that the Jews envied him for his wisdom and his miracles.

20-23: 'But the Chief Priests and the elders persuaded the crowds to ask for Barabbas and to put Jesus to death. But the governor said to them, 'Which of the two do you want me to release for you?' And they said, 'Barabbas.' Pilate said to them, 'Then what shall I do with Jesus who is called Christ?' They all said, 'Crucify him!' And he said, 'Why, what evil has he done?' But they kept shouting all the more, saying, 'Crucify him.'

The Priests were highly wealthy and influential, and they would have certainly prepared a crowd to gather before the seat of judgement to petition Pilate as they wished. Having taken so much trouble over the arrest they would not have left Jesus' fate to the whim of a fickle festival crowd. John (19:12) records that the Jews at this point played

222

their ace - threat of a report to Rome - pointing out that to recognize Jesus as a king was to discredit the rule of Rome. This seems to have swayed the natural sympathy that Pilate seems to have felt for Jesus - his job was on the line.

24-26; 'When Pilate saw that he was accomplishing nothing, but rather that a riot was starting, he took water and washed his hands in front of the crowd, saying, 'I am innocent of this man's blood; see to that yourselves.' And all the people said, 'His blood shall be on us and on our children!' Then he released Barabbas for them; but after having Jesus scourged, he handed him over to be crucified.'

A riot involving the adherents of the Chief Priests on the eve of Passover, would mean that Pilate would have to employ his troops who were there under the direct control of the Emperor, and so would mean that Pilate would have to answer to Rome for the bloodshed that would result. Was it worth it? Pilate had a history of local brutality already, from an occasion when he had seized some of the Temple's income to build a water aqueduct. Josephus records [171]: 'But Pilate undertook to bring a current of water to Jerusalem, and did it with the sacred money, and derived the origin of the stream from the distance of two hundred furlongs. However, the Jews were not pleased with what had been done about this water; and many ten thousands of the people got together, and made a clamour against him, and insisted that he should abandon his plan. Some of them also used reproaches, and abused the man, as crowds of such people usually do. So he placed a great number of his soldiers in their clothing, who carried daggers under their garments, and sent them to a place where they might surround them. So he bid the Jews himself go away; but they boldly casting reproaches upon him, he gave the soldiers that signal which had been beforehand agreed on; who laid upon them much greater blows than Pilate had commanded them, and equally punished those that were tumultuous, and those that were not; nor did they spare them in the least: and since the people were

223

unarmed, and were caught by men prepared for what they were about, there were a great number of them slain by this means, and others of them ran away wounded. And thus an end was put to this sedition.'

To have a complaint arising from his suppressing a riot resulting from siding with someone who had formally identified himself to the Roman court as a king would not help Pilate's political position. Given his history he would almost certainly be removed to Rome, as in fact later happened. As Josephus records: 'The nation of the Samaritans did not escape without tumults… Pilate prevented their going up (*to Tirathaba*), by seizing upon file roads with a great band of horsemen and foot-men, who fell upon those that were gotten together in the village; and when it came to an action, some of them they slew, and others of them they put to flight, and took a great many alive, the principal of which, and also the most potent of those that fled away, Pilate ordered to be slain. But when this tumult was appeased, the Samaritan senate sent an embassy to Vitellius, a man that had been consul, and who was now president of Syria, and accused Pilate of the murder of those that were killed; for that they did not go to Tirathaba in order to revolt from the Romans, but to escape the violence of Pilate. So Vitellius sent Marcellus, a friend of his, to take care of the affairs of Judea, and ordered Pilate to go to Rome, to answer before the emperor to the accusations of the Jews. So Pilate, when he had tarried ten years in Judea, made haste to Rome, and this in obedience to the orders of Vitellius, which he durst not contradict; but before he could get to Rome Tiberius was dead.' [172]

The pressure of the excited festival crowd finally told on Pilate; he capitulated to their demands and sent Jesus to be scourged as was normal prior to a crucifixion. The Romans used a short whip called a flagellum, consisting of several leather thongs with pieces of sheep bone and iron tied to them, which would sink into the victim's back and then be dragged down their body with each lash of the whip. A repeated application to the victim's back would cause deep lacerations, and the leather and bones would cut into the skin and muscle tearing the back into strips.

27-31: 'Then the soldiers of the governor took Jesus into the Praetorium and gathered the whole Roman cohort around him. They stripped him and put a scarlet robe on him. And after twisting together a crown of thorns, they put it on his head, and a reed in his right hand; and they knelt down before him and mocked him, saying, 'Hail, King of the Jews!' They spat on him, and took the reed and began to beat him on the head. After they had mocked him, they took the scarlet robe off him and put his own garments back on him, and led him away to crucify him.'

The soldiers take Jesus into their barrack hall to make sport of him. At this point none of Jesus' followers would have been present, but Mark records (15:39) that the Centurion responsible for the crucifixion came to believe in Jesus as the Son of God and so provide a possible source for these details. The Roman soldiery largely disliked the Jews, who despised them as pagan idolaters and resisted the influence of Roman culture by reason of their religion. The soldiers vent this anger upon Jesus, crowning him with a circle of brambles (*'akantha'* - from *'akmê'*, meaning a sharp point) [173] in contrast to the crown of oak leaves that their own emperors wore, and mocking him with the title that has been the official Roman cause of his receiving the death sentence on grounds of sedition against Caesar. They appear to be dressing him in the manner of their own Roman priestly augurs, i.e. in accordance with their own culture rather than Jewish culture. The role of the augur in Roman life encompassed a high ranking priestly function that included divining the future. They were important members of the Roman courts who gave advice concerning the likely success of proposed actions through observation of signs in the heavens, notably associated with the movement of birds. They carried a curved staff called a *'lituur'* (these are a commonly depicted feature of Roman coins from the period). The soldiers would most likely have fashioned such a staff from the long reeds native to the region, as is indicated by Mark's account (15:19). This mockery of Jesus included their blindfolding him and demanding that he prophesy to them who would hit him next (Luke 22:64). This indicates the role that the Roman soldiers perceived Jesus to hold within his own society, in other words a spiritual one which then made claims to kingship, but in a way which had so evidently failed. Augurs wore cloaks called '*trabea*', which are recorded as having scarlet and purple stripes.[174] This would explain Mark's comment (15:20) about the robe put on him by the soldiers being purple.

32-34: 'As they were coming out, they found a man of Cyrene named Simon, whom they pressed into service to bear his cross. And when they came to a place called Golgotha, which means 'Place of a Skull', they gave him wine to drink mixed with gall; and after tasting it, he was unwilling to drink.'

Roman law allowed civilians to be pressed into service (hence Jesus' teaching on going the 'extra mile' in Matthew 5:41). Jesus' weakness after the scourging and consequential blood loss meant that he was too dizzy to carry the cross far without falling. The soldiers therefore force a North African man from Cyrene (modern day Libya) to carry the cross. Mark (15:21) records that he was 'the father of Alexander and Rufus', indicating that this participation in Jesus' execution may have led Simon to faith and so to the involvement of members of his family in the life of the early Church. 'Golgotha' is the Hebrew word for 'skull' (as in Judges 9:53), which Luke (23:33) refers to as Calvary (Greek: '*kranion*') also meaning 'skull'. The place where Jesus was crucified was a Roman execution ground and the bodies of those executed were normally thrown into an open common grave. The uncovered bodies were then prey to wild dogs and birds, and the bones would have become scattered, hence it was known as the 'Place of the Skull' (Mark 15:22). Calvary is commonly referred to as a 'hill', but there is no evidence for this in the Gospel narratives. The place was adjacent to a main route into the city, because passers-by joined in the mocking of Jesus on the Cross. According to Hebrews 13:12 it was 'outside the city gate', which implies that it was not so far away as to be one of the surrounding mountains. It was not thought of a hill until the sixth century - the unnamed 'Pilgrim of Bordeaux' described it in A.D. 333 as a 'little mount'.[175] In any event it was a Roman execution ground and as such it would have been unclean for Jews to enter. Jesus tastes the drugged wine that the Roman's offered victims prior to nailing them to the execution stake, but does not drink it. He has already told his disciples that he will not drink wine again until he drinks it 'anew in the Kingdom of God' (Mark 14:25). He wishes to spend his final hours alert in mind, enabling him to pray and give directions to those of his followers brave enough to attend, e.g. concerning the care of his mother.

35-37: 'And when they had crucified him, they divided up his garments among themselves by casting lots. And sitting down, they began to keep watch over him there. And above his head they put up the charge against him which read, 'This is Jesus, the King of the Jews'.

Psalm 22:18 predicted that 'They divide my garments among them, and for my clothing they cast lots.' The Roman soldiers took possession of Jesus' clothing, which would have consisted of his shoes, his turban, under garment, tunic and his outer robe, and divided them among themselves. A crucifixion party consisted of four common soldiers, and John's account records that rather than tear up Jesus' inner tunic which was seamless and hence very valuable, they gambled for it. John 19:23-24: 'The soldiers, when they had crucified Jesus, took his outer garments and made four parts, a part to every soldier and also the tunic; now the tunic was seamless, woven in one piece. So they said to one another, "Let us not tear it, but cast lots for it, to decide whose it shall be." Thus they fulfilled the prophecy given one thousand years earlier. John (19:20-22) records that Pilate had written the formal Roman

227

charge against Jesus in three languages, Hebrew, Latin and Greek, and ordered it be erected above the cross despite the protests of the Chief Priests who requested in vain that it be changed to render it as simply a claim that Jesus had made. Pilate was determined to exert his authority to the extent that he was able to give offense to the Jewish leaders whom he had been forced to acquiesce to in crucifying Jesus.

38-44: 'At that time two robbers were crucified with him, one on the right and one on the left. And those passing by were hurling abuse at him, wagging their heads and saying, 'You who are going to destroy the Temple and rebuild it in three days, save yourself! If you are the Son of God, come down from the cross.' In the same way the Chief Priests also, along with the Scribes and elders, were mocking him and saying, 'He saved others; he cannot, save himself. He is the King of Israel; let him now come down from the cross, and we will believe in him. He trusts in God. Let God rescue him now if he delights in him, for he said, 'I am the Son of God.' The robbers who had been crucified with him were also insulting him with the same words.'

Pilate had come to Jerusalem to pronounce sentence on others as well, and it is probably two of Barabbas' followers who are on either side of Jesus. Both join in the insults of the Priests, before Luke records (23:40) that one repents and is promised eternal life by Jesus. The Priests quote Psalm 22:8 - 'He trusts in the Lord; let the Lord rescue him. Let him deliver him, since he delights in him.' They fulfill the role of the mockers of verse 7 - 'All who see me mock me; they hurl insults, shaking their heads.' The response of the Jewish authorities goes far beyond what would have been psychologically appropriate to a simple itinerant teacher, and shows a hatred reflective of what was considered an immense act of betrayal by someone they regarded as a peer.

45-50: 'Now from the sixth hour darkness fell upon all the land until the ninth hour. About the ninth hour Jesus cried out with a

228

loud voice, saying, 'Eli, Eli, lama sabachthani?' that is, 'My God, my God, why have you forsaken me?' And some of those who were standing there, when they heard it, began saying, 'This man is calling for Elijah.' Immediately one of them ran, and taking a sponge, he filled it with sour wine and put it on a reed, and gave him a drink. But the rest of them said, 'Let us see whether Elijah will come to save him.' And Jesus cried out again with a loud voice, and yielded up his spirit.'

The three hour period of darkness is too long for a normal solar eclipse, which in any event does not occur at the time of a full-moon, such as at Passover, and so the darkness may have been due to dark clouds gathering in the form of a storm that may have accompanied the earthquake described in verse 51. The fact that Jesus is praying Psalm 22 is not of itself an indication that he felt somehow abandoned by his Father at the point of his becoming the sin offering prophesied by Isaiah (53:10). Paul would subsequently write (2 Corinthians 5:19) that 'God (*i.e. the Father*) was in Christ reconciling the world to himself' (*italics mine*). Jesus would have prayed Psalm 22 often in the normal course of Jewish worship, and it describes very well what was happening to him at that point. It does not imply a sense of isolation from his Father. Psalm 22:14-16 reads: 'I am poured out like water, and all my bones are out of joint; my heart is like wax; it is melted within me. My strength is dried up like a potsherd, and my tongue cleaves to my jaws; and you lay me in the dust of death. For dogs have surrounded me; a band of evildoers has encompassed me; they pierced my hands and my feet.' The Roman soldiers, accustomed to crucifying Jews, confused 'Eli' with a cry for 'Elijah'. This prompts one of them to offer Jesus wine vinegar (a fulfillment of Psalm 69:21), which John (19:28) records was in response to Jesus' cry of 'I thirst'. At this point Jesus relinquished his spirit to his Father, being in control over the time of his death and having accomplished his Father's will and his own mission to be the perfect sacrifice for the sins of the whole world.

51-54: 'And behold, the veil of the Temple was torn in two from top to bottom; and the earth shook and the rocks were split. The tombs were opened, and many bodies of the saints who had fallen asleep were raised; and coming out of the tombs after his resurrection they entered the holy city and appeared to many. Now the centurion, and those who were with him keeping guard over Jesus, when they saw the earthquake and the things that were happening, became very frightened and said, 'Truly this was the Son of God!''

The disciples being in hiding meant that God would provide himself with new witnesses of a unexpected kind - devout Jews are raised back to life and Roman soldiers also now tell of what they have seen and heard. The Temple curtain, said to be a hands-breadth thick, separating the Holy of Holies from the Holy Place is torn in such a way as to be unattributable to man (torn from top to bottom).

55-61: 'Many women were there looking on from a distance, who had followed Jesus from Galilee while ministering to him. Among them was Mary Magdalene, and Mary the mother of James and Joseph, and the mother of the sons of Zebedee. When it was evening, there came a rich man from Arimathea, named Joseph, who himself had also become a disciple of Jesus. This man went to Pilate and asked for the body of Jesus. Then Pilate ordered it to be given to him. And Joseph took the body and wrapped it in a clean linen cloth, and laid it in his own new tomb, which he had hewn out in the rock; and he rolled a large stone against the entrance of the tomb and went away. And Mary Magdalene was there, and the other Mary, sitting opposite the grave.'

Jesus broke Rabbinic tradition by including women in the company of his disciples, and it was they who proved the most faithful of his followers, attending the execution and keeping watch over the grave rather than participating in the Passover service. John (19:39) records

230

that Joseph of Arimathea was accompanied by Nicodemus (a Sanhedrin council member) in taking the politically risky step of requesting the release of the body from Roman custody. In doing so they also made themselves unclean ceremonially (and so unable to celebrate Passover) by entering Pilate's house, the unclean site of execution and finally by touching a dead body. They also showed great faith by risking bringing on themselves any curse associated with the crucifixion (Deuteronomy 21:23). The proximity of the tomb to the unclean site meant that it was unused and so readily available - no Jew would wish to rise at the Day of Judgement with the many criminals and murderers buried nearby.

62-66: 'Now on the next day, the day after the preparation, the Chief Priests and the Pharisees gathered together with Pilate, and said, 'Sir, we remember that when he was still alive that deceiver said, 'After three days I am to rise again.' Therefore, give orders for the grave to be made secure until the third day, otherwise his disciples may come and steal him away and say to the people, 'He has risen from the dead,' and the last deception will be worse than the first.' Pilate said to them, 'You have a guard; go, make it as secure as you know how.' And they went and made the grave secure, and along with the guard they set a seal on the stone.'

If Joseph of Arimathea meant to house Jesus' body in his tomb until a more suitable burial place further from the Roman site became available, he was overtaken by events. The authorities are so concerned about the possibility of a fraud that they break their own Sabbath regulations and go to Pilate for permission to post some of the Roman guard (appointed to the Temple) at the tomb. Pilate even permits his official seal to be used to make moving the stone a criminal offense. In doing so he inadvertently provided the proof of the raising of Christ from the dead - it would have been quite impossible for Jesus' disciples to have taken the body from a guarded and sealed tomb. Rendering the tomb empty was therefore something that only God could accomplish.

Chapter 28

1-4: 'Now after the Sabbath, as it began to dawn toward the first day of the week, Mary Magdalene and the other Mary came to look at the grave. And behold, a severe earthquake had occurred, for an angel of the Lord descended from heaven and came and rolled away the stone and sat upon it. And his appearance was like lightning and his clothing as white as snow. The guards shook for fear of him and became like dead men.'

The two Mary's, being more conscientious of observing the Sabbath regulations than the Priests were, had gone home, but returned in time to witness to the stone being removed by an angel come down from heaven. The guards, perhaps not made of such stern stuff as these women, fall down in a faint. The angel then demonstrates his greater authority by breaking Pilate's seal and using the stone as a seat.

5-10: 'The angel said to the women, 'Do not be afraid; for I know that you are looking for Jesus who has been crucified. He is not here, for he has risen, just as he said. Come; see the place where he was lying. Go quickly and tell his disciples that he has risen from the dead; and behold, he is going ahead of you into Galilee, there you will see him; behold, I have told you.' And they left the tomb quickly with fear and great joy and ran to report it to his disciples. And behold, Jesus met them and greeted them. And they came up and took hold of his feet and worshipped him. Then Jesus said to them, 'Do not be afraid; go and take word to my brethren to leave for Galilee, and there they will see me.'

The women's faith means that they do not faint at either the sight or sound of the angel, who announces to them the first proclamation of Jesus' bodily resurrection. Their faithfulness is rewarded by meeting the risen Jesus before his male disciples do, in fact Luke (24:11) records that the men 'did not believe the women, because their words seemed to them like nonsense.' Jesus repeats his instructions (Matthew 26:32) that he is going ahead of him to their Galilean base - travel being rather easier for him in his resurrection body! The men's lack of faith does not prevent their being able to witness him themselves.

11-15: 'Now while they were on their way, some of the guard came into the city and reported to the Chief Priests all that had happened. And when they had assembled with the elders and consulted together, they gave a large sum of money to the soldiers, and said, 'You are to say, 'His disciples came by night and stole him away while we were asleep'. And if this should come to the governor's ears, we will win him over and keep you out of trouble.' And they took the money and did as they had been instructed; and this story was widely spread among the Jews, and is to this day.'

The Roman soldiers are under threat of execution for sleeping on duty, and also for losing the body, be it to an angel or to men, just as the jobs of the Priests are in jeopardy if news of what has happened gets out. The solution of bribing the guards is the best one available, even though the likelihood of a group of frightened and defeated men overpowering a Roman unit (60 men) and removing the stone without any loss of life is so remote as to be ludicrous.

16-20: 'But the eleven disciples proceeded to Galilee, to the mountain which Jesus had designated. When they saw him, they worshipped him; but some were doubtful. And Jesus came up and spoke to them, saying, 'All authority has been given to me in heaven and on earth. Go therefore and make disciples of all the nations, baptizing them in the name of the Father and the Son and the Holy Spirit, teaching them to observe all that I commanded you; and lo, I am with you always, even to the end of the age'.

233

The honesty of the Gospel writers to admit that some of the apostles (e.g. Thomas) doubted the evidence of their own eyes is good testimony of their truthfulness. Jesus, now in possession from his Father of all authority to rule on his Father's behalf, entrusts to them the 'great commission' of making disciples, just as they had been discipled by him. They were delegated the authority to baptize and pass on the teaching that so distinctly shaped their way of life with the help of him who said 'I will never leave you nor forsake you' (Hebrews 13:5). He says the same today.

Endnotes

1   Vine's Expository Dictionary of Old and New Testament Words
2   Published by Templehouse: www.templehouse-publishing.com
3   The Jewish historian to Caesar, who wrote 'The Antiquities of the Jews'
4   'Against Heresies' III.i.1
5   Nehemiah chapter 7 verse 64
6   Sanhedrin 11.1
7   Strong's Greek & Hebrew Dictionary
8   Strong's Greek & Hebrew Dictionary
9   Hegesippus, quoted in Eusebius' 'Church History' p71 (translator P Meier)
10   Strong's Greek & Hebrew Dictionary
11   NASB Greek-Hebrew Dictionary
12   Vine's Expository Dictionary of Old and New Testament Words
13   Strong's Greek & Hebrew Dictionary
14   Strong's Greek & Hebrew Dictionary
15   Flavius Josephus: 'The Jewish War', book 1, chapter 33, 5
16   Vine's Expository Dictionary of Old and New Testament Words
17   Strong's Greek & Hebrew Dictionary
18   Pirkei Avot 5:24
19   Strong's Greek & Hebrew Dictionary
20   Strong's Greek & Hebrew Dictionary
21   Strong's Greek & Hebrew Dictionary
22   Greek & Hebrew Dictionary
23   Strong's Greek & Hebrew Dictionary
24   Strong's Greek & Hebrew Dictionary
25   Vine's Expository Dictionary of Old and New Testament Words
26   Vine's Expository Dictionary of Old and New Testament Words
27   Vine's Expository Dictionary of Old and New Testament Words
28   Strong's Greek & Hebrew Dictionary
29   Strong's Greek & Hebrew Dictionary
30   Strong's Greek & Hebrew Dictionary
31   Strong's Greek & Hebrew Dictionary
32   Strong's Greek & Hebrew Dictionary
33   Strong's Greek & Hebrew Dictionary
34   Vine's Expository Dictionary of Old and New Testament Words
35   Vine's Expository Dictionary of Old and New Testament Words
36   Strong's Hebrew and Greek Dictionary
37   Strong's Hebrew and Greek Dictionary
38   Strong's Greek & Hebrew Dictionary
39   Strong's Greek & Hebrew Dictionary
40   Strong's Greek & Hebrew Dictionary
41   Strong's Greek & Hebrew Dictionary
42   Strong's Greek & Hebrew Dictionary
43   Strong's Greek & Hebrew Dictionary
44   Strong's Greek & Hebrew Dictionary

45 Strong's Greek & Hebrew Dictionary
46 Strong's Greek & Hebrew Dictionary
47 Strong's Greek & Hebrew Dictionary
48 Strong's Greek & Hebrew Dictionary
49 Strong's Greek & Hebrew Dictionary
50 Vine's Expository Dictionary of Old and New Testament Words
51 Strong's Greek & Hebrew Dictionary
52 Vine's Expository Dictionary of Old and New Testament Words
53 Strong's Greek & Hebrew Dictionary
54 Strong's Greek & Hebrew Dictionary
55 Vine's Expository Dictionary of Old and New Testament Words
56 Strong's Greek & Hebrew Dictionary
57 Strong's Greek & Hebrew Dictionary
58 Vine's Expository Dictionary of Old and New Testament Words
59 Strong's Greek & Hebrew Dictionary
60 Strong's Greek & Hebrew Dictionary
61 Strong's Greek & Hebrew Dictionary
62 Strong's Greek & Hebrew Dictionary
63 Talmud, Shabbat 31a
64 Strong's Greek & Hebrew Dictionary
65 Strong's Greek & Hebrew Dictionary
66 Nicomachean Ethics, 350 BC
67 Strong's Greek & Hebrew Dictionary
68 The Wars of the Jews, book 2, chapter 8, 4
69 Strong's Greek & Hebrew Dictionary
70 Strong's Greek & Hebrew Dictionary
71 Strong's Greek & Hebrew Dictionary
72 Strong's Greek & Hebrew Dictionary
73 Strong's Greek & Hebrew Dictionary
74 Strong's Greek & Hebrew Dictionary
75 Strong's Greek & Hebrew Dictionary
76 Vine's Expository Dictionary of Old and New Testament Words
77 Strong's Greek & Hebrew Dictionary
78 Strong's Greek & Hebrew Dictionary
79 Strong's Greek & Hebrew Dictionary
80 Strong's Greek & Hebrew Dictionary
81 Strong's Greek & Hebrew Dictionary
82 Strong's Greek & Hebrew Dictionary
83 Strong's Greek & Hebrew Dictionary
84 Strong's Greek & Hebrew Dictionary
85 Strong's Greek & Hebrew Dictionary
86 Sanhedrin 3:3
87 Sanhedrin 25b
88 Sanhedrin 6:10
89 Shabbatt 24:1

90 Strong's Greek & Hebrew Dictionary
91 Strong's Greek & Hebrew Dictionary
92 Strong's Greek & Hebrew Dictionary
93 Shabbatt 9. 3
94 Strong's Greek & Hebrew Dictionary
95 Strong's Greek & Hebrew Dictionary
96 Strong's Greek & Hebrew Dictionary
97 Strong's Greek & Hebrew Dictionary
98 Strong's Greek & Hebrew Dictionary
99 Strong's Greek & Hebrew Dictionary
100 Strong's Greek & Hebrew Dictionary
101 Strong's Greek & Hebrew Dictionary
102 Strong's Greek & Hebrew Dictionary
103 Strong's Greek & Hebrew Dictionary
103 Vine's Expository Dictionary of Old and New Testament Words
104 Strong's Greek & Hebrew Dictionary
105 Strong's Greek & Hebrew Dictionary
106 Strong's Greek & Hebrew Dictionary
107 Strong's Greek & Hebrew Dictionary
108 Strong's Greek & Hebrew Dictionary
109 Strong's Greek & Hebrew Dictionary
110 Strong's Greek & Hebrew Dictionary
111 Vine's Expository Dictionary of Old and New Testament Words
112 Strong's Greek & Hebrew Dictionary
113 Strong's Greek & Hebrew Dictionary
114 Strong's Greek & Hebrew Dictionary
115 Strong's Greek & Hebrew Dictionary
116 Strong's Greek & Hebrew Dictionary
117 Strong's Greek & Hebrew Dictionary
118 NASB Greek-Hebrew Dictionary
119 Vine's Expository Dictionary of Old and New Testament Words
120 Strong's Greek & Hebrew Dictionary
121 Strong's Greek & Hebrew Dictionary
122 Strong's Greek & Hebrew Dictionary
123 Vine's Expository Dictionary of Old and New Testament Words
124 Strong's Greek & Hebrew Dictionary
125 Vine's Expository Dictionary of Old and New Testament Words
126 Strong's Greek & Hebrew Dictionary
127 Strong's Greek & Hebrew Dictionary
128 Strong's Greek & Hebrew Dictionary
129 Strong's Greek & Hebrew Dictionary
130 Strong's Greek & Hebrew Dictionary
131 Strong's Greek & Hebrew Dictionary
132 Strong's Greek & Hebrew Dictionary
133 Strong's Greek & Hebrew Dictionary
134 Strong's Greek & Hebrew Dictionary

135   Strong's Greek & Hebrew Dictionary
136   Vine's Expository Dictionary of Old and New Testament Words
137   Strong's Greek & Hebrew Dictionary
138   Strong's Greek & Hebrew Dictionary
139   Vine's Expository Dictionary of Old and New Testament Words
140   Kritut 1:7
141   Strong's Greek & Hebrew Dictionary
142   'The Jesus Discovery' - www.templehouse-publishing.com
143   Strong's Greek & Hebrew Dictionary
144   Strong's Greek & Hebrew Dictionary
145   Josephus: 'The Antiquities of the Jews' book 15, chapter 11
146   Strong's Greek & Hebrew Dictionary
147   Strong's Greek & Hebrew Dictionary

148   The Odyssey Book 1, 43, 584-589
149   Strong's Greek & Hebrew Dictionary
150   Flavius Josephus: 'The Jewish War', book 1 chapter 5, 2
151   Flavius Josephus: 'Antiquities of the Jews' book 13, chapter 10
152   Aristotle: 'Historia Animalium', 350BC
153   Strong's Greek & Hebrew Dictionary
154   Ben-Dov: 'In the Shadow of the Temple'
155   Flavius Josephus: 'The Jewish War' book 2 chapter 13, 5
156   Flavius Josephus: 'The Jewish War' book 5 chapter 6, 1
157   Flavius Josephus: 'The Jewish War' book 5 chapter 12, 3
158   Strong's Greek & Hebrew Dictionary
159   Strong's Greek & Hebrew Dictionary
160   Strong's Greek & Hebrew Dictionary
161   Sanhedrin 4, 1
162   Strong's Greek & Hebrew Dictionary
163   Strong's Greek & Hebrew Dictionary
164   Strong's Greek & Hebrew Dictionary
165   Strong's Greek & Hebrew Dictionary
166   Sanhedrin iv. 1, f
167   Strong's Greek & Hebrew Dictionary
168   Flavius Josephus: 'The Jewish War' book 1, chapter 14, 4
169   Flavius Josephus: 'Antiquities of the Jews' book 18, chapter 3, 1
170   (Caesar) Augustus, Son of the Divine
171   Flavius Josephus: 'Antiquities of the Jews' book 18, chapter 3, 2
172   Flavius Josephus: 'Antiquities of the Jews' book 18, chapter 4, 1-2
173   NASB Greek-Hebrew Dictionary
174   'Roman Life', M Johnston, p 194
175   'Itinerarium Burdigalense', 333-334 AD

Lightning Source UK Ltd.
Milton Keynes UK

178472UK00001B/52/P